# The FILMS of
# SIDNEY POITIER

# The FILMS of
# SIDNEY POITIER

## by ALVIN H. MARILL

## Introduction by FREDERICK O'NEAL

THE CITADEL PRESS     •     SECAUCUS, N.J.

First edition
Copyright © 1978 by Alvin H. Marill
All rights reserved
Published by Citadel Press
A division of Lyle Stuart Inc.
120 Enterprise Ave., Secaucus, N.J. 07094
In Canada: George J. McLeod Limited, Toronto
Manufactured in the United States of America by
Halliday Lithograph, West Hanover, Mass.
Designed by William R. Meinhardt

**Library of Congress Cataloging in Publication Data**

Marill, Alvin H.
  The films of Sidney Poitier.

  1. Poitier, Sidney.  I. Title.
PN2287.P57M3    791.43'028'0924  [B]    77-28844
ISBN 0-8065-0612-1

# Acknowledgments

Gene Andrewski
Lewis Archibald
Robert Alan Aurthur
Alan G. Barbour
Dennis Belafonte
John Cocchi
Ken Darby
Ruby Dee
Guy Giampapa
William Greaves
Marilee Hastings
Stephen Klain
Stanley Kramer
Doug McClelland
Scott McDonagh
David McGillivray
Jim Meyer
Frederick O'Neal
Leo Pachter
James Robert Parish
Martin Ritt

The staff of the Theatre Collection
of the Lincoln Center Library for
the Performing Arts.

Johnson Publishing Company, NBC-TV, CBS-TV,
PBS, and the various studios for which Sidney
Poitier made movies.

# Contents

# Introduction by

# FREDERICK O'NEAL

Sidney Poitier and I go back a long way together—more than thirty years. It's a personal friendship that developed out of a professional acquaintanceship, and that in turn got off to a rather rocky start. Sidney never misses the chance to tweak me about being the heavy who told him to get into another line of work—that he'd never make it as an actor. I recall the first time I saw Sidney when he turned up at one of our auditions at the American Negro Theatre right after the war. Here came this lanky, nervous lad, sheepishly offering his partially completed application —with lots of blank spaces—to Abe Hill, Osceola Archer (Head of the American Negro Theatre School), Jeff Davis, Dr. Fred Carter, and myself. "Pwa-tyay," he told us his name was, I suppose trying to "Americanize" a decided West Indian accent. He was dressed in what seemed to be his formal wardrobe—an outlandish zoot suit with a gold chain hanging down to here and one end stuffed into the watch pocket.

I handed him a script and told him to go on the stage and start reading. The results were nearly unimaginable. He was perfectly dreadful, as well as nearly unintelligible. He read only haltingly with a sing-song accent of the islands. He never made much sense of the sentences nor grasp the essence of the character behind the lines. I told him that if he expected to become an actor, he must get rid of his West Indian accent, as he

would limit himself only to those jobs requiring such an accent; he should broaden his speech patterns to accommodate not only West Indian accents, but others as well.

Sidney was determined, if nothing else. I think my rebuff became a cause he had to avenge, and he presented himself to us again sometime later. He was not only eager. Succeeding as an actor had become an obsession with him. The second time around before the Auditions Committee proved only slightly better than his first audition. In a somewhat mannered speech, he recited a passage he had memorized from what seemed to me to be one of those "true confessions" magazines. And when we suggested that he improvise a war scene, he had no hesitation about groveling on the stage in his best suit.

We were more impressed with his drive than his reading, and after going into a huddle, we decided to take a chance on this earnest young hopeful. We told him we'd take him on for a training period—three months I think it was. Osceola took Sidney under her wing and put him through the rigors of diction, mime, stagecraft— the fundamentals of acting in general—in her company classes that included a remarkable future company of talents: Ruby Dee, Harry Belafonte, Gertrude Jeannette, Earl Hyman, playwright and actress Alice Childress, Hilda Simms, and Clarisse Taylor, who's in *The Wiz,* and others.

At the end of Sidney's three month tryout, we found that he had been listening to recordings of spoken dramatic works and had begun to disguise his West Indian accent, so we kept him, and he went on to prove how wrong we had been in our initial judgments.

When Sidney got to Hollywood several years later, I had already been doing some film work, and we found ourselves acting together in *No Way Out,* in which Sidney made such an impressive screen debut. We had done a couple of scenes with me playing his brother, but shortly after production began, I had to withdraw from the cast because of the death of my mother.

Sidney was a film veteran by the time we next worked with one another. The movie was Richard Brooks' *Something of Value,* and we were working on location. There was the extraordinary Juano Hernandez, William Marshall, and Ivan Dixon—all of us, Sidney, too, playing native Africans in Hollywood's time-honored tradition. Sidney and I were both Mau Mau fighters in that one, although my character was somewhat more hotheaded than his. Sidney's sizzling performance as Kimani in the Brooks film drove home to me all over again the natural acting skills that a decade earlier at his ANT audition had remained hidden while he was doggedly battling his island accent. By *Something of Value,* though, his screen presence was almost singlehandedly shaping the movies he was in, even though he still was getting secondary billing, usually below the title.

It wasn't long before superstardom found Sidney and later the power—as producer and director—which brought with it the responsibility for making films that reflected more sharply the black consciousness. Sidney met this responsibility and has dedicated himself, in recent years, to creating positive films for general audiences, both black and white. It has been my privilege to have known Sidney since back when—and to have marveled at his growth as an actor, and to have been a good friend, over the past thirty-odd years.

A sequence deleted from his first movie, *No Way Out*. Poitier with his "family," Frederick O'Neal, Mildred Joanne Smith (back to camera), Maude Simmons, Ruby Dee and Ossie Davis.

# SIDNEY POITIER:
## Long Journey from Cats

"Twenty-five years ago," Sidney Poitier told a bicentennial symposium for the American Film Institute's Center for Advanced Film Studies, "I was there by myself in films. There was no Gordon Parks; there was no Michael Schultz; there was no Jim Brown, no Fred Williamson, no young actors, no young actresses, no assistant directors, no editors. I walked across the Twentieth Century-Fox lot and I was there with the shoeshine boy. There were only two blacks there. I worked at Columbia Pictures when there wasn't another black person to be *seen*. We have a hell of a long way to go—we black people—but don't go too long without realizing that, over the last twenty-five years, we've come a hell of a long way! Do you *hear* me?"

Sidney Poitier's rise to the top in Hollywood happened to coincide with the American civil rights movement which, as Poitier was making his debut in films, was itself working up its initial head of steam that would propel it into the consciousness of America during the next two decades. That movement, in the arts, at least, quietly attached itself to Poitier's coattails. The struggle,

in films, was to be Poitier's alone. To the movement, however, he was to be the symbol, the first black superstar, the ebony saint, as he frequently has been called, the personification of the black man on the screen.

He came to films on the crest of Hollywood's wave of postwar movies with controversial racial themes, but prestigious films such as *No Way Out* and the British made *Cry, the Beloved Country,* and programmers like *Red Ball Express* brought him little opportunity and what seemed to be a dead end. It would take later films—like *Blackboard Jungle, Edge of the City,* and finally *The Defiant Ones*—to turn the corner for him, define his screen persona, and make movie audiences aware of the magnetism of an exciting talent who, only ten years earlier, had been advised by knowledgable artistic figures to get out of the business and look for another line of work.

In the mid-Seventies, Sidney Poitier retains his mantle not only as the leading black actor in Hollywood but also as a major power behind the scenes (as producer, director, and packager of important, *money-making* movies). From this

Poitier's initial film publicity portrait.

With wife, Juanita, in the mid-1950s.

position, he has had to fend off challengers to his crown—ex-athletes turned action stars like Jim Brown and Fred Williamson, matinee idols such as Billy Dee Williams (who does nothing to discourage his promotion as the black Clark Gable); versatile light-comedy-to-heavy-Shakespeare actors represented by James Earl Jones; comics Bill Cosby and Richard Pryor; all-around show business types personified by Sammy Davis Jr.; and others.

"I've had job opportunities partly because there were black actors before me who died and never had a shot," Sidney Poitier has said. "I am here partly because of the dues they paid—and I'm talking about Frank Wilson, Canada Lee, Rex Ingram, Hattie McDaniel, Louise Beavers. *Way* back, they were here, and they endured." They, however, were degraded in films—playing menials: the sambos, the Toms, the Mammies, shoeshine boys, waiters—"niggers," as Poitier puts it, who "were lazy, shiftless, screwed around a lot." Poitier came along as a new stereotype: the saint, who remains clear-eyed, nonviolent despite enormous provocation, superior in skills and ability, while cognizant, as one writer put it, of the limitations society imposes on him, and posing no threat to the established mores, sexual as well as social.

The Poitier saga makes him the Horatio Alger of the film industry—that of a boy making good beyond anyone's wildest dreams. Despite the urgings of Bill Cosby to his buddy Sid Porter (as Cos calls Poitier) about recanting the long familiar tale about how he grew up with a poor family of tomato farmers in the Caribbean and admitting that he was a product of an upper class Westchester, New York, background,* the Poitier story begins on the tiny, dirt poor Bahamian Island of Cat, a dot on the map approximately one hundred miles from Nassau. Actually, an accident of birth made Sidney Poitier an American

---

* The *outré* suggestion was offered during an appearance by the two on the Merv Griffin Show where they were promoting Poitier's film, *Let's Do It Again.*

Taking a break with Rock Hudson during the filming of *Something of Value.*

citizen. His parents, Reginald and Evelyn Poitier, had sailed to Florida to sell their tomato crop, although Mrs. P. was eight months pregnant at the time. Their youngest son, Sidney, came into the world in Miami on February 24, 1924 (or, according to various publicity releases and other sources, three years later). He was the eighth Poitier child. Before him: Cyril, who became a handyman in Miami and later helped raise a teenage Sidney; Cedric, a truck driver in Nassau who was asphyxiated when he stopped for a nap one day and left the motor running; Ruby, the oldest girl, who married a waiter and moved to Miami; Reginald Jr., who worked his way up from dishwasher to maître d' of the British Colonial Hotel in Nassau; Teddy, Sidney's other sister, who became a housewife and mother in Nassau; and brothers Redis and Carl, both waiters.

Like the other Poitiers, Sidney worked the fields beside his parents, hauling dirt, lugging water, dragging heavy baskets. "We were poor, man. I mean we were *busted*. We were so poor we didn't even own dirt. But my parents were outstanding people. My father was a fine and just man, and my mother wanted what he wanted. They were very happy, happier than any of us

With producer David Susskind between takes of
*A Raisin in the Sun.*

ever were." On Cat Cay, there was no electricity, no running water, no automobiles or schools, and a primitive thatched-roof stone hut was home to all ten Poitiers, crammed into three rooms. The kitchen was outside, and Mrs. P. cooked on an open grill. Their backyard was the entire island, fifty miles long and ten wide—"like walking from Brooklyn to the Bronx," Sidney recalls.

The Poitier flock began to disband when Cyril, the oldest, went to Miami and sent back glowing letters about life in America. When the Depression swept through the Bahamas, the Poitiers lost their farm when the wholesale price of tomatoes— at a nickel a bushel—made even the cost of shipping prohibitive. Reginald, only in his early fifties, became a white-haired old man, plagued by arthritis. In 1938, the decision was made to uproot the family, and Sidney and his mother, it was agreed, would go to Nassau to find lodging and work—an advance guard, so to speak. The journey by small sailboat took a good, stomach-churning twenty-four hours. Life in Nassau on the island of New Providence—after the initial adventure of seeing automobiles, for instance, for the first time, had worn off—was not more fulfilling than on Cat Cay. The family had been reunited in one ramshackle, two-room wooden hut

The Poitiers at home in 1959: with wife Juanita and daughters Sherry (on lap), Pamela and Beverly (right).

after another, scrounging for food, living from hand to mouth. Sidney's formal education—first at Western Senior High, later at Governors High—ended after eighteen months, and he was back working as a dollar-a-day water boy to laborers on a construction gang, then as a laborer himself—a two-dollars-a-day pick swinger.

Though lacking in self-discipline and incapable of applying himself, Sidney had developed a subconscious desire to succeed—at something. Unfortunately, he fell in with several companions —his first real friends—who subsequently ended up in prison for petty thievery. Sidney's father, though chronically ill, had no intention of seeing his youngest son go the way of the boy's "best friends," and he appealed to Cyril in Miami to take Sidney and bring him up in America. The year was 1942, and Sidney, with boatfare sent by brother Cyril, returned to the city where he was born. "In Miami, I got my first taste of racism. I was unprepared for it," Sidney remembers. "You see, in New Providence, there was a color line but the white community was a minority and my contacts with it were rather remote. Now the line was all over the place like barbed wire, and I kept running into it and lacerating myself. My brother had gotten me a job as a delivery boy, and one of my first deliveries was in an all-white neighborhood. There I made the mistake of knocking on the front door instead of at the service entrance."

Sidney was a Negro who did not know his place, and there apparently were any number of Miami whites who were willing to teach him.

"I couldn't let it beat me. You see, all my life, although it was only a poor one and a fierce one, I have always had great pride. My parents taught me I was as good as anyone. In the Caribbean, a young Negro is never robbed of his pride, as he is in some parts of the southern U.S. So I never go into the South anymore."

As yet, he had not left the South, and he lived with Cyril and his family for nearly two years, not knowing where his talents lay. He worked as a garbageman, parking lot attendant, busboy, Fuller Brush salesman, petty gambler. He had the equivalent of just a second grade education and was hampered by a West Indian patois that was nearly incomprehensible.

In 1943, he tried to enlist in the Navy but was turned off by racial prejudice—and that was only in the recruiting office! Discouraged, he felt that more desperate measures were warranted, and virtually without funds, he headed North to New York City—working his way slowly toward the Greyhound Bus Terminal on Eighth Avenue at 50th Street in Manhattan, arriving in the dead of winter. He had a dollar fifty in his pocket and not much more than the clothes he was wearing. He was directed to Harlem by a Negro at the terminal, and with a nickel for the subway and two pairs of pants under his arm (the rest of his wardrobe—a jacket and an extra pair of shoes—had been stolen five minutes after he had hit New York), Sidney went uptown to hunt for a hotel room. "I thought I could get one for a dollar a week, but they wanted $2.50 for a single night." He found a place that would rent him one for a

On the set of *A Raisin in the Sun* with director Daniel Petrie, producer Philip Rose, and co-star Diana Sands.

[ 14 ]

buck fifty, but now he was a nickel short after his subway ride. So he asked directions to Forty-second Street, the only other place in New York that struck a familiar note, and he went back downtown, surfacing in the carnival atmosphere of Times Square.

"I was stupefied by the noise. And I had never seen so many whites—or so many Negroes—in my life. I want to tell you, I was confused. I didn't know how I would eat or sleep. A few minutes later, I saw a sign in the window of the Turf Restaurant on Broadway: 'Dishwasher wanted, $3.00 per night.' Man, I said to myself, I'm in!" Sidney was in an apron and slaving over a stack of dishes piled head high before he had the chance to list his rather meager qualifications for the night manager.

"By the next morning, I'd eaten two square meals and had three dollars, plus the $1.40 I'd started with, and I went back to 'my place'—the Greyhound Terminal." There he invested another nickel in a pay toilet, put the seat down and his feet up against the wall door, and fell asleep. He called it the Executive Suite. It was Sidney's home during the next five months.

Poitier augmented the three-bucks-a-night from the Turf with a stint plucking chickens at the Waldorf (Astoria, not the cafeteria), and by being a semi-regular blood donor at a Times Square blood bank for two dollars a pint. With the warm weather of spring, Sidney moved outdoors from the Executive Suite to the rooftop of a building across the street from the Capitol Theatre at 51st and Broadway. By now he had

Receiving the Prix du Gary Cooper Award from Danielle Darrieux in Paris in 1961.

Relaxing with Alan Ladd, James Darren, Glenn Corbett, director Hall Bartlett, and Paul Richards while a new set-up is readied for *All the Young Men*.

[ 15 ]

Accepting his Oscar for *Lilies of the Field* from Anne Bancroft.

perusing it from front page to back, pronouncing the words phonetically with his still heavy West Indian accent, and then putting the paper to use as a blanket. If nothing else, he had fresh sheets every night and was reasonably well informed. And he enlarged his repertoire of job skills: dockhand, truckdriver, busboy, porter. What drove him? "I was poor. I mean, being poor is bad enough, but being poor and a Negro—well, there was just nothing, man, *nothing*. And I felt things. I wanted people to notice me. It was important."

Eventually, in the summer of 1944, Sidney took the "A" train back up to Harlem and moved into a closet sized cubicle on 127th Street at eight dollars a week, which he managed by working two jobs at once. After a year in New York, frustrated by his inability to find nothing more than manual labor and deciding he needed companionship, he enlisted in the Army and was quickly on his way to Camp Upton for basic training. "In the Army," he remembers, "I was very rebellious—always restless—and the restlessness manifested itself in a violent thrashing about—something I still have as a carryover today. The minute I have to do something and I don't really want to do it, I become quite rebellious."

At Upton, Sidney was trained in the rudiments of physiotherapy and then assigned to the 1267th Medical Detachment, an all-Negro company stationed at a veteran's hospital for psychiatric cases in Northport, Long Island. He found he was no

invested some of his earnings on the latest in zoot suits—pegged trousers, padded-shoulder jacket, black patent leather shoes, a snappy fedora, a neon-striped tie—and had become a regular reader of *The New York Times* at 3¢ a copy—

With director Martin Ritt and Diahann Carroll during the filming of *Paris Blues*.

more suited to Army life than to the schools back in Nassau, and was the butt of jokes and racial slurs of the primarily hip New Yorkers in his outfit. "I was oddball number one and the kick-off joke was my accent." He coped for a year and was discharged with $800 in his pocket, and soon found himself among the civilian hipsters "with the peggiest pair of pants you ever saw—a wide-brimmed hat, a three-yard chain—the works."

He went through his eight bills and it was back to the dreary routine of manual labor, as dock walloper and ditchdigger with other tedious jobs in between. His reading habits switched from *The New York Times* to the *Amsterdam News,* and there he came across an ad, next to one for a dishwasher: "Actors Wanted. Apply the American Negro Theatre." Sidney made his way to the basement of the New York Public Library on 135th Street where the auditions were being held that November day in 1945 and joined the other hopefuls. " 'Poyteeair!' I heard them call. 'Pwa-tyay. Sidney Pwa-tyay,' I corrected them. 'You an actor, Poyteeair?' I was asked. 'I'd like to be,' I answered. I was handed a script from a play that was being cast, shown a passage in the middle of the page, and asked to read." The request came from Frederick O'Neal, one of the founders of the ANT as well as a distinguished actor who later went on to become, for many years, the president of Actors Equity.

The Poitier audition took less than thirty seconds. "I read very poorly, and O'Neal escorted me to the door. He was very bugged. 'Look, boy,' he told me, 'don't waste our time. You're no actor and you can't be one. Go get a job somewhere else.' " The O'Neal rejection provided Poitier with a goal. "The way he said 'Forget it!' made me feel as if I had been attacked. I have never been so forcefully rejected. I was going to make him retract his prediction." Poitier's goal: unremitting war on his accent. He invested fourteen dollars on a radio—trifling to what it symbolized—and embarked on a crash program. "I'd take my supper—a loaf of raisin bread, usually, and a bottle of Pepsi-Cola—up to my room, and I'd lie on my bed listening to the news, to plays, to commentators, to everything. I'd start at the top of the dial and work my way down to the bottom, studying the pronunciation of broadcasters. Then I'd turn it off and drill for an hour or so, aping

Sharing a word with director Federico Fellini at the Academy Award ceremonies.

their diction. It became an obsession with me."

He put in a sixteen hour workday—eight in the garment district, eight in his room, listening for an hour, talking for an hour. The diligence paid off. Slowly he succeeded in erasing the broadest parts of his accent, reading aloud from magazines and newspapers, continuing his studies in snatches at off moments. Within six months, Sidney was back at another ANT school audition, armed with a new voice and a true confessions magazine. "I had memorized a long passage of purple prose that I was going to recite. I got through the passage, although O'Neal thought he had remembered me from before. He and Abe Hill and Osceola Archer weren't exactly indulgent. They were cold—cold and exacting."

Then he was given a situation to improvise—a sniper in the jungle whose buddy is killed. "So I did my improvisation. I got down on the floor and got my famous brown suit, the one I'd worn when I first came to Manhattan, all dusty. Then

With daughters Pamela (left) and Sherry in 1964.

they sent me home, and a week later, I got a postcard asking me to stop by the theatre. They said they'd take me into the school for a three month trial. I was able to pay the school a few dollars a week, and for the rest of the tuition, I pushed a broom backstage."

At the end of the three months, Poitier was told he was being released because the school had its quota of promising students. "ANT felt it could not devote anymore time to me because they didn't think I was very good. Frantically, I begged for an extension—and put on the greatest performance of my life." He won his newest audition and became part of one of the most respected resident companies of the day, acting in student productions of *Strivers Road, You Can't Take It With You, The Fisherman, Rain, Riders to the Sea* and *Hidden Horizon,* among others. One of the plays being cast, *Days of Our Youth,* had in its lead Poitier's acting classmate and new found friend, Harry Belafonte. Belafonte, already making money as a nightclub singer, suggested Sidney for the understudy role, and Sidney was playing the part one night while Harry was doing one of his club dates, when Broadway director James Light chanced to visit. Light liked what he saw and offered the young lead—Sidney Poitier, he learned the actor's name was—a small role in an upcoming all-Negro production of *Lysistrata* at the Belasco Theatre.

The "official" Academy Award photo in 1964. With Gregory Peck, Annabella (who accepted for Patricia Neal), and Anne Bancroft.

With Harry Belafonte in 1954.

Sidney went downtown and, on the night of October 17, 1946, he opened in the tiny role—a mere twelve lines—of Polydorus, a courier who breaks in on a group of Athenian women staging a sex strike to bring their warring husbands to their senses, and tells them that the women of Sparta have just embarked on a similar scheme. The actors' occupational disease, stage fright, afflicted Poitier, and he recalls: "I think I managed to get six of my twelve lines out. I couldn't talk above a whisper and I was shaking all over. Finally, I ran off stage before I was supposed to. I stopped the show cold."

*Lysistrata* was rapped by the critics—it folded after just four performances—but Sidney was noticed. Brooks Atkinson, for one, thought that he brought "enormous comic insight" to his part, Polydorus, while Ward Morehouse, of the *New York Sun,* observed that "Sidney Poitier has a few comic utterances as the sex-starved Polydorus."

His stage fright, it turns out, was exactly what the role called for, and although his Broadway debut was short-lived, "people were asking about the young actor who played Polydorus. I was offered a job right away, at sixty-five dollars a week, as understudy to all the actors in the national company of *Anna Lucasta*." He found himself on a tour of the U.S.—Washington, D.C., Philadelphia, Detroit, Cincinnati, St. Louis, Chicago, Minneapolis, Denver, Salt Lake City, San Francisco, Los Angeles—and then for thirty-two performances in the role of Lester back on Broadway at the National Theatre in late August of 1947. Then there were no more performances to give and Sidney was back in Harlem with a modest bankroll and a pocketful of reviews. There he did a one-act play, as Lottie in Kenneth White's *Freight,* for the ANT at the Harlem Children's Center on West 134th Street in early 1949 with his friends, William Greaves and Dots Johnson. *Freight* deals with a group of Negro laborers fleeing in a railroad box car from a lynch mob.

Shortly thereafter at a Negro Actors Guild party, Bill Greaves introduced Sidney to a lovely girl named Juanita Hardy. A college graduate, model and dancer, daughter of a noted dress designer, she was to be named Miss Press Photographer of 1950. Her sister Joan was married to fighter Archie Moore, who would become world light heavyweight champion. Sidney and Juanita soon became regulars at the restaurant Harry Belafonte had purchased in Greenwich Village.

In addition to doing some acting in Negro productions of current Broadway plays such as *John Loves Mary* and *Detective Story* with Ruby Dee and others at the Apollo Theatre in Harlem, Sidney got a film job in the fall of 1949, an Army Signal Corps documentary entitled *From Whence Cometh My Help* made in New York and New Jersey. It was a push for religion among the troops, and marked Poitier's screen debut. Professionally, however, Sidney was at liberty when he found himself suddenly with two jobs from which to choose. The Playwright Company wanted him for the juvenile lead, a non-singing part, in the musical drama, *Lost in the Stars,* which Kurt Weill and Maxwell Anderson had adapted from Alan Paton's *Cry, the Beloved Country.*

Accompanied by Diahann Carroll at the 1965 Oscar gala.

At the 1965 premiere of *Ship of Fools* with Julie Robinson Belafonte.

At virtually the same time, Sidney was contacted by 20th Century-Fox to come to Hollywood to take the pivotal role of Luther Brooks, the young Negro intern in a white hospital, in Darryl F. Zanuck's *No Way Out*—friends Ruby Dee, Ossie Davis, Hilda Simms and Frederick O'Neal already were signed for the film. *Lost in the Stars,* Poitier concluded, was certain to receive widespread attention from the critics, while *No Way Out* provided an opportunity to broaden his horizons. The play would give him $100 a week; the movie a flat $7500.

Poitier opted for Hollywood, got Juanita to give up her career for him, and married her on April 26, 1950, after returning from Hollywood and *No Way Out*. The film came at the end of the cycle of black problem movies which occupied the major studios immediately after the war. Its prime development: the treatment of the black protagonist with Poitier projecting a conscientious, hardworking, straight-A intern who takes enormous abuse without ever losing his cool. Although Poitier received better notices than the film itself, his option was not picked up and he once again was at liberty. Then British producer Zoltan Korda signed him for an important role in the film version of *Cry, the Beloved Country*. One way or another, Poitier seemed to have been destined to play a role in the property—with music or without.

In the time-honored Hollywood tradition, signing in at Grauman's Chinese Theatre in 1967.

He was flown to England where he initialed an agreement that made him Zoltan Korda's slave—literally. It was the only way he'd be allowed to work in South Africa, which permitted only "indentured" blacks to enter the country. In some quarters, he never was forgiven for signing that paper. In defense, Poitier has said: *"Cry, the Beloved Country* gave me the chance to say some things about apartheid that needed saying. There are few roles that I've prepared harder for. I wanted to project what it was like to be black and under the iron heel of a vicious racist white minority. I think how I felt came across in the film. Sure, it was a humiliation to have to indenture myself, but sometimes you have to take a punch to land a harder one." Poitier's quiet, dignified performance as the young minister who helps an aging parish priest (Canada Lee, in his last screen role) was greeted with the same acclaim that came his way with *No Way Out,* but three more years would pass before another worthwhile role was presented to him.

In the interim, he gained film experience with a pair of routine "B" movies—Budd Boetticher's potboiler, *Red Ball Express,* a war movie in which racial antagonism, a minor part of the story, is represented by a running feud between a black corporal (Poitier) and a redneck private (Hugh O'Brian), and the underrated curio directed by James Wong Howe, the noted cinematographer, *Go, Man, Go!,* a pseudo-documentary about The Harlem Globetrotters, with Poitier

Preparing for a scene in *Guess Who's Coming to Dinner* with Roy Glenn, Sr., and Beah Richards, as director Stanley Kramer gives final instructions.

playing Inman Jackson. "For in spite of Hollywood's wind of change," writer Dennis John Hall said in *Films and Filming,* "leading film roles for colored actors were still as elusive as straws in the wind."

"Hollywood as a rule still doesn't want to portray us as anything but butlers, chauffeurs, gardeners or maids," Sidney told a reporter in 1951—when he had been unemployed for more than six months. His enforced inactivity following *Cry, the Beloved Country* caused him to look elsewhere for an income, and with an actor friend, John Newton, and brother-in-law Archie Moore, he opened a Harlem restaurant, Ribs in the Ruff, in 1953. Its doors were not exactly battered in, despite the "secret Caribbean barbeque sauce" Poitier had "invented." Undaunted, Sidney and associates quickly expanded with another ribs joint in Queens, and soon they were losing money at five separate locations. When he wasn't mixing his secret sauce, Poitier was picking up work in live TV until the second call from Hollywood came along. Most notably, he was cast in *Parole Chief* on NBC's Philco Playhouse (11/16/52), playing a harassed but dignified Negro on the parole board (Delbert Mann directed), and he acted on the Sunday morning religious series, *Look Up and Live* (then hosted by Merv Griffin), among other shows.

Sidney and Juanita Poitier began their family during his out-of-work-as-an-actor days in New York. Daughter Beverly was a Fourth of July baby in 1952, and sisters Pamela (4/12/54)

With Joanna Shimkus in 1969.

and Sherry (7/4/56) followed, with Gina coming along in 1961. The fortunes of the now sometime actor and somewhat disillusioned restaurateur finally changed when Hollywood rediscovered him and Richard Brooks cast him as Gregory Miller, the black teenager (Sidney was then 31!) whose natural leadership abilities are awakened by teacher Glenn Ford, in *Blackboard Jungle.* His compelling performance, which generated much of the movie's force, brought him the expected critical acclaim but failed to convince Hollywood of his star potential. Only an offer to act in *The Phenix City Story,* a film exposé to be made independently, came his way, sent by Martin Baum, an actor's agent who had been impressed by Poitier's work in *Blackboard Jungle.* He also was approached with a part in a unique film project, *The Mark of the Hawk,* financed by the United Presbyterian Church, made in 1955,

With Katharine Houghton while director Stanley Kramer discusses a sequence for *Guess Who's Coming to Dinner.*

Preparing to announce formation of First Artists Production Company, with Paul Newman and Barbra Streisand in 1969.

Poitier in mid-career.

but not released until after he had attained stardom several years later.

Poitier said of *The Phenix City Story*: "The role was a cheat, in the context of what the film dealt with. The part was a cheat and a compromise. It was a lie, an absolute out-and-out lie, and they used it in an uncourageous manner. It was the part of a young Negro father, during the political and criminal holocaust in Phenix City, Alabama—an open city of gambling and corruption." He noted: "This father, because he worked for somebody or did something, his daughter was killed and thrown on the lawn. And the father goes out hunting for the killer, and toward the end of the film, he comes across him and he's got him in a shed and he's going to kill him. And they put in his mouth the most ugly compromise. If it had been a change of heart the man had, it could have been beautiful because it would have shown great growth, you see. But they put in his mouth—crappy words like 'I suddenly realize the Lord doesn't want me to do this.' "*

* *The Phenix City Story* subsequently was filmed under Phil Karlson's direction. The role Poitier had been sought to play was pared down substantially and taken by James Edwards.

The First Artists Production Company partners: Steve McQueen, Paul Newman, Barbra Streisand and Sidney Poitier.

[ 23 ]

With Brock Peters, Ruby Dee and Cab Calloway at a benefit for the Dance Theater of Harlem in 1972.

With Joanna Shimkus in London in 1972.

Despite his imperiled financial situation caused by the failure of his restaurant venture, Poitier returned the script to agent Baum, who, amazed and somewhat annoyed, said: "The job would have paid $1250 a week for four weeks and cleared up some of his debts." Later Baum professed admiration for Sidney's integrity and admitted: "I decided that was the kind of talent I wanted to represent," and he convinced Poitier to sign with him. Their business arrangement spanned the next twenty years. Initially, however, Baum had no more luck scouting up roles for Poitier than the actor had had on his own—merely a small part, at first, in *Goodbye, My Lady,* a gentle, lyrical "boy meets dog" movie which William Wellman was making in Georgia. Then it was back to New York.

Robert Alan Aurthur, one of the coterie of distinguished television writers during the medium's Golden Days of the '50s, had spotted Poitier in *Blackboard Jungle* and subsequently in a television drama, as Clifford Hill in a version of Booth Tarkington's *Fascinating Stranger* on the ABC Pond Theater (6/23/55), and the "boy playwright"—as Aurthur refers to himself—saw in Poitier the young Negro he (Aurthur) remembered from his own days as a stevedore on the New York waterfront years before. He also recalled a short story, *On the Docks,* which had gotten him ten dollars from a magazine just after the war. "With certain changes, I could rewrite it as a TV play," Aurthur related not long ago, "and Sidney Poitier, whom I had never met, would be the living Tommy Tyler." Aurthur recalls approaching Gordon Duff, producer of the Philco-Goodyear Playhouse, about getting his script on the air. "Gordon couldn't remember a Negro ever playing the lead in a TV drama, and told me: 'Write it without describing the guy as a Negro. Then after we cast Poitier, it'll be too late for anyone to complain.'"

Aurthur continues: "Then we were told that the Playhouse was being cancelled. Duff resolved that my play, now called *A Man Is Ten Feet Tall,* would be our farewell." Sidney was contacted and signed for $1000—the top money paid for TV in those days. "Whatever the underlying motives," Aurthur remembers, "word came to us that Sidney was unacceptable because of the political blacklist. Bolstered by my anguished screams, Gordon Duff answered that this was nonsense, that he refused to accept the decision. Sidney was distressed, recalling his association with Canada Lee, and bolted. When I phoned Poitier's home, his wife said he wouldn't speak to me. I said I'd call back every fifteen minutes until he did, and on the third try, Sidney answered. Whatever I said, beyond abject apologies, took fifty minutes, and for most of the call, Bob Mulligan, the show's director,* paced my office as I begged and cajoled, pleading with Sid to read my play. Were he then to dislike it, I would accept a refusal."

Martin Baum called back the following day to say that Sidney would play the part only if the salary were doubled. "A little revenge for Sid, and cheap enough for us," Aurthur said. Ten days of rehearsal followed, and at 9:00 on Sunday night, October 2, 1955, *A Man Is Ten Feet Tall* went on the air. One hour later, a landmark TV series faded into history. The eight year run of the Philco Playhouse was ended. Not without acclaim, however: *A Man Is Ten Feet Tall* won seven television awards, including the Sylvania Award to Sidney Poitier as Best Actor of the Year for his performance.

David Susskind had Poitier repeat the role of Tommy Tyler in the film version of the Robert Alan Aurthur teleplay—this time with John Cassavetes, Ruby Dee and Jack Warden in the roles originally played by Don Murray, Hilda Simms and Martin Balsam. *Edge of the City,* as the movie adaptation was called, marked the film directing debut of Martin Ritt, another TV alumnus, and was an artistic if not a financial success. For Sidney Poitier, it marked a turning of the

---

* Mulligan went on to Hollywood fame as director of such films as *Fear Strikes Out, Inside Daisy Clover, To Kill A Mockingbird, Summer of '42, The Other,* etc.

Directing a scene for *Buck and the Preacher.*

corner. His services suddenly were in demand in Hollywood, and he would do no further TV acting.

Richard Brooks, who had engaged Sidney to play the troubled Gregory Miller in *Blackboard Jungle*, next gave him the role of Kimani in the filming of Robert Ruark's sensational best-seller of the then topical Mau Mau uprising in Kenya, *Something of Value*. Poitier's intelligent portrayal of the young African (his last Hollywood style "native" part for two decades) who is raised alongside British colonial Rock Hudson and later becomes a top man in the Mau Mau movement, earned him another scrapbook full of critical praise and admiration from director Brooks, who attributed Sidney's strength to "an amazingly profound and sympathetic understanding of human virtues and weaknesses, and to an astonishing lack of prejudice as an artist for one who has encountered so much bigotry."

Poitier then was cast as Rau-Ru, the retainer of ex-slaver-turned-plantation-owner Clark Gable in Raoul Walsh's melodrama, *Band of Angels*. The film version of Robert Penn Warren's epic novel was roundly criticized as, at best, a cut-rate *Gone with the Wind*, and was considered only a temporary setback in Sidney's accelerating movie career. With film work becoming steadier, however, he moved his wife and daughters out of Harlem, not to Hollywood, but to the well-integrated upperclass New York suburb of Mount Vernon. "I have an interest in not losing my balance and I also have an interest in keeping my children in a certain kind of multiracial culture milieu. And I fear antiseptic living. I *fear* it. It leads to alcohol and nicotine and a kind of stagnation intellectually, and I'm not interested in that," he told a reporter at the time.

Poitier's best remembered role—the part that made him a superstar—followed: that of Noah Cullen in Stanley Kramer's *The Defiant Ones*. He etched an extraordinary performance as a tough-minded Negro convict who manages to escape from a southern prison work gang with a bigoted, blustering white man shackled to him by a two-foot chain. Surmounting formidable physical obstacles and their own mutual antagonism, the two scramble across the countryside ahead of the sheriff's posse and gradually form a grudging friendship through their common trials, deciding after their wrist chain has been severed to share, at the climax, their fate together. Poitier and co-star Tony Curtis both received Academy Award nominations for their acting, but lost that year to David Niven. Sidney, however, won the prestigious Golden Bear Award at the Berlin Film Festival for his towering performance—and praise from director Stanley Kramer: "Sidney Poitier is the only actor I've ever worked with who has the range of Marlon Brando—from pathos to great power."

Stardom, Poitier was to discover rather

Joining Harry Belafonte and Bill Cosby to inaugurate "The New Bill Cosby Show" on TV in 1972.

With Harry Belafonte in 1972.

quickly, brought with it an arsenal of problems which manifested themselves in his next film role and tested his moral convictions. Before *The Defiant Ones* went into release, word of Sidney Poitier's ascending star reached Samuel Goldwyn, then preparing his sumptuous screen version of *Porgy and Bess*. Having been rebuffed in his attempts to sign Harry Belafonte to play Porgy, Goldwyn summoned Poitier and persuaded him to take one of the film's two starring roles. Although Belafonte at the time was *the* black matinee idol (then, it turned out, on the verge of abandoning his film career), it fell to Poitier to become the symbol for his race. When he was announced for the role of Porgy in early November of 1957, black pressure groups—led by the N.A.A.C.P.—descended on him, hoping that by prevailing upon him to withdraw, the Goldwyn project might be abandoned. Torn by the dilemma, Poitier boldly requested script approval from Goldwyn, who in response was said to have uttered another of the classic Goldwynisms: "No one looks at my movies before they are made but me."

At the risk of jeopardizing his film career—Goldwyn's still powerful industry clout could have assured that Poitier never again would work in Hollywood—Sidney withdrew from the production one week after signing to star as Porgy, and others in the cast followed him off the project. Still others, who had been considering roles in

*Porgy and Bess,* suddenly were no longer interested. Goldwyn's spokesmen issued a statement from the boss: "It is my money that is going to finance *Porgy and Bess,* and I will decide how it will be made."

Sidney, meanwhile, had left town and was signed by British Lion to make a movie in the Virgin Islands—called, in a creative bit of titling, *Virgin Island*—with his *Edge of the City* co-stars, John Cassavetes and Ruby Dee, and a new British actress, Virginia Maskell. From location, Poitier responded to the *Porgy and Bess* flap raging in Hollywood. "It is a classic and Mr. Goldwyn will do it justice. But for me, as a creative artist, I just do not have sufficient interest in the piece. I am not enthusiastic about the part. Still I'm sure that Mr. Goldwyn will assemble a superb cast and produce an excellent film."

Goldwyn, of course, was a determined man and he turned every setback in his long career into a personal crusade. Unwilling to accept Poitier's decision not to play Porgy, a persistent Sam Goldwyn once again called Sidney to his court, and pleaded, cajoled and strongly urged (and possibly hinted at an industry blackball) that Poitier once again change his mind. To the dismay of the N.A.A.C.P. and others, Sidney reconsidered, telling the press that he was "confident that Mr. Goldwyn, with his characteristic good taste and integrity, will present the property in a sensitive manner." *The New York Times*

Director Poitier awaiting the next set-up during the filming of *A Warm December.*

confirmed the story: "Hollywood rumors of a quiet boycott by Negro entertainers of Samuel Goldwyn's *Porgy and Bess* were squelched with an announcement that Sidney Poitier had agreed, for the second time, to star in the role of Porgy." Quickly, a company was put together—Dorothy Dandridge as Bess, Pearl Bailey as Maria, Brock Peters as the deadly Crown, Sammy Davis Jr. as Sportin' Life. Diahann Carroll as Clara. Production was set for July 2, 1958 under Rouben Mamoulian's direction.

Shortly before cameras were set to roll, the Catfish Row set and the *Porgy and Bess* costumes went up in flame. The mysterious fire caused only a temporary if costly delay as the undaunted Goldwyn ordered everything replaced, and then decided on August 27 for the new starting date. Before then, however, Goldwyn replaced Rouben Mamoulian (citing the standard "artistic differences") with Otto Preminger, whose qualifications for the assignment included the direction of the all-Negro musical film, *Carmen Jones,* with many of the same players now prepared to make *Porgy and Bess.* The naming of Preminger rekindled the simmering controversy over the filming of the Gershwin folk opera classic.

Ken Darby, the associate music director of *Porgy and Bess,* has recalled: "I truly believe that the cast would have revolted *en masse* had it not been for Sidney, Pearl Bailey and Clarence Muse. Preminger, under contract to deliver the film in a given number of shooting days, designed each day's work as one complete ten-minute sequence— an entire reel of film. This required endless rehearsals, a continuous flow of camera movement, a flawless lighting of the entire set, and a total performance by all the actors. Stormy confrontations between director and stars would take place, tears would be shed, doors would slam, and then, the whistle would blow, lights would be lit, and the cast would be hustled in for another take. But never once did I ever witness Sidney lose his cool, and I was on the set every day."

Poitier's few comments about the filming of *Porgy and Bess,* then and subsequently, reenforce the impression that he considers it the low point in his career. The high point quickly followed. Taking a hiatus from moviemaking, he returned to the Broadway stage as star of Lorraine Hansberry's powerful *A Raisin In the Sun*. His interest in the play was sparked by his friend Philip Rose, and it was Sidney who suggested Lloyd Richards, his acting buddy from the ANT days, as director. Richards thus became the first black director of a major Broadway production, and Sidney Poitier himself, a decade later, would be only the second. Nearly a year was needed to bankroll the project, cast it and complete the rehearsals, and it was still quite an unknown quantity when it began its shakedown performances (two weeks in New Haven beginning on January 21, 1959, followed by a month in Chicago). Poitier himself was uncertain as to how it would be received and he signed a contract to do a movie the following September.

All expectations were brilliantly realized when *A Raisin In the Sun* opened on March 11, 1959 at the Ethel Barrymore Theatre on Broadway. It was greeted with critical raves and, later, the Pulitzer Prize. *The New York Times'* Brooks Atkinson found that "(it) is likely to destroy the complacency of anyone who sees it" and then called Poitier "a remarkable actor with enormous power that is always under control. Cast as the restless son, he vividly communicates the tumult of a highstrung young man. He is as eloquent when he has nothing to say as when he has a pungent line to speak. He can convey devious processes of thought as graphically as he can clown and dance." And *Life* Magazine wrote of Poitier: "He is already accepted almost without question as the best Negro actor in the history of the theatre—whenever (he) walks on stage, excitement walks with him. He seems to be taking it easy most of the time, but with the hidden tension of a coiled spring."

Poitier acted the role of Walter Lee Younger 198 times on Broadway, then withdrew from the show on August 29 to fulfill his movie commitment: Hall Bartlett's *All the Young Men,* in which he co-starred with Alan Ladd. For the first time, he was cast simply for the drawing power of his name. Of this wartime potboiler, a routine action film with a racial prejudice theme grafted on, Poitier had this observation: "Pointless, innocuous, a complete waste of time." The critics, in general, agreed. He then was approached to appear in Mervyn LeRoy's action drama, *The Devil At Four O'Clock,* acting opposite Spencer Tracy. His decision not to play the role and the subsequent casting of Frank Sinatra in the part gave rise to the legendary Hollywood axiom, "If you can't get Poitier, then rewrite the part for a white actor." His symbolic popularity with white audiences and his proven bankability, together with the marquee value of his name, gave Poitier an unsought emotional identification to millions

At the premiere of *Uptown Saturday Night* on Broadway, with beauty queens Earlene Phipps (Miss St. Thomas) and Sevena Steinmann (Miss St. Croix), plus Coretta King.

of moviegoers who may very well never have really known another Negro. His films could routinely play movie houses in the Deep South, while other pictures, made by blacks with all black casts, were relegated to either minor theatres or out-and-out "Negro houses." (Even the handful of movies in which Harry Belafonte had starred in the Fifties had trouble obtaining playdates in many parts of the country, primarily because his striking good looks and insinuating sexiness made small town officials and local movie exhibitors extremely nervous, noting a real or imagined effect he was having on their women folk—white as well as black.) Poitier had become *the* Negro in films; other fine actors, like Brock Peters, Juano Hernandez, James Edwards and Ossie Davis, remained resolutely in the background.

Various projects began tumbling out of the hopper, all scheduled for Sidney Poitier. Most went unrealized; most notable among them, *The Iron Man,* a variation on the Othello theme, centering on the exploits of the 99th Pursuit, a WW II Negro fighter squadron. John Cassavetes was to have directed and Claudia Cardinale to have co-starred. Another, *Synanon,* subsequently was made with Bernie Hamilton in the part for which Poitier originally had been sought. Instead, Sidney played Walter Lee Younger in the screen version of *A Raisin In the Sun* with the original stage cast. The David Susskind-Philip Rose film adaptation, under the direction of Daniel Petrie, making his screen directing debut, came just two years after the play had begun its successful run. Originally to have been shot in Chicago, despite the virtual lack of outdoor sequences, but finally made in Hollywood, this (practically) one set movie is a literal transcription of the Broadway play, preserving on celluloid the vivid, moving performances with which Poitier, Claudia McNeil, Ruby Dee, Diana Sands and the other players had electrified so many theatre-goers.

Poitier next worked once again with Martin Ritt (of *Edge of the City*) in *Paris Blues,* sharing above-the-title billing with Paul Newman and Joanne Woodward. The movie, made on location on the Left Bank, for the first time permitted him

Limbering up for a scene from *The Wilby Conspiracy.*

to play a romantic role—opposite Diahann Carroll. A discreet relationship that had begun when they worked together on *Porgy and Bess* became more overt when they were reunited in *Paris Blues*. Her marriage to entrepreneur Monte Kay was just ending, while the marital ship of the Poitiers had been drifting toward the rocks for some time, and Juanita, it seems, had been aware that her husband had been dating others. Sidney and Diahann were constant though circumspect companions against the real life as well as reel life Paris backdrop, and despite the continuing press releases from producer Sam Shaw stressing how innocuous the pair's relationship was, it had become obvious how serious their affair was.

Once the four months of shooting in Paris was ended, Sidney flew back to Hollywood to begin *Pressure Point* for Stanley Kramer—playing a prison psychiatrist treating a racial bigot—and Diahann Carroll went to Broadway to star in the Richard Rodgers musical, *No Strings,* for which she won both a Tony Award and stardom. Fol-

lowing *Pressure Point,* Sidney returned to the East Coast and found that his feelings for Miss Carroll had not diminished (she still was working on Broadway). He quietly moved out of his Mount Vernon home and into an apartment on Manhattan's West Side, and picked up the romance with renewed intensity. The sole problem in the way of a probable marriage: she refused to abandon a promising career on the musical stage and in supper clubs. And with a suddenness, their relationship once again cooled.

In 1961, Sidney's father—ill for some time—died in Nassau. Sidney and Juanita flew to the islands for the funeral. Then, giving their marriage another chance, the two purchased a fourteen-room Tudor mansion in Pleasantville, New York, where their three girls were soon joined by baby sister Gina. Poitier took time, amidst his personal turmoil, to then testify before Adam Clayton Powell's House Committee on Education and Labor, which was investigating discrimination in the entertainment industry, assailing the "lily-white Broadway theatre" while ignoring the fact that he could have worked on Broadway more times than he did rather than opting for Hollywood. He then went back to reading movie scripts and discarding dozens before finding the role he wanted to play—a footloose handyman who, against his better judgement, agrees to help a group of German nuns build a chapel in the Arizona desert. Poitier laid his reputation on the line for this low budget movie and worked for a

percentage of the profits. The only recognizable name in the small cast, he gambled on his attempt to carry the picture on his presence alone.

In *Lilies of the Field,* Poitier's Homer Smith is again only incidentally a Negro, and the role presented the definitive example of his "good-guy" persona. The film became his greatest hit, and on April 14, 1964, Sidney Poitier became the first (and, to date, only) black artist to be honored with an Academy Award as Best Actor of the Year. "It's been a long journey to this moment," he told the audience emotionally after the Oscar was thrust into his grasp by Anne Bancroft, the previous year's Best Actress Award winner. Juanita was not with him to relish the moment. Instead, he celebrated his award quietly at a small dinner with Diahann Carroll and mutual friends.

Several weeks later, with Juanita and their youngest daughter, Gina, Sidney returned to the Bahamas to accept a hero's welcome. Thousands of cheering Bahamians waved flags along the ten mile motorcade into the city, where he found banners streamed across intersections, calypso bands playing colorfully and energetically, and storefront decorations and signs that read: "Our Hero Sidney! Hail Sidney, the Greatest Actor in the World! Welcome Home Sidney! We Love You—Your Glory Is Ours!" The Poitiers were feted at a Governor's House where he stood imperially with the acting Governor and received more than 200 guests—cabinet ministers, senators, members of Parliament, and the Premier, Sir

With director Ralph Nelson on location for *The Wilby Conspiracy.*

Wrapping up filming on *Let's Do It Again* as Denise Nicholas, one of the leading ladies, prepares to record the moment.

Roland T. Symonette. Politely he answered questions about his acting and his Hollywood career—the standard routine, aware all the time that all of the servants were black and that the white uniformed military band was playing familiar airs from *Porgy and Bess.*

More informal and far more relaxed was the later party the Poitiers attended in the comfortable surroundings of a small cabaret in the Negro quarter of Nassau, where Sidney moved easily among the crowd, greeting most of the patrons, shaking their hands, inquiring after their families. Then he had three graves to visit—his father's, his brother Cedric's, and his mother's. Evelyn Poitier had not lived to see her son win the Oscar. She had died three months too soon.

As so often in his career, Sidney found that the peaks were followed by a series of routine assignments, and his first less-than-challenging parts after winning his Oscar were as a Moorish sheik in *The Long Ships* and a photojournalist covering NATO operations in *The Bedford Incident,* both with Richard Widmark, reuniting the two, long years after playing antagonists in *No Way Out.* Sidney acted in these films to take advantage primarily of the value of his Academy Award and make money while it was offered, and he later confessed: "They were made for reasons of greed and selfishness and corruption." On *The Long Ships:* "To say it was disastrous is a compliment." On *The Bedford Incident:* "It was a bad movie, but it didn't start out a bad movie." He then made a cameo appearance in George Stevens' biblical extravaganza, *The Greatest Story Ever Told.* The only black face among the massive cast, Poitier gave a brief, dignified portrayal of Simon of Cyrene.

Next came Guy Green's tearjerker, *A Patch of Blue,* playing a smooth Prince Charming to a pretty, white Cinderella—who happens to be blind. "I had never worked in a man-woman relationship that was not symbolic," he has argued. "Either there were no women, or there was a woman but she was blind, or the relationship was of a nature that satisfied the taboos." *The Slender Thread* followed—a two-hour telephone conversation in which he tries to keep would-be suicide Anne Bancroft on the line until help arrives.

Then came his first Western, *Duel At Diablo,* an overly violent exercise that reunited him with *Lilies of the Field* director, Ralph Nelson. About the six, Poitier has said: "I didn't do them just because they came along, but because I wanted to do them. Still, they were in fairly easy range, and I did not have to gird the old artistic loins, you know?"

During the post-*Lilies of the Field* period, Poitier made a few rare television appearances, joining Harry Belafonte in several specials about black entertainers and their contribution to American culture. As the two best known black personalities, Harry produced and performed in, and Sidney was host/narrator of *The Strollin' 20s,* recapturing Harlem's past, on February 11, 1966, and *A Time For Laughter,* a review tracing the history and significance of Negro humor in American life, on April 6, 1967. Diahann Carroll also appeared in both shows. Another side of Sidney Poitier also became evident around the same time with the release of a record album for Warner Bros. that featured Poitier reading Plato against a jazz background. (*Variety* reviewed it as

"one of the most hip readings of Plato probably ever delivered.") And he had been announced for a television version of *Othello* opposite George C. Scott's Iago, under Tony Richardson's direction. Later Poitier would say: "I used to think I wanted to play Othello. It was a classic and had authority, and I was in awe of it. No more, man! It's a bad part. I was just victimized by the timelessness of it. It still stands by itself, but reading it, I now see that the character is a little wanting." Other projects which never came to fruition: the lead in a stage production of *Blues For Mr. Charlie* and a "guest appearance" as Willie Shakespeare, Crown Prince of the Jolliqinki, in the filming of *Doctor Dolittle* (Geoffrey Holder took the role).

In his private life, Poitier's romance with Diahann Carroll again was ablaze and had reached the stage where he confirmed to the press that a marriage would take place in the fall of 1967. Autumn came and went with no further mention of the nuptials—perhaps because Juanita had refused to give Sidney a divorce—and the

At the inauguration of the Motion Picture Academy's new home with fellow Oscar winners: (front row) Claire Trevor, Harold Russell, Red Buttons and Patty Duke; (second row) Eva Marie Saint, Walter Matthau, Ginger Rogers, Rod Steiger and Maximilian Schell; (third row) Jack Lemmon, Shelley Winters, Karl Malden, Laurence Olivier and Peter Ustinov; (top row) Sidney Poitier and Ben Johnson.

Greeting fans at the New York premiere of
*Let's Do It Again.*

affair once again cooled. Sidney then shifted his screen career into high gear and found himself in three of 1967's biggest grossing films, in many cities competing with one another, and he was named by *Motion Picture Herald* and by *Fame* as the Number One Star of the Year in their annual theatre owners' poll. His performances as Virgil Tibbs in Norman Jewison's hard hitting *In the Heat of the Night,* Mark Thackeray in James Clavell's heartwarming schoolroom drama *To Sir, With Love,* and John Prentice, the brilliant physician who falls in love with (and actually kisses on screen!) the daughter of Spencer Tracy and Katharine Hepburn in Stanley Kramer's then controversial romantic comedy *Guess Who's Coming To Dinner,* apparently split his supporters enough to deny him even an Oscar nomination, despite his critical plaudits.

Although many of his friends, like writer James Baldwin, were critical of the Kramer film, Poitier (who received $400,000 plus 10% of the net) defended it. "I happen to be one of the millions who *loved* it, and I'll work for Stanley Kramer anytime he calls. Unfortunately that film became a football with the critics." The three million dollars Sidney Poitier was said to have earned from *Guess Who's Coming To Dinner* might have had as large an impact as his professed sincerity on his "love" for the movie, but it afforded him the luxury and the power to begin the latest phase of his career—as producer and director. "I'm a fairly intelligent man," he later told Martin Le-

vine of *Newsday,* "and in 1968 when those three films hit, and all year long were No. 1, No. 2, and No. 3, they were jockeying with each other and I know then that that was the peak of my career in terms of fame. I used to sit and evaluate the decline, the quality of the decline, the rapidity of the decline, and how I would try to engineer the rest of my career with dignity and integrity, so that I level off, ultimately possibly into oblivion, with grace."

First he gave in to the urge to return to Broadway, but not as an actor. His friend, Robert Alan Aurthur, who had written *A Man Is Ten Feet Tall* for him, had based a play partially on Poitier's life, and Sidney jumped at the opportunity to direct *Carry Me Back To Morningside Heights.* Described as "a meaningful comedy about a liberal 28-year-old Jew from Brooklyn and Greenwich Village who sells himself as a slave to a black Columbia law student," *Carry Me Back* starred David Steinberg and Lou Gossett. Also in the cast were Cicely Tyson, Johnny Brown and Diane Ladd. On the eve of the play's premiere, Sidney told *The New York Times:* "I allow my actors to come in and give full expression to whatever interpretation, concept and impulses they have. My ideas are introduced afterward. I have worked with dozens of directors and I have an instinctive response to every circumstance that a character I'm playing is caught in, and those instincts sometimes are very good and very sound. If a director is so insecure that he cannot examine the validity of these impulses, the actor tends to become withdrawn and cautious."

The play opened on February 27, 1968. Martin Gottfried, then critic for *Women's Wear Daily,* spoke for most of his first-nighter confreres: "Sidney Poitier makes his Broadway debut as a director with this production, and you don't need the program notes to realize he is a beginner. His staging is straight forward enough, but without the confidence that would add any kind of life or even make the general performances definite. The company seems pretty much left on its own, and with the script giving nobody any help, each player more or less does his own thing. Unfortunately, Lou Gossett wound up imitating the whole collection of Poitier acting mannerisms."

Participating at the royal visit of Sweden's King Gustaf in Hollywood, with Charlton Heston, King Gustaf, Liv Ullmann, Clint Eastwood, Edgar Bergen, Warner Bros. board chairman Ted Ashley, and Warner Bros. president Frank Wells, in 1976.

*Carry Me Back To Morningside Heights* lasted only a week, and Poitier was quick to assume the blame. "If this play, however brilliantly written, is a failure, then it is due to my inadequacies and I need to know that." And so it was back to films, where Poitier fulfilled an ambition to set up his own production outfit when, despite his current track record at the box-office and his status as the No. 1 moneymaker in the movies, he could find no backing for a project called *For Love of Ivy,* based on a storyline he had conceived. He got Robert Alan Aurthur to flesh out a screenplay, and then made arrangements with the newly formed Palomar Productions to undertake its financing and filming.

Aware of growing restlessness, particularly by the black press, about his screen image as the Ebony Saint, the persona that had made him the dominant image of the black onscreen no longer being pertinent, Sidney attempted to adjust by making his own films. And he told the press, at a news conference to announce *For Love of Ivy:* "I'm the only one, the only Negro actor who works with any degree of regularity. I represent ten million people in this country and millions more in Africa. I'm the only one for these people to identify with on the screen, and I'm not going to do anything they can't be proud of. Wait till there are six of us; then one of us can play villains all the time."

His portrayal of a gambler and bon vivant represented his first effort to alter the Poitier image the screen had come to know—in some cases, too well. His aim was to offer the alternative view to the image of the black man on the screen, and to create a love story to be symbolic of Negro women in America, that most could identify with, and to, in Poitier's words, "allow my daughters to see themselves on the screen." Rather than striving for any type of social significance with *For Love of Ivy,* he turned out a romantic comedy ("Doris Day and Rock Hudson in blackface," one black writer grumbled). Author Donald Bogle felt that "despite its corn, *For Love of Ivy* distinguished itself because it offered the first love scene between blacks in a popular

movie. Otherwise, it seemed hopelessly out of time and tune, and leading man Poitier seemed almost obsolete." The success of the film at the boxoffice (where it grossed more than $5 million) confirmed Poitier's initial judgement. His next project following the carefree *For Love of Ivy,* however, proved that his fans would accept an image change only up to a point. They would not buy Poitier, though, as the black militant he portrayed in *The Lost Man,* which was updated from the old James Mason classic, *Odd Man Out.*

Joining forces with Robert Alan Aurthur, here not only as writer of the screenplay but also making his directorial debut, Poitier is cast opposite a white woman, played by Joanna Shimkus. And, as several discerning critics noted, the scenes this time were not shown through the rear view mirror of a taxicab. Filmed in Philadelphia, *The Lost Man* tells of a black revolutionary who commits a robbery to help "the brothers." His attempts to adjust to the changing nature of the civil rights movement in America and to reflect its more militant aspects in his screen work were not wholly successful. "The supercool, superdecent, superstar" *(The New York Times'* words) as a sullen, doomed revolutionary who dies in the arms of a white, liberal chick failed to capture the imagination of the day's moviegoers, who were more attuned to the black exploitation bloodbaths being filmed by Jim Brown and others. More lasting than Poitier's performance as Jason Higgs in *The Lost Man* has been his relationship with his leading lady. Joanna Shimkus, a Canadian model-turned-actress, had been hailed by critics for her work in the movie, *Zita,* which turned out to be the highlight of her screen career. The romance between Sidney and Joanna continued long after the cameras had stopped rolling, and the two became inseparable, with Joanna abandoning her acting. The couple had two daughters, Annika born in 1972, and Sidnee Taiia, in December of the following year.

In mid-1969, Sidney Poitier joined Paul Newman and Barbra Streisand to form First Artists Production Company, Ltd., to finance, arrange distribution and control all facets of their films (other than those each still had the option of making for the established studios). Each was committed initially to produce and star in three films, while sharing in the profits of those the others made. Poitier and Newman at the time rated first and second as the nation's top box-office stars, and Streisand already was on her way to becoming the screen's most bankable actress. Subsequently, Steve McQueen added his name to the partner list of FAPC, and several years later, Dustin Hoffman signed aboard.

After the misfire of *The Lost Man,* Poitier again assumed the familiar guise of Virgil Tibbs in *They Call Me MISTER Tibbs* in 1970 and *The Organization* in 1971, and for his own production company, E & R Pictures (for his parents, Evelyn and Reginald), he played a superhero Jesus-like figure with the power to predict death, in *Brother John,* best described as "an obtuse mystical melodrama" that dismayed those critics who had hoped that Poitier had retired his halo.

Poitier understandably resented this sort of criticism, nearly as much as he was troubled by the type of films blacks then were making with increasing regularity and, it seemed, fervor—the "get whitey, get the man!" blaxploitation movie with shootings, stabbings, dopepushing, whippings, semi- and total nudity, gutter language, and the other elements that, moviemakers learned, sold tickets. Militants had been criticizing him more strongly than any of his predecessors, because, as one writer noted, he was carrying other people's hopes and dreams, a rough experience. Poitier answered: "There were so many people whose dreams weren't realized in the kind of films I made, and their frustrations were so overwhelming in terms of what kind of relief they required, that I became a symbol, a target, and that was a terribly difficult period. Now, I can't tell you how relieved I am. I have Jim Brown and Fred Williamson and Calvin Lockhart and Harry Belafonte—I have all these guys out there—they're getting their heads smashed in now, you see. The parts I did were the parts I wanted to do. They were the kinds that were being written at that time in relation to black people."

With longtime buddy Harry Belafonte, he then starred in a western comedy/drama called *Buck and the Preacher.* Joseph Sargent was the original director, but Poitier and Belafonte, for whose production companies the film was being made, had him removed and Poitier himself took over the reins. *Buck and the Preacher,* dealing with a little publicized aspect of post-Civil War American history during which freed slaves were tracked down by sadistic bounty hunters and forced to return to unofficial slavery in the South, opened another vista to Sidney—as director as well as executive producer and star. "My greatest difficulty came on the very first day I directed," he told the Greystone filmmakers seminar (held by the American Film Institute) in 1976. "I had seen the camera, and I knew what it was about. I knew lens sizes. But how to use the camera as an instrument of your own creative process was all new to me. I felt the panic building within me when I made my first setup. I had very sympathetic actors to work with [old colleagues Harry Belafonte and Ruby Dee among them] and they were very nice, but I felt that my setup was organic to the material, even though I was scared. Then I began to watch the actors unfold in the frame that I had structured, and they began to make sense. They seemed to be real. What they were doing had some kinship to my view of reality as an actor, and I began to relax."

Poitier, who had not worked with a strong director since Stanley Kramer in 1968, would call the shots on all of his subsequent starring features—with the exception of *The Wilby Conspiracy* that his agent, Martin Baum, produced in 1974 and reunited him with Ralph Nelson. And all of the Poitier films through the mid-1970s, with that one exception, would be made for FAPC by Sidney's own Verdon Cedric Productions (for his deceased sister Verdon and his brother Cedric). His *A Warm December,* made in Great Britain, was the first bearing the personal Poitier imprint. A black *Love Story,* it had him playing the familiar supersmooth hero that long had dismayed the black press and even led Vincent Canby of *The New York Times* to question: "Is Sidney Poitier becoming obsolete?"

In May of 1975, a surprisingly vicious comedy by black playwright Imamu Amari Baraka (the former LeRoi Jones) opened in New York at the Henry Street Settlement's New Federal Theatre. Entitled *Sidnee Poet Heroical,* it was staged eight times—admission free! The play dealt with an ambitious but uneducated West Indian black who comes to America and decides to become a moviestar. His sidekick is a glib, outgoing calypso singer named Lairee Elefant. The play then proceeded to parody Poitier's movies: a black convict looks out for the honky who's chained to him, a Negro carpenter dances with a nun, a "nigger helper" aids a blind girl, and so on. Also portrayed (by black actors) in the Baraka satire were Katharine Hepburn, Spencer Tracy, Otto Preminger and Katharine Houghton. Critic Mel Gussow called it, in *The New York Times,* "a corrosive indictment of the American dream, and the plundering of that dream by the expectations of society."

Despite the snipings of Baraka and others in the anti-Poitier camp, Sidney continued on his quest to make only positive pictures—or none at all. Consolidating his power as well as his many friends in the profession—veteran actors, up and coming talents and promising young black writers and behind the camera craftsmen—he then set about making the biggest, most entertaining black movie ever, featuring the largest black all-star cast assembled on the screen (a total black employment, *Ebony* Magazine judged, of 1300). Overflowing with talent, Poitier's *Uptown Saturday Night,* an outrageous comedy in which he even cast himself against type doing slapstick, bucked the contemporary blaxploitation trend by providing family entertainment as a showcase for the versatilities of dozens of well known black personalities and veteran character actors. The film's unqualified success encouraged Sidney to produce, direct and romp through a slightly less star-laden follow-up (not really a sequel) called *Let's Do It Again*—which went on to outgross *Uptown Saturday Night* and become one of Warner Bros.' top dollar movies of 1975.* That in turn led to *A Piece of the Action* two years later.

Sidney and Juanita Poitier, long separated, were officially divorced in July of 1975, and six months later, on January 23, 1976, with Harry and Julie Belafonte standing up for them, he and Joanna Shimkus were married in Santa Monica, California. In a curiously worded notice in its

* *Let's Do It Again* has brought in more than $10.6 million, *Uptown Saturday Night* $7.2 million, according to *Variety.*

With Joanna Shimkus

weekly listing of show business marriages, *Variety* observed: "Bride is an actress; groom is an actor-director." That line might well have sent chronologers scurrying to Actors Equity listings to determine whether another Sidney Poitier was posted!

Television producer-director William Greaves, Poitier's longtime friend and colleague from their acting days back in Harlem, has felt that "Sidney reemerged in black comedies like *Let's Do It Again*. He really didn't get into that whole black exploitation genre of the early '70s, and for a while he was shunted aside because of the whole rise of black militancy on the screen. He was considered, perhaps, too conservative, doing all those mainstream integration movies, and maybe his image was viewed as too placid. His recent comedies certainly have been successful by any standard, although they and he might not necessarily have assisted his stardom. He's really at his best as a serious dramatic actor—he was superb in *No Way Out,* superb in *Blackboard Jungle,* superb in *The Defiant Ones* and *In The Heat of the Night,* and it's evident that he'll be superb in future serious roles. At the present time, of course, Sidney is more interested, I guess, in the bottom line, because in Hollywood you'll get your throat slit if you don't pay attention to it."

As the reigning still young elder statesman of the black film colony, Sidney Poitier admits to being distressed that there is not an appreciable number of black producers being developed nor is there real breakthrough in high earnings among the blacks in films. "Stars like Jim Brown and Fred Williamson deserve every penny they get," he has said, noting that there are a few making a good buck. "Any actor who can turn in a profit on a film is worth his salary, whatever his salary may be." He adds, though, "The only people who will get rich in this business are those who will make pictures and own them. There are a lot of talented people out here in Hollywood, but we all wait at home for the phone to ring."

*Ebony* Magazine writes: "For Sidney Poitier, home is still the Bahamas, although he is a recognizable force in Hollywood. Most other black actors say he is the most powerful among them. After years of stardom, and salaries that sometimes approached a million dollars a picture, he now usually works for a percentage of the film, which is even better. But most of all, Sidney Poitier is making films."

# The FILMS of
# SIDNEY POITIER

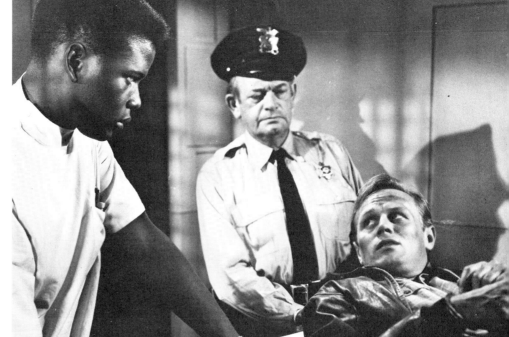

With Ken Christy and Richard Widmark.

# No Way Out

20th Century-Fox                    1950

## THE CAST:

*Ray Biddle*, RICHARD WIDMARK; *Edie Johnson*, LINDA DARNELL; *Dr. Daniel Wharton*, STEPHEN McNALLY; *Luther Brooks*, Sidney Poitier; *Cora Brooks*, Mildred Joanne Smith; *George Biddle*, Harry Bellaver; *Dr. Moreland*, Stanley Ridges; *Lefty,* Dots Johnson; *Gladys,* Amanda Randolph; *Johnny Biddle,* Don Hicks; *Connie,* Ruby Dee; *John,* Ossie Davis; *Whitey,* George Tyne; *Rocky,* Bert Freed; *Luther's Mother,* Maude Simmons; *Kowalski,* Ken Christy; *Mac,* Frank Richards; *Assistant Deputy,* Robert Adler; *Deputy Sheriff,* Jim Toney; *Day Deputy,* Ray Teal; *Dr. Cheney,* Will Wright; *Jonah,* Wade Dumas; *Ambulance Driver,* Fred Graham; *Ambulance Doctor,* William Pullen; *Henry,* Jasper Weldon; *Polish Husband,* Ruben Wendorf; *Polish Wife,* Leiola Wendorf; *Landlady,* Kitty O'Neill; *Interns,* Stan Johnson and Frank Overton; *Joe,* Emmett Smith; *Terry,* Ralph Hodges; *Priest,* Thomas Ingersoll; *Man,* Jack Kruschen; *Bailiff,* Howard Mitchell.

## CREDITS:

*Producer,* Darryl F. Zanuck; *director,* Joseph L. Mankiewicz; *screenplay,* Joseph L. Mankiewicz and Lesser Samuels; *photography,* Milton Kras-

With Richard Widmark.

[ 43 ]

With Linda Darnell and
Stephen McNally.

ner; *music,* Alfred Newman; *assistant director,* William Eckhardt; *art directors,* Lyle R. Wheeler and George W. Davis; *editor,* Barbara McLean. Running time: 102 minutes.

Moviegoers first saw Sidney Poitier on the screen in *No Way Out,* Joseph L. Mankiewicz's brutal racial drama which Darryl F. Zanuck had ordered made in the waning days of 20th Century-Fox's cycle of gritty, black-and-white social documentaries on (primarily) anti-Semitism, law enforcement, and the problems of the American Negro. Among the era's wave of realistic films concerning themselves with controversial racial themes were 20th's own *Pinky* (Elia Kazan directed), Stanley Kramer's *Home of the Brave* (Mark Rob-

son), independently-made *Lost Boundaries* (Alfred J. Werker), and, rather unexpectedly, MGM's *Intruder in the Dust* (Clarence Brown)—an off-beat item from the studio whose glossy output generally had been geared to family entertainment rather than social comment.

*No Way Out* rode the crest of the wave in the summer of 1950, going into release without much fanfare (and boasting an advertising campaign which disclosed absolutely nothing about its content) while most Americans were off enjoying the sea and surf. Critical appraisal of the film was reasonable but not overly enthusiastic. Invariably, though, Sidney Poitier was singled out for his thoughtful, compelling performance as the young doctor who, as the only non-white prac-

With Mildred Joanne Smith.

With Richard Widmark.

With Richard Widmark and
Linda Darnell.

ticing medicine in a county hospital, suffers the professional tolerance of the staff and humiliating indignities at the hands of one of his patients, a pathological bigot. *Variety* was among the first to spot the actor, noting that "Poitier is splendid." *Hollywood Reporter* similarly praised him, saying "Sidney Poitier is a young, talented Negro actor whose quiet dignity and persuasive style mark him for an important future." In its review of the film, *Time* Magazine called Poitier "likeable," while critic Thomas M. Pryor, reviewing for *The New York Times,* felt that "Sidney Poitier gives a fine, sensitive performance of quiet dignity."

Sidney Poitier, who, the year before, had appeared in a documentary on religion, *From Whence Cometh My Help* (see appendix), for the Army Signal Corps, was given featured billing just below the title in his first major Hollywood film, and was listed fourth in the cast. His impressive performance, critical acclaim notwithstanding, failed to skyrocket him to stardom (as the sensational debut of his co-star, Richard Widmark, had done for him several years earlier), simply—as more than one cinema historian and film critic has concluded—because his skin was the wrong color. The motion picture industry of the late Forties and early Fifties might have lowered its barriers slightly to focus on the colored problem but the cinematic emancipation of the

Negro had not yet been extended to outright movie stardom.

The setting for *No Way Out* is a large county hospital where a young Negro intern, Luther Brooks (Poitier), labors professionally under the kindly eye of Dr. Daniel Wharton (Stephen McNally), the chief resident and his only friend on the staff. When the Biddle brothers, a pair of toughs, are brought into the prison ward with gunshot wounds from a bungled filling station holdup, Brooks is assigned their examination. He determines that the wounds are minor but diagnoses symptoms in Johnny Biddle (Don Hicks), who has lapsed into a coma, that indicate something more serious—possibly a brain tumor. Brooks orders a spinal tap but is unable to save the patient.

Ray Biddle (Richard Widmark), a paranoid with a pathological hatred for Negroes, screams murder, blaming the "nigger doctor" who had examined Johnny—the doctor who Ray had assumed was the janitor who mopped the hospital floors. Biddle's warped mentality convinces him to charge the doctor with deliberately killing his brother, and he refuses to permit an autopsy that might vindicate Brooks. Handcuffed to his hospital bed, Ray mercilessly baits Brooks. When George Biddle (Harry Bellaver), his mute brother, and Edie Johnson (Linda Darnell), Johnny's ex-wife, visit him, Ray sees the chance to accuse the college bred Brooks of murder in order to precipitate a race riot, and dupes Edie and George into helping.

Meanwhile, the correctness of his fellow workers and the prison police, together with the invectives being hurled at him by Biddle and his followers, begin causing Brooks to seriously question his future. His wife (Mildred Joanne Smith), his mother (Maude Simmons) and Dr. Wharton all urge him to persevere, and the latter contacts Edie Johnson and tries to persuade her to reason with Biddle about allowing the autopsy on her ex-husband to clear Brooks. Biddle, though, convinces her that it is simply a trick, and impresses on her the importance of having his white buddies beat up on the blacks. Impulsively, Edie grasps at the opportunity to escape, at last, from the stifling life of Beaver Canal, the slum section which Ray and Johnny had made their personal territory. Behind her back, however, Ray instructs his brother George to keep an eye on her to make sure she stays in line.

Rumors of the impending rumble reach the Negro gangs, giving them the chance to surprise Biddle's followers from Beaver Canal who have assembled in an abandoned warehouse. The riot is under way, moving along the back alleys and into a dump for junked subway cars. The bloody battle rapidly fills the county hospital, and Brooks has his hands full, working shoulder to shoulder with the all-white staff. When the mother of one of the white victims spits in Brooks' face, though, he walks out, and, against Wharton's better judgement, forces an autopsy on Johnny

Biddle by surrendering to the police with a false murder confession.

With Wharton's help, Brooks proves his diagnosis during a court ordered autopsy, but Ray Biddle's closed mind refuses to accept the verdict of the coroner, and with the aid of his brother George, he manages to escape from the prison ward, despite his crippled leg, and vows to get Brooks. He grabs Edie and forces her to help set up an ambush on the doctor who, he is still convinced, murdered Johnny.

Unwillingly, Edie calls Brooks and asks him to meet her at Dr. Wharton's house, knowing that Wharton is away for a few days. After Ray leaves for the meeting with Brooks, Edie manages to break away from George and notify the police. She then rushes after Ray in an attempt to save Brooks' life, and manages to sneak into Wharton's house unseen and pull the light switch as Ray is about to shoot Brooks. Ray then collapses from his loss of blood as Brooks, wounded himself when Biddle fired, makes his way to Ray's side and saves him from bleeding to death, cradling the sobbing psychopath in his arms and calming him: "Don't cry, white boy, you're gonna live!"

In Poitier's role of Luther Brooks many have seen, in retrospect, the archetype for many of the actor's subsequent screen characterizations—the clean-cut, sensitive, black loner who fights prejudice and/or evil with sharp-eyed understanding. In only a few of the almost forty films Poitier has done since has he deviated from this particular motion picture image.

With Richard Widmark and Linda Darnell.

With Canada Lee.

# Cry, The Beloved Country

London Films/Lopert                    1952

THE CAST:

*Stephen Kumalo*, CANADA LEE; *James Jarvis*, CHARLES CARSON; *Rev. Msimangu*, Sidney Poitier; *Margaret Jarvis*, Joyce Carey; *Father Vincent*, Geoffrey Keen; *Mary*, Vivien Clinton; *Martens*, Michael Goodliffe; *Mrs. Kumalo*, Albertina Temba; *John Kumalo*, Edric Connor; *Kumalo's Friend*, Charles McCrae; *Absalom*, Lionel Ngakane; *Farmer Smith*, Bruce Anderson; *Capt. Jaarsveldt*, Bruce Meredith Smith; *Mary Jarvis*, Berdine Grunewald; *Harrison, Sr.*, Cecil Cartwright; *Harrison, Jr.*, Andrew Kay; *Father Thomas*, Max Dhlamini; *Father Tisa*, Shayiwa Riba; *Gertrude Kumalo*, Ribbon Dhlamini; *Gertrude's Child*, Tsepo Gugushe; *Young Man*, Daniel Adnewmah; *Mrs. Ndele*, Emily Pooe; *Taxi Driver*, Reginald Ngcobo; *First Reporter*, Michael Golden; *Second Reporter*, Clement McCallin; *Judge*, Stanley Van Beers; *Prison Warden*, John Arnatt; *Superintendent*, Scott Harrold.

CREDITS:

A Zoltan Korda/Alan Paton Production. *Producer/director*, Zoltan Korda; *screenplay*, Alan Paton from his novel; *photography*, Robert Krasker; *music director*, Dr. Hubert Clifford conducting the London Symphony Orchestra; *music*, R. Gallois Montbrun; *assistant director*, John Bremer; *art director*, Wilfrid Shingleton; *editor*, David Eady. Running time: 105 minutes.

Sidney Poitier went to South Africa—as an indentured servant to producer Zoltan Korda—to act in *Cry, the Beloved Country*, an absorbing adaptation of Alan Paton's impassioned novel about the post-war social conditions in Johannesburg. Ironically, this was the straight, dramatic version of *Lost In the Stars*, the Broadway musical which Poitier had turned down in favor of a film career.

In *Cry, the Beloved Country*, Poitier plays the

As Reverend Msimangu.

young Anglican priest, Reverend Msimangu (technically the film's second lead), who helps a country pastor find his son in the bewilderment of the big city. The distinguished Canada Lee, in his last role, is the simple, God-fearing preacher who comes down from the hills of rural Natal to prowl through Johannesburg seeking his missing sister and wayward son, and finds them both in the crime-ridden slums.

With the aid of the more sophisticated Msimangu, Reverend Stephen Kumalo (Lee) learns that his sister (Ribbon Dhlamini) has become a prostitute and his son, Absalom (Lionel Ngakane), is involved with a gang of thieves and has

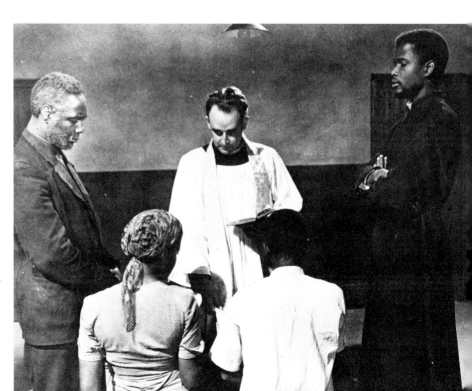

With Canada Lee and Geoffrey Keen.

With Canada Lee and Scott Harrold.

murdered a white man, the son of James Jarvis (Charles Carson), the powerful, bigoted, white landowner from Kumalo's village of Ixopo.

At Absalom's trial, Kumalo and his brother John (Edric Connor) hear the young man admit that he had fired the fatal shot during a robbery because of fear. The other defendants deny having been at the scene of the killing, and Absalom is sentenced to death, after being married to the girl who had had his child. Overwhelmed by the tragedy, the aging preacher sadly returns to his village where he discovers that he has been ordered to leave his beloved parish because of the scandal. In his darkest hours, Kumalo strikes up an unexpected friendship with farmer Jarvis in a demonstration of the ironies that touch human lives, and the two fathers, black and white, come to a better understanding of each other and the conditions in which they live, and Jarvis promises Kumalo every help that he can extend to the natives.

Of Poitier's quiet, dignified performance, the *St. Louis Post-Dispatch* applauded: "Sidney Poitier emerges as an actor of the first rank." *Film Daily* enthused: "Performances throughout are splendid with American actor Sidney Poitier standing out as a young Negro preacher." *Variety* viewed *Cry, the Beloved Country* (later known

With Edric Connor, Geoffrey Keen and Canada Lee.

[ 49 ]

With Michael Goodliffe.

With Canada Lee.

as *African Fury)* as "a very moving film, full of simplicity and charm" and thought that "Sidney Poitier is manly and striking as the young preacher."

In *The New York Times,* Bosley Crowther described the film as "a motion picture of comparable beauty and power," and noted that "Sidney Poitier makes evident deep conflicts in the role of a young Negro priest."

The acclaim for the film and for Canada Lee's profoundly moving performance was generally universal and in most cases praise also was found for Sidney Poitier's acting. Critic Otis L. Guernsey, Jr., though, hedged slightly in his review in the *New York Herald Tribune,* granting that "Canada Lee gives a nearly monumental performance . . . [but] the acting in general is a little too stiff for realism." And viewing the film more than two decades later, one tends to agree with the somewhat unusual performing styles of

most of the cast, with only the Poitier performance typical of the distinctive acting method to which moviegoers long since have become accustomed.

*"Cry, the Beloved Country* gave me the chance to say some things about apartheid that needed saying," Poitier later admitted. "There are few roles that I've prepared harder for. I wanted to project what it was like to be black and under the iron heel of a vicious racist white minority. I think how I felt came across in the film. Sure, it was a humiliation to have to indenture myself, but sometimes you have to take a punch to land a harder one."

In 1974, the musical *Lost In the Stars* was brought to the screen, with Brock Peters as Kumalo, Clifton Davis as Absalom and Paul Rogers as Jarvis. There was no role comparable to the one of the young priest played by Poitier in *Cry, the Beloved Country.*

# Red Ball Express

Universal-International                1952

THE CAST:

*Lt. Chick Campbell,* JEFF CHANDLER; *Sgt. Red Kallek,* ALEX NICOL; *Pvt. Ronald Partridge,* CHARLES DRAKE; *Joyce McClellan,* Judith Braun; *Antoinette DuBoise,* Jacqueline Duval; *Corp. Andrew Robertson,* Sidney Poitier; *Kitty Walsh,* Cindy Garner; *Sgt. Max,* John Hudson; *Pvt. Wilson,* Hugh O'Brian; *Pvt. John Heyman,* Jack Kelly; *Tank Lieutenant,* Palmer Lee (Gregg Palmer); *Major,* John Pickard; *Gen. Gordon,* Howard Petrie; *Pvt. Taffy Smith,* Bubber Johnson; *Pvt. Dave McCord,* Robert Davis (Davis Roberts); *First Mechanic,* David Friedman; *Jones,* Syl Lamont; *Pvt. Higgins,* Frank Chase; and Howard Negley, Thomas B. Henry, Arthur Space, Walter Reed, Robert Karnes, Ted Ryan, Douglas Evans, Eugene Borden, Yola D'Avril, Sid Clute, Clark Howat, Emmett Smith, Robert Dane, Nan Boardman, Don Hicks, Harry Lauter, Harold Dyrenforth, Peter Michael, George Dee, James McLaughlin, Roger McGee, Mike Dale, Jack Hyde, Douglas Bank, Tommy Long, Murry Olshansky, Richard F. Gaston.

CREDITS:

*Producer,* Aaron Rosenberg; *director,* Budd Boetticher; *screenplay,* John Michael Hayes; *story,* Marcel Klauber and Billy Grady, Jr.; *photography,* Maury Gertsman; *music director,* Joseph Gershenson; *editor,* Edward Curtiss. Running time: 83 minutes.

A formula action drama offered Poitier his third screen role, a patronizing film with the authors paying lip service to better race relations. *Red Ball Express,* which rolled off Universal-International's assembly lines, took an exciting, true, wartime incident and buried it beneath backlot banalities, cliche situations and stereotyped characters. During World War II, the famed Red Ball Express, the non stop, high-speed trucking outfit

Brawling with Hugh O'Brian as Charles Drake watches.

which was the pride of the Army Transportation Corp and was a mostly black outfit led by white officers, was ordered to resupply General Patton's tanks that had outrun their supply lines following the allied breakthrough at St. Lo in France and were in danger of being annihilated. The real story of how the Express caught up with Patton's men and prevented the collapse of the allied offensive offers thrilling adventure. What emerged in *Red Ball Express,* filmed at Fort Eustis in Virginia, was a B-movie wartime potboiler given "A" status simply by the presence of the company's stalwart Jeff Chandler in the lead.

Under the guidance of director Budd Boetticher, then doing workhorse duty for Universal-International, the film managed to have some pacing, a sense of humor and the standard heroics, plus an intense, dedicated Sidney Poitier performance while he was marking time until his Hollywood career got its needed and inevitable impetus.

The screenplay which John Michael Hayes turned out on demand from producer Aaron Rosenberg offered the predictable frontline look at men in war, with the Red Ball Express unit inexplicably converted to an almost completely lily-white outfit under Jeff Chandler's hardline command. The company included the expected soldier types—the griping goldbricks, the enlisted men who ogle the U.S.O. girls, the top-kick who gains his men's grudging respect, etc. Sidney Poitier is cast as an excessively race-conscious corporal who anticipates prejudice both from his tough C.O. (Chandler), whose brusqueness is caused simply by the pressures of command, and his first sergeant (Alex Nicol), a redneck who works off his long imagined grudge against Chandler by venting his hatred of blacks on Poitier and the other Negroes in the outfit.

In the course of the simplistic story, Chandler manages to whip his unit into shape, save Patton's advance, reconcile his differences with his sergeant, and win over the disgruntled blacks in his command. Reviewing for *The New York Times,* critic Oscar Godbout said: "There is nothing in this film to recommend, with the possible exception of Sidney Poitier and Jeff Chandler. The director, for the record, was Budd Boetticher, and we imagine this film is one he'd prefer to forget."

Joe Pihodna, writing in the *New York Herald Tribune,* found more merit, calling *Red Ball Express* "a unique film because it frankly discusses the question of color prejudice in the service. The Negro's attitudes and his treatment by certain of his fellow soldiers are brought into sharp focus here." *Films and Filming* observed that "Poitier and Jeff Chandler grapple gamely with an unimaginative script which relies too heavily on stock American military movie cliches."

In the opinion of *Variety*'s critic: "There is nothing new in the story to bolster the good idea behind the pic. However it does have the pace of good pulp fiction . . . and is cloaked in enough standard action for less discriminating audiences." *Hollywood Reporter* spoke of Aaron Rosenberg's "fine production," Budd Boetticher's "excellent direction," the screenplay's "smooth handling of the delicate race question, which is treated with such good taste that it never becomes a soapbox oration." The paper concluded: "Sidney Poitier adroitly commands sympathetic understanding as the colored soldier."

Sidney strikes Hugh O'Brian, as Cindy Garner, Jacqueline Duval, Bubber Johnson and Frank Chase react.

With Patricia Breslin, Dane Clark and Bram Nossen.

# Go, Man, Go!

United Artists                              1954

THE CAST:

THE HARLEM GLOBETROTTERS as Themselves,* and *Abe Saperstein*, DANE CLARK; *Sylvia Saperstein*, Patricia Breslin; *Inman Jackson*, Sidney Poitier; *Zack Leader*, Edmon Ryan; *James Willoughby*, Bram Nossen; *Irma Jackson*, Ruby Dee; *Papa Saperstein*, Anatol Winogradoff; *Mama Saperstein*, Celia Boodkin; *Appraiser*, Lew Hearn; *Slim*, Slim Gaillard; *Fay Saperstein*, Carol Sinclair; *Master of Ceremonies*, Mort Marshall; *Sam*, Ellsworth Wright; *Secretary*, Jean Shore; *Ticket Seller*, Frieda Altman; *Bathing Beauties*, Jule Benedic and Jerry Hauer; *Sports Announcers*, Marty Glickman and Bill Stern.

CREDITS:

A Sirod Production. *Producer*, Anton M. Leader; *associate producer*, Mike Shore; *director*, James

With Dane Clark.

---

* Reece "Goose" Tatum, Marques Haynes, "Sweetwater" Clifton, Ermer Robinson, Joshua Grider, J. C. Gipson, Willie Gardner, Walter Dukes, Joel McRae, Bill Garrett, Clarence Wilson, Bill Brown.

Wong Howe; *screenplay*, Arnold Becker; *photography*, William Steiner; *music*, Alex North; *title song*, Sy Oliver and Mike Shore; *sung by* Slim Gaillard; *art director*, Howard Bay; *editor*, Faith Elliott. Running time: 83 minutes.

As dramatic fiction told in pseudo-documentary style, *Go, Man, Go!*, an independent, shoestring production tracing the rise of the famed Harlem Globetrotters, is a well-intentioned little item which generally was sloughed off to the bottom half of double bills (although it did get a Broadway showcase, premiering in the spring of 1954). The film is memorable in cinema history for a variety of reasons: it offers an early Sidney Poitier performance (as center Inman Jackson, one of the original Globetrotters); it marked the directing debut of veteran cinematographer James Wong Howe, and remains his only feature film as

With Dane Clark and Patricia Breslin.

a director; it features an interesting, if forgotten, score by composer Alex North; it spotlights the actual stars of the amazing Harlem Globetrotters,

With Dane Clark, Edmon Ryan and Celia Boodkin.

demonstrating their mastery of the game as well as their astounding ball-juggling and inimitable clowning.

In addition to the Globetrotters themselves (given, as a group, top billing), *Go, Man, Go!* stars Dane Clark in a first-rate portrayal of Abe Saperstein, the driving force behind the team. And in Arnold Becker's somewhat romanticized screenplay, the story of Saperstein's struggles to guide his boys to fame and success develops cleanly without preachment while clearly implying that the main opposition to the Globetrotters' participation in professional basketball is because of the team's color.

*Go, Man, Go!* follows Saperstein's tireless efforts to guide the Globetrotters to fame and success, beginning in the late 1920s when he loads his scraggly group of players into a broken down Pierce Arrow and, as the only substitute player, barnstorms through the country, hustling pick-up games, tenaciously striving to get his boys into big arenas in major cities. With the encouragement of his wife, Sylvia (Patricia Breslin), and his sportswriter friend, Zack Leader (Edmon Ryan), Saperstein single-mindedly vows to make a place in organized basketball for an all-Negro team. After a series of rebuffs, he manages to book a crowded, ambitious schedule against the toughest opposition in the minors, but finally is compelled to cancel date after date because of team injuries and fatigue.

To overcome the problem, Saperstein arranges with his men to work a platoon system, having the players take turns at clowning with the ball during games so that the others can rest. The clowning is a stroke of genius, catching the public's fancy and rapidly establishing the Globetrotters as a unique box-office attraction. Despite the team's success, however, pro basketball officials, led by James Willoughby (Bram Nossen), refuse to recognize the Globetrotters and try to squeeze Saperstein out of organized basketball by banning the team from a series of professional tournaments on technicalities and pressuring arena operators into canceling dates arranged by Saperstein.

To retaliate, the team's scrappy manager/promoter comes up with independent financing and books a series of games in football stadiums in direct competition with the big league games, intimidating Willoughby and his operators. In a change of tactics, Willoughby sends out word to

With Dane Clark and The Harlem Globetrotters.

With Edmon Ryan, Dane Clark, Patricia Breslin, Anatol Winogradoff and Lew Hearn.

allow the Globetrotters to enter the championship tournament, and despite unfair handicaps, the team battles its way through elimination rounds and beats the Chicago Majors in the final game in 1940. The championship assures the Globetrotters' future and international fame.

Unlike a previous film on the Harlem Globetrotters, entitled unimaginatively *The Harlem Globetrotters* (1951), the James Wong Howe version of the team's rise was well received by the critics. *Time* Magazine felt that it was "probably as interesting a movie as can be made about the game of basketball . . . a good, fast script by Arnold Becker hits only the biggest bumps on the Globetrotter's road to glory." Critic Bosley Crow-ther referred to it as "a lively little independent picture . . . spiced with a lot of colorful action by the actual stars of the famous ball-juggling team, this effort rates solid approval as a creditable professional sports romance."

*Variety* was one of the few papers which took note of Sidney Poitier's participation, calling him "good as Inman Jackson, an original 'Trotter' star who sticks with the coach through all the trouble." Writer Dennis John Hall, surveying Poitier's career in *Films and Filming* in 1971, felt that "the film is of considerable interest . . . for Sidney Poitier's spirited efforts to rise above some of the worst dialogue he has ever had to contend with."

With Patricia Breslin, Edmon Ryan, Dane Clark and Anatol Winogradoff.

With Glenn Ford.

# Blackboard Jungle

Metro-Goldwyn-Mayer                 1955

THE CAST:

*Richard Dadier*, GLENN FORD; *Anne Dadier*, ANNE FRANCIS; *Jim Murdock*, LOUIS CALHERN; *Lois Hammond*, Margaret Hayes; *Mr. Warneke*, John Hoyt; *Joshua Edwards*, Richard Kiley; *Mr. Halloran*, Emile Meyer; *Prof. A. R. Kraal*, Basil Ruysdael; *Dr. Bradley*, Warner Anderson; *Gregory Miller*, Sidney Poitier; *Artie West*, Vic Morrow; *Belazi*, Dan Terranova; *Pete V. Morales*, Rafael Campos; *Emmanuel Stoker*, Paul Mazursky; *Detective*, Horace McMahon; *Santini*, Jameel Farah (Jamie Farr); *DeLica*, Danny Dennis; *Levy*, Chris Randall; *Tomita*, Yoshi Tomita; *Carter*, Gerald Phillips; *Lou Savoldi*, David Alpert; *Miss Panucci*, Dorothy Neumann; *Miss Brady*, Henny Backus; *Mr. Lefkowitz*, Paul Hoffman; *George Katz*, Robert Foulk; and Tom McKee, John Erman, Richard Deacon, Manuel Paris.

CREDITS:

*Producer*, Pandro S. Berman; *director*, Richard

As Gregory Miller.

[ 58 ]

With Glenn Ford.

Brooks; *screenplay,* Richard Brooks; based on the novel by Evan Hunter; *photography,* Russell Harlan; *music adaptation,* Charles Wolcott; *song* "Rock Around the Clock" performed by Bill Haley and His Comets; *assistant director,* Joel Freeman; *art directors,* Cedric Gibbons and Randall Duell; *editor,* Ferris Webster. CinemaScope. Running time: 101 minutes.

*Blackboard Jungle* rekindled Hollywood's interest in Sidney Poitier, who had been "back East" dabbling in television and trying to hustle a living running a ribs joint in Harlem. The film's release in the spring of 1955 brought a steady stream of producers pounding on Poitier's door. He had been discovered at last and was to become a permanent fixture on the screen, initially, despite his sincere efforts, the film industry's showcase— as one screen historian noted—for its integration intentions.

A crisp, ugly-but-honest melodrama-cum-social document about juvenile delinquency, strikingly directed by Richard Brooks who also had culled the taut screenplay from Evan Hunter's best-seller, it was realistically acted by Glenn Ford and several other veterans in addition to a cast of chillingly authentic-appearing young actor "hoods." *Blackboard Jungle* quickly joined Stanley Kramer's *The Wild Ones* of the year before as the two prime examples of the screen's fifties preoccupation with the youth rebellion.

Excitingly unreeling to the staccato beat of "Rock Around the Clock," the pioneer rock-n-roll classic by Bill Haley and His Comets, the film burst across the screen with accurate (but screen-laundered) dialogue, relentless hoodlum terror, and standout performances by Sidney Poitier, remarkably effective even past 30 in his portrayal of a teenaged Negro who has had no stimulus to awaken his leadership abilities simply because of his color, and by Vic Morrow, sickeningly vicious as the hopped-up leader of the classroom bullies. Hardly less convincing is Glenn Ford as their embattled teacher, "endowed with the endurance of St. Sebastian, the ingenuity of Horace Mann, and the in-fighting techniques of a Marine commando," as described by critic Robert Hatch in *The Nation.*

Ford is Richard Dadier, who to his classroom of truculent hoodlums becomes "Daddy-O" and "Teach"—both terms becoming part of the day's real life jargon. A young navy vet tackling his first teaching job, he quickly finds himself face to face with a roomful of teenaged savages in a bloody battleground masquerading as a technical high school. Rapidly, he learns of his inability not only to control his class but even to stir the slightest interest in his pupils. Idealistic fellow teacher Joshua Edwards (Richard Kiley) befriends him and tries to warn him of the obstacle course pitfalls; sexy English instructor Lois Hammond (Margaret Hayes, in a sensuous perform-

With Vic Morrow, Glenn Ford and
John Erman.

ance) becomes attracted to the good-looking newcomer to the staff; cynical, sarcastic, Jim Murdock (Louis Calhern), a veteran teacher, provides less encouragement about Dadier's professional abilities; and Warneke (John Hoyt), principal of the jungle, sees his job merely to keep the
animals occupied during school hours.

Early on, Dadier makes the mistake of in-
terrupting a rape attempt on Lois Hammond in a
dimly-lit stairwell by knife wielding Artie West
(Vic Morrow), the self-styled gang leader, and
only arouses the contempt of Artie's followers.
Dadier's halting attempts to break through to his
students leads only to frustration, and soon his
pregnant wife Anne (Anne Francis) is being per-
secuted with obscene phone calls and anonymous
letters hinting that Dadier has been seeing far too
much of Lois after school hours.

Gradually, the incredibly patient Dadier and
Gregory Miller (Poitier), one of his Negro students, develop a mutual respect and somewhat
uneasy accord. In Miller, Dadier spots a certain
alertness, an undeveloped intellect lying dormant
because of a lack of self-confidence, and definite
leadership possibilities. It is in the final showdown, in which Dadier is forced to take Artie
West's switchblade away from him and humiliate
him in front of his gang, when only Miller comes

With Glenn Ford.

to his teacher's aid. Whether Dadier really could gain the respect of his whole class or just a temporary truce simply by unarming the school's toughest hood is problematical, but the film ends on a positive note.

In a basically unsympathetic part, Poitier went against precedent, at least by screen standards, by playing a bad guy (though repentant) in a multiracial film, while offering a stunningly intelligent and strangely compelling performance. "As a straight melodrama of juvenile violence," critic Bosley Crowther observed, "this is a vivid and hair-raising film . . . as hard and penetrating as a nail." About the actors, Crowther said: "Vic Morrow, as the most rebellious pupil, is a sinister replica of a Marlon Brando roughneck, and Sidney Poitier, as the approachable Negro, is exceedingly sharp and alert. As individuals, these two performers would seem superlatively realistic types."

In *Saturday Review,* Otis L. Guernsey, Jr., referred to the film's Gregory Miller as "an enigmatic Negro boy played skillfully by Sidney Poitier," while Herb Rau, in the *Miami Daily News,* called Poitier "outstanding" and felt that "much of the suspense value in the film is due directly to his fine performance." *Newsweek,* calling *Black-board Jungle,* "a bitter pill coated with excitement," wrote: "Particularly good are Ford as the embattled teacher, Vic Morrow as the enemy, and Sidney Poitier as the lonely Negro boy who becomes the ally."

In the *New York Herald Tribune,* reviewer William K. Zinsser found that "Sidney Poitier does a sensitive job as a Negro of great promise, whose truculent manner turns every class into a nightmare," and Marjorie Adams, critic for the *Boston Globe,* cheered: "Sidney Poitier is fine . . . outlining what is certainly the most dimensional portrait of a Negro ever seen in an American movie."

The film's instant fame as a violent treatise on American teen violence, however, also had its backlash effects. The industry was pressured into helping suppress its release abroad because of its "distorted" views of this country, and the State Department even had it banned from the 1955 Venice Film Festival. In addition, several critical sources, while generally praising the performers, concurred with the findings of *Films In Review* that "it has cinematic power but a seriously confused viewpoint, as its idealistic teacher finds *all* of his students are overtly contemptuous and *all* are either vicious or criminal or both."

With Glenn Ford.

[ 61 ]

With Brandon DeWilde.

# Goodbye, My Lady

Warner Bros.                    1956

THE CAST:

*Uncle Jesse,* WALTER BRENNAN; *Cash Evans,* PHIL HARRIS; *Skeeter,* BRANDON DE WILDE; *Gates Watson,* SIDNEY POITIER; *Waldon Grover,* William Hopper; *Aunt Bonnie Dew,* Louise Beavers; and George Cleveland, Joe Brooks.

CREDITS:

A Batjac Production. *Producer/director,* William A. Wellman; *screenplay,* Sid Fleischman; based on the novel by James Street; *photography,* William H. Clothier; *music,* Laurindo Almeida (guitar) and George Field (harmonica); *song* "When Your Boy Becomes a Man" by Don Powell and Moris Erby; *second unit photography,* Archie Stout; *art director,* Donald A. Peters; *editor,* Fred MacDowell. Running time: 94 minutes.

William Wellman's heartwarming, family oriented film version of James Street's 1954 bestselling novel offered Sidney Poitier to moviegoers in his last minor role—as the college-educated confidante of young Brandon De Wilde, the backwoods lad who finds a rare Basenji hound in the heart of the swamp behind the small cabin he shares with his weatherbeaten uncle (Walter Brennan).

Hoping to create a boy-and-his-dog adventure in a league with *The Yearling* or *My Friend Flicka,* Wellman turned out a gentle, magnificently photographed (by William Clothier) little film for John Wayne's Batjac Productions. A small cast, working on location in Georgia's Pascagoula Swamp, held its own in the presence of the extraordinary animal around which the story revolves—a dog that sheds tears when unhappy and laughs rather than barks. In the 1950s, however, as in virtually every film era, the so-called "family movie" was firmly in the Disney domain, and, as Wellman later wrote, "I am just not Disney." *Goodbye, My Lady* was dismissed as a laudable failure, despite a passel of awards from a diversity of groups, from the D.A.R. onward. In Manhattan, in fact, the Wellman film was unable even to receive a first-run play date.

The story finds Skeeter (De Wilde), a tow-headed lad, enjoying a shiftless, easygoing existence with his kindly, illiterate Uncle Jesse, who spends his days teaching the boy the proper moral values of life. The teenaged youth one day comes upon a strange looking dog lost in the swamp, and boy and dog soon become inseparable. Skeeter begins the task of breaking his new pet, Lady, of the useless instinct to kill swamp rats and the outlaw impulse of preying on chickens. Over the months, he develops Lady into a first-rate hunting dog whose phenomenal powers of scent enable her to point quail at sixty yards.

Through his friend, Cash Evans (Phil Harris), the gruff storekeeper, Skeeter discovers that Lady is more than merely a swamp hound. A newspaper ad in the lost-and-found column describes the dog as a Basenji, a rare breed that goes back to Biblical times, and offers a handsome reward for its return. Skeeter's pal, Gates Watson (Sidney Poitier), a farmer from across the river, also has read the ad and wants the reward being offered, but is unwilling to disappoint Skeeter even when he learns that it was Lady who has been raiding his chicken coop.

The Basenji becomes the symbol for Skeeter's first adult decision when Waldon Grover (William Hopper), manager of the kennels of a wealthy sportsman from up North, shows up to claim Lady, and Uncle Jesse leaves the choice of returning the dog in the hands of his nephew. The idea of parting with Lady breaks Skeeter's heart, but Uncle Jesse's training prompts him to do the honest thing. When he returns to Cash's store after giving Lady back to Grover, Skeeter is offered a cup of black coffee, indicating he has become a man—in the eyes of both Cash and Uncle Jesse—and able to take emotional punishment.

Critic Philip T. Hartung, writing in *Commonweal,* thought that "director William Wellman . . . merits considerable praise for his careful handling of his touching story . . . which might easily have become an exercise in sentiment instead of an honest study of a boy's development." Less satisfied was Britain's *Films and Filming,* which felt that "the experienced cast and director have little to show for themselves, and the film takes 95 minutes to unfold what is essentially a story of second-feature proportions."

*Variety* alone even mentioned Poitier's participation, saying simply "Sidney Poitier and Louise Beavers score as Negro friends" (they played nephew and aunt), and judging: "Besides posing a good moral lesson, it is film entertainment that can be enjoyed by all, but is particularly recommendable for family audiences."

Writing of *Goodbye, My Lady* years later, William Wellman confessed: "It was a financial fiasco. I don't know why. The story was beautiful, the performances superb: Walter Brennan, Brandon De Wilde, Phil Harris, Bill Hopper, Sidney Poitier, and the cutest, gamest little dog you ever saw. How could you miss? But I did . . . I am proud to have made the best children's picture of the year, but why didn't the kids go see it? Why didn't they drag their mothers and fathers to the theater?" And why did Wellman fail to include it in the filmography at the end of his autobiography? Nor is the film mentioned in the several published biographies of Sidney Poitier. Poitier himself never has made a published comment on his role in the film.

With Yvonne DeCarlo and Clark Gable.

# Band of Angels

Warner Bros.                                    1957

THE CAST:

*Hamish Bond,* CLARK GABLE; *Amantha Starr,* YVONNE DeCARLO; *Rau-Ru,* SIDNEY POITIER; *Ethan Sears,* Efrem Zimbalist, Jr.; *Charles de Marigny,* Patric Knowles; *Seth Parton,* Rex Reason; *Captain Canavan,* Torin Thatcher; *Miss Idell,* Andrea King; *Mr. Calloway,* Ray Teal; *Jimmee,* Russell Evans; *Michele,* Carolle Drake; *Aaron Starr,* William Forrest; *Mr. Stuart,* Raymond Bailey; *Dollie,* Tommie Moore; *Sukie,* Zelda Cleaver; *General Butler,* Marshall Bradford; *Shad,* Joe Narcisse; *Budge,* Juanita Moore; *Manty (as a child),* Noreen Corcoran; *Runaway,* Jack Williams; *Helper,* Charles Heard; *Gillespie (overseer),* Roy Barcroft; *Jacob (coachman),* Curtis Hamilton; *Sheriff,* Jim Hayward; *Mrs. Hopewell,* Riza Royce; *Minister,* Guy Wilkerson; *Mrs. Morton,* Ann Doran; and Mayo Loizeaux, Carla Henry, June-Ellen Anthony, William Fawcett, Jean G. Harvey, Alfred Meissner, Dan White, Larry Blake, Ewing Mitchell, Forbes Murray, Joe Gilbert, Robert Clarke, Maurice Marsac, Gizelle D'Arc, Bob Steele, Zon Murray, Morgan Shean, Myron Cook, X Brands, William Hudson, William Schallert, Charles Horvath, Anthony Ghazlo, Madame Sul-te-wan.

CREDITS:

*Director,* Raoul Walsh; *screenplay,* John Twist, Ivan Goff and Ben Roberts; based on the novel by Robert Penn Warren; *photography,* Lucien Ballard; *music,* Max Steiner; *art director,* Franz Bachelin; *editor,* Folmar Blangsted. WarnerScope and WarnerColor. Running time: 127 minutes.

With Patric Knowles.

In Raoul Walsh's wobbly costume epic adaptation of Robert Penn Warren's old South novel, *Band of Angels,* Sidney Poitier turned up resolutely—forty-five minutes into the proceedings—as Clark Gable's high-steppin' "boss nigger," brought back from Africa as an infant by then-slaver Gable, reared as his son, and educated beyond his station.

A lackluster melodrama about miscegenation which strove mightily to duplicate the scope if not the popularity of *Gone With the Wind,* the film was completely miscast with an aging (then 56) Clark Gable, still quite dashing, however, as a Southern gentleman; fading glamour girl Yvonne DeCarlo, rather unconvincing in her mid-thirties trying to pass as a teenaged Kentucky belle; and Sidney Poitier, suppressing his obvious acting talents, as the strong-willed slave. "Fanciers of awful movies won't want to miss this choice specimen," wrote William K. Zinsser in the *New York Herald Tribune.* "It's like a parody of antebellum dramas. There are a hundred laughs in the florid speeches, the incredible acting, the bland direction, the bombastic music, the involuted plot."

Hamish Bond (Gable), a reformed slave trader turned New Orleans plantation owner, buys at auction a stunning octoroon, Amanda Starr (Yvonne DeCarlo). She was the daughter of a wealthy Kentucky planter who, returning from finishing school to attend his funeral, learns that her mother had been a Negro slave, and, according to custom, is sold as chattel with her

With Patric Knowles and Yvonne DeCarlo.

dead father's plantation to pay off his debts. Degraded by Calloway (Ray Teal), a lecherous slave trader who tries to rape her, she threatens suicide but is rushed to the auction block. Bond's $5000 offer for her, to calm his own guilt complex about being a former slaver and to save her from a humiliating future, is too rich for the other bidders, and he brings her to his home to join his creole mistress Michele (Carolle Drake) and the other slaves in fairly elegant living.

At Bond's walled home in the center of New Orleans, Amanda meets Rau-Ru, Bond's handsome Negro retainer. He had been rescued from certain death years before by Bond but resents his master's kindness and patiently awaits the day when troops from the North will come to

With Yvonne DeCarlo and
Patric Knowles.

With Carolle Drake.

free the slaves. Amanda, meanwhile, is surprised at not being relegated to Bond's slave quarters but rather treated as a lady. Nevertheless, she takes the opportunity, during a shopping trip in town with Michele, to make an escape attempt.

With Clark Gable.

Rau-Ru brings her back. Eventually, Amanda lets herself succumb to Bond's charms during a flashing (symbolic) thunderstorm.

When the War Between the States erupts, Rau-Ru goes North and joins the Union army, returning when New Orleans is taken. Circumstances force a confrontation between Rau-Ru and his former benefactor, but the ex-slave cannot forget his debt to Bond and is unable to turn him in. With his help, Bond and Amanda are able to escape together.

Warner Bros.' advertising department, after serious discussions, chose to sell the film with this copy campaign: "He bought her . . . she was his! He bought a beautiful slave and made her mistress of his giant plantation! He knew greed at Rio Bongo, the debauchery at Pointe du Loup, the treachery at Belle Helene—but nobody really knew him!" Gable himself undoubtedly chuckled. So did many of the critics. *Newsweek* wrote: "Here is a movie so bad that it must be seen to be disbelieved . . . the plot, originally conceived by the novelist Robert Penn Warren, was delivered by the electric typewriters of no less than three Hollywood scriptwriters . . . Look away, look away!"

Bosley Crowther called the film "flamboyant melodrama in big, juicy, WarnerColored blobs, with nary a thoughtful reflection at any point in the vast, romantic scene . . . Sidney Poitier is lofty and aggressive in the badly balanced role of a favored slave." Archer Winsten, critic for the *New York Post,* noted that "there are side issues concerning slavery and the pride of an educated slave, nobly played by Sidney Poitier, that indicate a picture trying to elevate itself above soap opera histrionics." And in *The New Yorker,* reviewer John McCarten felt: "Mr. Poitier, playing a noble and educated slave, is so lofty in attitude that he couldn't be touched, spiritually speaking, by Tenzing."

*Variety* found: "As co-star, Sidney Poitier, young Negro actor, impresses as Gable's educated protege." And Dorothy Masters, in the New York *Daily News,* merely said: "Sidney Poitier lends his talents to the difficult role of a Negro in rebellion against his status as a pampered slave."

With Rock Hudson.

# Something of Value

Metro-Goldwyn-Mayer                    1957

THE CAST:

*Peter McKenzie,* ROCK HUDSON; *Holly Keith,* DANA WYNTER; *Kimani,* SIDNEY POITIER; *Elizabeth Newton,* Wendy Hiller; *Njogu,* Juano Hernandez; *Leader,* William Marshall; *Jeff Newton,* Robert Beatty; *Henry McKenzie,* Walter Fitzgerald; *Joe Matson,* Michael Pate; *Lathela,* Ivan Dixon; *Karanja,* Ken Renard; *Witch Doctor,* Samadu Jackson; *Adam Marenga,* Frederick O'Neal; *Kipi,* Paul Thompson; *Game Warden,* Lester Matthews; *Little Henry,* Gary Stafford; *Little Jeff,* Duncan Richardson; *Midwife,* Madame Sul-te-wan; *Crown Consul,* Leslie Denison; *Wanjiru,* Barbara Foley; *Cook,* Carl Christian; and Bob Anderson, Bruce Lester, Wesly Bly, Pauline Myers, Kim Hamilton, Barry Bernard, John Dodsworth, Ottola Nesmith, Morgan Roberts, Tommie Moore, Juanita Moore, Barbara Morrison, Anna Mabry, John Alderson, Charles R. Keane, Jack Lynn, Ike Jones, Myrtle Anderson, Darby Jones, Naaman Brown.

CREDITS:

*Producer,* Pandro S. Berman; *director,* Richard Brooks; *screenplay,* Richard Brooks; based on the novel by Robert C. Ruark; *photography,* Russell Harlan; *music,* Miklos Rosza; *art directors,* William A. Horning and Edward Carfagno; *editor,* Ferris Webster. Running time: 113 minutes.

While Richard Brooks' *Blackboard Jungle* never made it to the Venice Film Festival because of outside pressure, his *Something of Value* did, and Sidney Poitier's performance won him a special citation. Poitier went native for the second time, accepting third billing (in type one-third the size of Rock Hudson, and even just half as large as the film's female lead, Dana Wynter), in this potent dramatization--with a few soap opera touches--of Robert Ruark's 1955 bestseller about racial turmoil in East Africa. Strong, vivid, in some scenes uncomfortably graphic, *Something of Value* proved harrowing screen fare while

As Kimani.

offering another electrically charged Poitier characterization as a native youth, reared by colonial whites and driven into violence by desperation and to his death by treachery after having been robbed of his land and traditions and left without things to cherish and esteem—without something of value.

"If only to watch one startling performance," *Newsweek* enthused, *"Something of Value* is worth a visit. The actor: Sidney Poitier, who plays Kimani, a Kikuyu torn between his respect for the British family he grew up with and his allegiance to the cult that promises an end to white supremacy . . . With his role in *Something of Value,* Poitier has turned into a full-fledged star."

In Brooks' film, which straddles the thin line between entertainment and sermon, Kimani and Peter McKenzie (Rock Hudson), a native boy and a white youth, are raised almost as brothers, but are torn apart when Kimani is humiliated by the intolerance of the settlers, and his aging, witchcraft worshipping father (John Akar) is jailed by the whites. Kimani falls in with a Mau Mau group, headed by Njogu (Juano Hernandez), whose sworn intention is to drive the British from Kenya. As the violence escalates, however, Kimani's hatred of the whites is gradually offset by his disgust at the bestiality of the Mau Mau movement, especially after his first test: to massacre the white family that had reared him. He is unable to slaughter McKenzie's

With Juano Hernandez and
Frederick O'Neal.

sister, Elizabeth (Wendy Hiller), although his men kill her husband and children and seriously wound her.

The fearful Mau Mau carnage also has taken its toll on McKenzie himself. He has changed from a man with respect and sympathy for the natives to an avenging fighter determined to match terror for terror, a transformation which brings about a rift with his wife, Holly (Dana Wynter), who has implored him to take her away from Africa. After the Mau Mau attack on his sister, McKenzie assumes the task of tracking down the band of killers and convincing Kimani to surrender and make peace. He locates Kimani in the mountain wilderness and talks his old friend into bringing his followers down from the hills, but a group of hot-headed colonials, led by Joe Matson (Michael Pate), ambushes the natives. Kimani's wife is killed, but he manages to escape with his infant son.

Once again, McKenzie takes up the chase and ultimately finds Kimani, but is unable to convince the latter that he (McKenzie) was not responsible for the ambush. In desperate hand-to-hand struggle, Kimani is killed when he falls into a spiked elephant pit. Tortured by the events, McKenzie takes Kimani's son and returns to Holly, who is in Nairobi with Elizabeth, awaiting the birth of the latter's child. If it is a boy, McKenzie vows, Kimani's son will be raised as his brother.

"It misses being a great film," said Bosley

With Wendy Hiller.

With Frederick O'Neal and
Ken Renard.

[ 69 ]

As Kimani.

Crowther, "because its story follows conventional lines. It is more sentimental than realistic—and because its contours are somewhat studio-blurred." *The New York Times* critic continued: "Sidney Poitier gives a stirring, strong performance as the emotion-torn black friend. It is his display of pounding passions and the frequent bursts of shocking savagery that throw shafts of sharp illumination through this notably black-and-white film."

*Variety* found that "the cast generally is good, with Sidney Poitier . . . delivering an outstanding portrayal. He carries the picture and gives it power and strength as one watches his resentment grow and finally explode into an orgy of killing. The performance has depth and great understanding, and rates plenty kudos."

Robert Hatch wrote in *The Nation:* "It is not a remarkable picture, though exciting as a story and well enough acted by Rock Hudson, Sidney Poitier, William Marshall, Wendy Hiller and the others, but it does make a commendable effort to show what the issues are and to divide the human decency evenly between the whites and blacks." *Time* commented that "[it] makes an intelligent effort to live up to its title," while *Commonweal*'s critic, Philip T. Hartung, considered it "forceful though hard-to-take . . . expertly played by Rock Hudson and Sidney Poitier" but felt that "it covers too complex a subject and it depends too often for its effect on cruelty that is almost unbearable to watch."

The harshest criticism came from *Films in Review,* which called the movie "anti-West propaganda . . . not only a prejudiced aspersion of the white man, and a worthless report on the Mau Mau, but an unbelievable piece of clap-trap melodrama."

*Something of Value* was reissued a half dozen years after its initial release. It then was retitled, for no special reason, *Africa Ablaze.*

As Kimani holding his infant son.

With John Cassavetes.

# Edge of the City

Metro-Goldwyn-Mayer                    1957

THE CAST:

*Axel North,* JOHN CASSAVETES; *Tommy Tyler,* SIDNEY POITIER; *Charley Malik,* Jack Warden; *Ellen Wilson,* Kathleen Maguire; *Lucy Tyler,* Ruby Dee; *Mr. Nordmann,* Robert Simon; *Mrs. Nordmann,* Ruth White; *Davis,* William A. Lee; *Brother,* Val Avery; *Detective,* John Kellogg; *Wallace,* David Clarke; *Lucy's Mother,* Estelle Hemsley; *Old Stevedore,* Charles Jordon; *Night Boss,* Ralph Bell; *Tommy's son,* Perry Green.

CREDITS:

A Jonathan Production. *Producer,* David Susskind; *associate producer,* Jim DiGanci; *director,* Martin Ritt; *screenplay,* Robert Alan Aurthur; based on his *television play "A Man Is Ten Feet Tall;"\*photography,* Joseph Brun; *music,* Leonard Rosenman; *art director,* Richard Sylbert;

---

\* Telecast on Philco Playhouse (NBC 10.2.55) with Don Murray and Sidney Poitier in the leads.

*assistant director,* Don Kranze; *editor,* Sidney Meyers. Running time: 86 minutes.

Long deserved star status came at last to Sidney Poitier in *Edge of the City* in which he recreated the TV role of the Negro railway yard worker which had won him the Sylvania Award as the Best Actor on Television during 1955-1956. (On television, as the final production of the prestigious, fondly remembered Philco/Goodyear Playhouse, it was called *A Man Is Ten Feet Tall,* the title by which the movie was known outside of the United States.)

The film, displaying Poitier's special ability to create a character of nobility and humanity, marked the theatrical feature debut of both director Martin Ritt and writer Robert Alan Aurthur, who had perfected their respective crafts in the television vineyards. It also brought producer David Susskind to filmmaking. Poitier, however, was the only actor from the original teleplay to appear in the film (the TV roles played by Don

With Jack Warden and John Cassavetes.

As Tommy Tyler.

Murray and Martin Balsam were taken in the movie by John Cassavetes and Jack Warden).

Poitier is Tommy Tyler, a gangling, bop-talking, full-of-life freightcar loader in New York City's railroad yards, who befriends a sullen white neurotic, Axel Nordmann (Cassavetes), a down-and-out army deserter at odds with his father and plagued by a nagging guilt about his brother's death. The good-humored Tommy takes it upon himself to redeem Axel, and with his wife, Lucy (Ruby Dee), Tommy welcomes Axel into his home and introduces him to school teacher Ellen Wilson (Kathleen Maguire). The friendship be-tween the two men, however, antagonizes Charley Malik (Jack Warden), their brutal, bigoted gang boss, who resents the fact that Axel would rather work alongside a Negro than on his (Charley's) own crew, especially after Charley had gone out on a limb to get Alex the job in the first place. Tossing constant epithets at Tommy and goading Axel mercilessly, Charley eventually forces a showdown, but when Axel refuses to fight, Tommy takes his place, and in a vicious, cold blooded battle with loading hooks, is killed by Charley. Then threatening to expose Axel as a deserter, Charley forces him to remain silent

With Kathleen Maguire,
John Cassavetes and Perry Green.

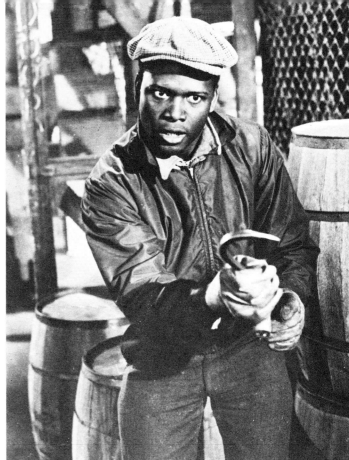

With John Cassavetes.

As Tommy Tyler.

about the fight when the police make their investigation.

When Axel refuses to do anything to avenge Tommy's killing, the latter's widow berates him for deserting a friend and suggests that the reason for his decision not to act is that her husband had been black. Following much soul searching, Axel goes to his dad (Robert Simon) for a reconciliation, tells Ellen of his plans, and then seeks out

Charley Malik, confronts him in a desperate struggle, turns him over to the police, and surrenders on the desertion charges, knowing that his family and Ellen are standing by him.

Various critics (among them Bosley Crowther) noted the many similarities between *Edge of the City* and *On the Waterfront*—the tongue-tied hero, the bullying boss, the shy girlfriend, the fighting priest (here a Negro), the knockdown

With John Cassavetes, Ruby Dee and Kathleen Maguire.

With John Cassavetes.

climactic battle between star and antagonist—as well as how patronizing the film was, especially in its interracial discourse in the various sequences in Tommy's apartment, in the park across the street, on the loading docks, etc. Oversimplified as it was—and as well-intentioned—*Edge of the City* still impresses as a courageous, literate film, beautifully acted by both Poitier and Cassavetes, with Jack Warden and Ruby Dee, in lesser roles, not far behind, and effectively directed by Martin Ritt.

In her four star rave in the New York *Daily News,* critic Dorothy Masters wrote of Poitier: "The superb sensitivity and projection apparent in *Edge of the City* offers a challenge few can hope to equal in a long, long time . . . [and] his splendid characterization is also a triumph of craftsmanship and synchronization." *Variety* called the movie "a courageous, thought provoking and exciting film [that] marks a milestone in the history of the screen in its presentation of an American Negro," and then noted: "Sidney Poitier turns in the most distinguished of his many first-rate characterizations."

In the *New York Herald Tribune,* William K. Zinsser enthused that Poitier "is so engaging . . . that it's impossible not to believe in him completely. With this performance, Poitier matures into an actor of stature. His Negro is a man of deceptive simplicity with his quick smile and exhilarating talk, he can cajole [Cassavetes] out of deep gloom; with a joke, he can stop an ugly fight

before it begins. But underneath he is a man of serious faith and deep strength, and when it's time for him to listen sympathetically or to say something important, he is the finest kind of a friend in need."

Critic Arthur Knight used most of his *Saturday Review* review to praise Cassavetes as the next Marlon Brando, and then concluded simply: "Sidney Poitier is impressive as the Negro freight walloper." *Hollywood Reporter,* on the other hand, cheered: "The young Negro actor, Sidney Poitier, gives an outstanding performance . . . [he] is very moving mostly because he possesses an extraordinarily expressive face and because he is a resourceful and skillful actor."

*Time* viewed: "Surprisingly enough in a Hollywood movie, the Negro is not only the white man's boss, but becomes his best friend and is at all times his superior, possessing greater intelligence, courage, understanding, warmth and adaptability. The mystery is why so engaging a Negro would waste time on so boringly primitive a white man."

One of the few adverse notices came from *Films In Review,* which thought: "Sidney Poitier is not at all believable as the Negro foreman. It's true he is given ridiculous things to say, but this is not his fundamental trouble. The basic truth is Poitier tries more to imitate a white man than to act a part."

With Jack Warden.

With Tony Curtis.

# The Defiant Ones

Stanley Kramer/United Artists        1958

THE CAST:

*John "Joker" Jackson,* TONY CURTIS; *Noah Cullen,* SIDNEY POITIER; *The Woman,* Cara Williams; *Sheriff Max Muller,* Theodore Bikel; *Capt. Frank Gibbons,* Charles McGraw; *Big Sam,* Lon Chaney, Jr.; *Solly,* King Donovan; *Mac,* Claude Akins; *Editor,* Lawrence Dobkin; *Lou Gans,* Whit Bissell; *Angus,* Carl "Alfalfa" Switzer; *The Kid,* Kevin Coughlin; *Joe,* Boyd (Red) Morgan; *Wilson,* Robert Hoy; *State Trooper,* Don Brodie.

CREDITS:

A Stanley Kramer Production. *Producer/director,* Stanley Kramer; *screenplay,* Nathan E. Douglas and Harold Jacob Smith; *photography,* Sam Leavitt; *music,* Ernest Gold; *song* "Long Gone" by W. C. Handy and Chris Smith; *production design,* Rudolph Sternad; *art director,* Fernando Car-

rere; *editor,* Frederic Knudtson. Running time: 97 minutes.

Sidney Poitier's performance as Noah Cullen in *The Defiant Ones* firmed his status at last as a star of the first magnitude. With an unforgettable portrayal in a memorable, and for its time, cou-

With Lon Chaney, Jr. and Tony Curtis.

With Tony Curtis and Cara Williams.

rageous motion picture, both moving and literate, Poitier creates a strong portrait which mirrors, through the pent-up frustrations of one man, the agonies of an entire race. His towering acting job, of course, in no way diminishes the one done by Tony Curtis, the white man on the other end of the two-foot chain which is their common bond. Both actors won Academy Award nominations for their roles (but lost to David Niven that year), and Poitier was named Best Actor at the Berlin Film Festival. The film itself was chosen Best Picture of the Year, and Stanley Kramer as Best Director, by the New York Film Critics.

*The Defiant Ones* was marked with an indelible social significance in its blunt lesson in brotherhood, unfolding against a grim background of hate and prejudice. In the now familiar narrative, Poitier is angry Noah Cullen, a Southern Negro, taunted all of his life and jailed for assaulting a white man who had insulted him. Tony Curtis is sullen, boastful Joker Jackson, a redneck bully who hated saying "Thank you" to anyone. Both are being trucked with fellow prisoners to a work detail, but when the van crashes

With Tony Curtis and Cara Williams.

With Tony Curtis.

into a ditch, the two, shackled together at the wrist by a heavy chain, make a frantic bid for freedom. Slashing at each other with bitter accusations and racial epithets, their only common goal is to escape the sheriff's posse relentlessly pursuing them.

Gradually, the fugitives are forced to set aside personal hatreds and reluctantly work together if they are to survive, as one harrowing experience follows another in their flight. First they must rely on teamwork to clamber out of a clay pit, then ford a turbulent stream and finally attempt to steal food from a small turpentine settlement, where they are captured by an angry mob and only escape being lynched when a former chain gang member named Big Sam (Lon Chaney) sets them free.

With the posse still hot on their heels, Joker and Noah come across a lonely farm inhabited by a lonely, sex starved woman (Cara Williams) and her 11-year-old son (Kevin Coughlin). The woman, whose husband had deserted her eight months earlier, gives them food, lodging and a chisel to break their chain. That night, she seduces Joker and persuades him to take her and her son with him. Noah, still intent on fleeing northward, is directed to a short cut through a swamp by the woman, who then admits to Joker that she has sent the Negro to sure death in quicksand. Realizing that there still is a strong bond between him and Noah, despite the absence of their chain, Joker rejects the woman and his

With Tony Curtis.

chance for freedom, and goes after his comrade. As he heads for the swamp, the boy shoots him in the shoulder.

Joker finds Noah in the swamp and they make their way to a railroad track on the high ground, the posse only minutes behind. Noah grabs onto a freightcar rumbling slowly by, hoists himself up, and then reaches back to grasp Joker's outstretched hand. Joker is too weak from loss of blood, though, and falls to the ground. Noah leaps from the northbound train that guarantees freedom and, crooning the bluesy lament, "Long Gone," awaits the sheriff's men while cradling Joker in his arms.

Director Stanley Kramer has said: "This was a film which was able to fully exploit Sidney Poitier's acting range—from extreme violence to the most utter pathos. Chained together with Tony Curtis, it was Poitier who made the chain a symbol which tied not only the fugitives but also all human beings. He, at first, rebelled against singing in the film—he has the voice of a flat-footed kangaroo. But this worked for us—it was a chain gang voice—and in the end, it broke your heart with its bravado."

The reviews for the film, its two actors, and virtually everything about the production were dazzling. Paul V. Beckley, critic for the *New York Herald Tribune,* called it "one of the finest dramatic films of our time [and] Poitier and Curtis by these roles are undeniably set in the first rank of our screen actors." In *Saturday Review,* Arthur Knight wrote of *The Defiant Ones* as "a distinguished motion picture, a film that Stanley Kramer, the motion picture industry, and every American citizen can be proud of . . . Poitier invests his sympathetic role with dignity, power and overwhelming conviction."

Bosley Crowther described the film in *The New York Times* as "a remarkably apt dramatic visualization of a social idea . . . between the two principal performances, there isn't much room for a choice. Mr. Poitier stands out as the Negro convict and Mr. Curtis is surprisingly good. Both men are intensely dynamic. Mr. Poitier shows a deep and powerful strain of underlying compassion."

*Variety* felt that "the performances . . . are virtually flawless. Poitier, always a capable actor, here turns in probably the best work of his career . . . a cunning, totally intelligent portrayal that rings powerfully true and establishes Poitier as one of the best actors on the screen today." Similarly, Rose Pelswick, reviewing for the *New York Journal-American,* said: "Poitier . . . once again proves himself one of the finest actors on the screen."

*Time* called the movie "savory cinema, free of froth and sharply seasoned" and decided that "if Sidney Poitier's wildeyed, bare-fanged portrayal of Noah Cullen is overwrought, it has at least prodded teen-agitator Tony Curtis into the first performance of his career."

With Tony Curtis.

With Eartha Kitt.

# The Mark of the Hawk

Universal-International                      1958

THE CAST:

*Obam*, SIDNEY POITIER; *Renee*, EARTHA KITT; *Amugu*, JUANO HERNANDEZ; *Bruce Craig*, JOHN McINTIRE; *Steve Gregory*, Patrick Allen; *Prosecutor*, Earl Cameron; *Governor General*, Gerard Heinz; *Kanda*, Clifton Macklin; *Barbara Craig*, Helen Horton; *Sundar Lai*, Marne Maitland; *Inspector Hall*, Ewen Solon; *Magistrate*, Lockwood West; *Dr. Lin*, N. C. Doo; *Ming Tao*, David Goh; *Overholt*, Francis Matthews; *Ben*, Phillip Vickers; *Fred*, Bill Nagy; *First Officer*, Harold Siddons; *Second Officer*, Frederick Treves; *African Doctor*, Lionel Ngakane; *Chinese Officer*, Andy Ho; *Chinese Soldier*, John A. Tinn.

CREDITS:

A Lloyd Young and Associates Production for Film Productions International and World Horizons, Inc. *Executive producer*, W. Burton Martin; *producer*, Lloyd Young; *director*, Michael Audley; *screenplay*, H. Kenn Carmichael; *story*, Lloyd Young; *photography*, Erwin Hiller; *music*, Matyas Seiber; *music director*, Louis Levy conducting the Associated British Studio Orchestra; *song* "This Man Is Mine" by Ken Darby; *sung* by Eartha Kitt; *assistant director*, Rene Dupont; *art director*, Terence Verity; *African location unit director*, Gilbert Gunn; *photography*, Toge Fujihara; *editor*, Edward Jarvis. Superscope and Technicolor. Running time: 84 minutes.

The least seen Sidney Poitier movie is a curious color-and-SuperScope "message" film produced in 1955 by the United Presbyterian Church, with an multiracial cast topped by four actors from the United States and several English performers. *The Mark of the Hawk* is a sincere drama on racism in modern Africa, extolling the teachings of Christ as a solution to the turmoil and arguing that Christianity is the answer to the challenge of Communism. It mixes religious and interracial politics against the rampant Mau Mau terrorism of the day.

    Filmed in Nigeria by an independent, church backed group headed by producer Lloyd Young (who also wrote the original story), it stars Sidney Poitier as Obam, an ambitious young native legislator in colonial Africa who is torn between his ancient background and modern ways. His wife, Renee (Eartha Kitt), his pastor, Amugu (Juano Hernandez), and an American missionary, Bruce Craig (John McIntire), urge him to curb his impatience and use peaceful means in seeking independence for his people. His younger brother, Kanda (Clifton Macklin), and a white agitator, Steve Gregory (Patrick Allen), pressure him to violence, though, and when a dead hawk is found after a terrorist raid, Obam (whose African name means "The Hawk") is accused of being behind it.

Scorning the pleas for restraint by both Reverend Craig and the conservative Governor General (Gerard Heinz), Obam becomes increasingly militant, until the gentle missionary discloses that he previously had faced the same problems as a clergyman in Red China, where his adopted Chinese son was murdered. He convinces Obam that killing is not the answer, and at the urging of Amugu, Obam curbs his anticolonial hatred but is arrested while attempting to stop an outbreak of hostilities between the natives and the colonial settlers, during which Reverend Craig is slain. At Obam's trial, his brother Kanda steps forward and confesses to being the terrorist leader. Obam apologizes to his people and pledges himself to Christianity.

William K. Zinsser, in the *New York Herald Tribune,* called the film "a mature and honest portrait of Africa today. It achieves an almost impossible feat: it sees all sides of the situation fairly and with compassion . . . the picture is astonishing in its thoroughness and balance [and] its actors are strong and earnest. Poitier and Her-

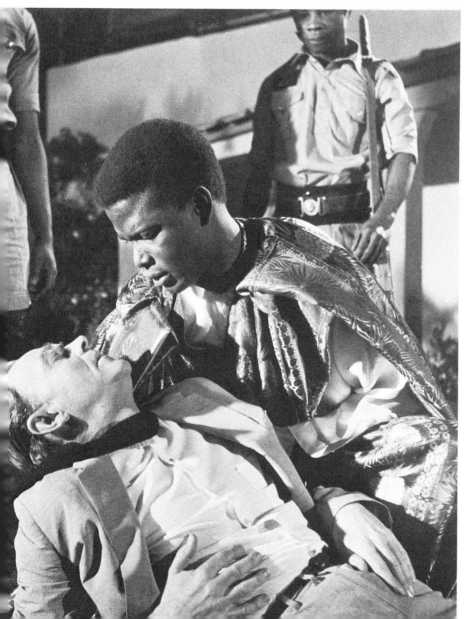

With John McIntire.

As Obam.

nandez are sober and thoughtful Negroes."

Reviewing for the *Chicago Daily Tribune,* Mae Tinee found the leading role "well portrayed by the talented Sidney Poitier" and thought that "the script is a wordy one, but it is intelligent and persuasive, and the acting throughout is excellent." Critic Howard Thompson's opinion in *The New York Times* was that "There have been trimmer and more dramatic films on racism in modern Africa . . . but one moviegoer has yet to hear a better suggestion on the subject: simple adherence to the teachings of Christ . . . The picture's saving grace, literally, is Mr. McIntire, as the producer's mouthpiece for the 'African Church' . . .

Mr. Poitier and Clifton Macklin, as the two symbols of violence, are just as earnest."

*Variety* saw the film as "a weakly scripted political yarn of African yearning for freedom," but observed that "Poitier delivers strongly as the confused legislator."

Most critics commented on the choice of Eartha Kitt, moaning an out-of-place torch song, *This Man Is Mine,* near the film's fade-out, and stunningly attired despite living on the fringes of the wild. Her performance as Poitier's wife, while brief, generally was considered appealing and thoughtful, if rather extraneous. Incredibly, she managed to obtain top billing over Poitier!

With Clifton Macklin and Lockwood West.

With Ruby Dee.

# Virgin Island

Films-Around-the-World                    1958

THE CAST:

*Evan,* JOHN CASSAVETES; *Tina,* VIRGINIA MASKELL; *Marcus,* SIDNEY POITIER; *Mrs. Lomax,* Isabel Dean; *Commissioner,* Colin Gordon; *Prescott,* Howard Marion Crawford; *Captain Jason,* Edric Connor; *Ruth,* Ruby Dee; *Mrs. Carruthers,* Gladys Root; *Band Leader,* Julian Mayfield; *Doctor,* Reginald Hearne; *Heath,* Arnold Bell; *Grant,* Alonzo Bozan.

CREDITS:

A Countryman Production for British Lion. *Producers,* Leon Clore and Grahame Tharp; *associate producer,* Leigh Aman; *director,* Pat Jackson; *screenplay,* Philip Rush and Pat Jackson; based on the novel *Our Virgin Island* by Robb White; *photography,* Freddie Francis; *music,*

Clifton Parker; *conductor,* Marcus Dobbs; *art director,* William Hutchinson; *assistant director,* Dennis Bertera; *editor,* Gordon Pilkington. Eastman Color. Running time: 94 minutes.

Poitier's flair for screen comedy first was demonstrated in *Virgin Island,* a balmy English-made frolic filmed in the Caribbean. It reunited him with John Cassavetes, his buddy from *Edge of the City,* and introduced to the screen actress Virginia Maskell. Ruby Dee, who frequently was cast as Poitier's sister, girl friend, mistress or spouse, is his wife in this one.

Richly photographed by Freddie Francis, this pleasant comedy romance "with sparkling performances by John Cassavetes and Sidney Poi-

As Marcus.

tier" *(Variety)* is fluff about an American writer vacationing in the Virgin Islands, a well-bred young English girl he meets and falls for on one of its sandy beaches, and a friendly islander who helps them set up housekeeping. After sweeping Tina Lomax (Virginia Maskell) off her feet and selling her a bill of goods about living their own lives away from it all, Evan (Cassavetes) marries her, to the dismay of her wealthy mother (Isabel Dean), buys a deserted island for $85, and with only a brass bedstead and Man Friday, Marcus (Poitier), starts a life of comparative bliss.

Tina placates her disapproving mother, Evan rides out a brief skirmish with the local governor (Colin Gordon), and Marcus and his wife, Ruth (Ruby Dee), help in the housebuilding and in-laws entertaining. Tragedy almost touches the couple when Evan and his pregnant wife become stranded in a boat as Tina goes into labor. Evan swims for help, returns with Marcus, and the baby is safely delivered.

Evan and Tina decide to partially return to civilization, after having established their claim to the island. For six months of the year, Marcus

With Virginia Maskell.

and Ruth will be the caretakers, and for the other six, Evan and Tina will live on their virgin island.

*Virgin Island,* filmed in the spring of 1958, was reviewed in *Variety* in late October. "The plot is pure woman's magazine hokum," the paper's critic thought. "A standout performance is given by Sidney Poitier as a gentle, comic islander who helps the couple through their problems." Another 18 months or so elapsed before the film found an American release, and opened in New York City on the bottom half of a double bill. Howard Thompson wrote in *The New York Times:* "This little film may be as thin as a palm frond, but by dint of good-natured acting, easy dialogue, and the feeling that it is being made up as it goes along, it does point a disarming, unpretentious compass toward that isle we all dream about. And the fade-out, a small example of racial color blindness, has a very sweet sound indeed."

Wanda Hale gave the film two-and-one-half stars in her New York *Daily News* review, calling it "a naive little number" and feeling that "Sidney Poitier gives brightness and efficiency as a native friend of the couple, a role he must have taken for the fun of making a color picture in the Virgin Islands."

Britain's *Monthly Film Bulletin* observed that "Sidney Poitier's outrageous caricature of the laughing West Indian hovers constantly on the verge of the sinister, but his ebullience, and the crisp, clean-living appeal of Miss Maskell in her less serious moods, are the film's two undeniable assets." In a long piece on Poitier in *Films and Filming,* Dennis John Hall considered: ". . . the film has an engaging charm that defies criticism.

As Marcus.

As far as Poitier is concerned, for the first time his considerable flair for light comedy is exercised to the full, and he obviously enjoys himself hugely as does the rest of the small but excellent cast." And in its standard mini-review, *Parents' Magazine* informed that "There is something engagingly amateurish about this film set in the Caribbean, like children 'playing house.' "

Poitier, in his wide-brimmed Panama hat, island-tinged dialect and ingratiating smile, romped through *Virgin Island* giving a broad, spirited characterization, and, following this obvious Caribbean vacation, then returned to more serious filmmaking in Goldwyn's (and Gershwin's) *Porgy and Bess*.

With Virginia Maskell and John Cassavetes.

With Sammy Davis, Jr., Brock Peters and Dorothy Dandridge.

# Porgy and Bess

Samuel Goldwyn/Columbia Pictures          1959

THE CAST:

*Porgy,* SIDNEY POITIER; *Bess,* DOROTHY DANDRIDGE; *Sportin' Life,* SAMMY DAVIS, JR.; *Maria,* PEARL BAILEY; *Crown,* Brock Peters; *Jake,* Leslie Scott; *Clara,* Diahann Carroll; *Serena,* Ruth Attaway; *Peter,* Clarence Muse; *Annie,* Everdinne Wilson; *Robbins,* Joel Fluellen; *Mingo,* Earl Jackson; *Nelson,* Moses LaMarr; *Lily,* Margaret Hairston; *Jim,* Ivan Dixon; *Scipio,* Antoine Durousseau; *Strawberry Woman,* Helen Thigpen; *Elderly Man,* Vince Townsend, Jr.; *Lawyer Frazier,* Roy Glenn; *Undertaker,* William Walker; *Detective,* Claude Akins; *Coroner,* Maurice Manson.

Principal Singing Voices: *Porgy,* Robert McFerrin; *Bess,* Adele Addison; *Sportin' Life,* Sammy Davis, Jr.; *Maria,* Pearl Bailey; *Crown,* Brock Peters; *Clara,* Loulie Jean Norman; *Serena,* Inez Matthews.

CREDITS:

A Samuel Goldwyn Production. *Producer,* Samuel Goldwyn; *director,* Otto Preminger; *screenplay,* N. Richard Nash; based on the musical play by George Gershwin from the novel *Porgy* by DuBose Heyward and the play *Porgy* by DuBose and Dorothy Heyward; *photography,* Leon Shamroy; *music director,* Andre Previn; *associate,* Ken Darby; *choreography,* Hermes Pan; *production design,* Oliver Smith; *art directors,* Serge Krizman and Joseph Wright; *costumes,* Irene Sharaff; *editor,* Daniel Mandell. Todd-AO and Technicolor. Running time: 146 minutes, plus intermission.

Sidney Poitier's engaging portrayal of Porgy, the crippled beggar who worked Catfish Row from the back of a goat cart and worshipped the beautiful, loose living Bess, confirmed his full-fledged stardom despite his misgivings about the role initially and the doubts that he still harbors about

With Dorothy Dandridge.

With Dorothy Dandridge.

playing Porgy in the perspective of the succeeding two decades. In its day, as the Civil Rights movement was shifting into high gear, *Porgy and Bess* was steeped in controversy (as opposed to the acclaim it has received during its mid-1970s renaissance, highlighted by its Broadway revival in 1976), and Poitier, on the threshold of becoming a major star, was caught in the middle.

In 1957, when veteran producer Samuel Goldwyn announced his intention to film with an all black cast the Gershwin folk opera in his typically lavish, damn-the-cost style, he was bombarded with objections from such groups as the NAACP on grounds that the story contributed to the denigration of the American Negro. Despite the opportunity to work in a class production—and no one made them with more style than Goldwyn—black performers were urged to boycott the filming of *Porgy and Bess,* and led by the movies' black star of the day, Harry Belafonte, who turned down the role of Porgy (despite the fact that he previously had chosen to act in *Carmen Jones,* another all-black musical), they chose not to accept Goldwyn's offers. Not an industry legend for lack of courage or persistence, Goldwyn turned *Porgy and Bess* into a personal crusade. He had vowed to make it; it *would* be made.

Goldwyn had been aware of the excitement generated by Sidney Poitier in the completed but as yet unreleased *The Defiant Ones,* and he sent for Poitier and sold him on the role of Porgy. After agreeing to play the part, though, Poitier apparently was reached by various groups (some, it is reported, camped on his doorstep in Mount Vernon) and talked into reconsidering. With regrets, he asked Goldwyn to release him from his contract, and he flew off to the Bahamas to work instead in the British-made film, *Virgin Island.* Goldwyn was not to be deterred, however, and in late 1957, Poitier was summoned to the mogul's inner sanctum where Goldwyn and director Rouben Mamoulian did another sell job on the actor. Once again, Poitier consented to star as Porgy—to the dismay of the Civil Rights group—and Goldwyn quickly began gathering a cast for the

With Dorothy Dandridge and Pearl Bailey.

project. Many were alumni of *Carmen Jones:* Dorothy Dandridge as Bess, Pearl Bailey as Maria, Brock Peters as Crown, Diahann Carroll as Clara. And to play Sportin' Life, Sammy Davis, Jr., who actively campaigned for the role.

The company was assembled but problems continued to plague the project. On the eve of production, a mysterious fire destroyed the Catfish Row set and the costumes. While these were being replaced on Goldwyn's orders, a dispute over interpretation forced Goldwyn to dismiss Mamoulian, whose own association with *Porgy and Bess* spanned its history (he had staged the original dramatic production on Broadway in 1927 and the musical version by Gershwin in 1935, as well as another company in Los Angeles and San Francisco three years later). Otto Preminger was then brought in to direct, bringing with him whatever experience was needed from his efforts on *Carmen Jones.* Preminger's interpretation only provoked further disputes, bordering, it was reported, on a cast mutiny.

Ken Darby, who shared an Academy Award with Andre Previn for the scoring of *Porgy and Bess,* recalls working with Poitier: "He was brought to my office on the Goldwyn lot by Rouben Mamoulian to 'learn' the physical actions that go along with 'singing'—Robert McFerrin, the Metropolitan Opera baritone, would sing the role. Poitier admitted, with a broad smile, that he 'couldn't carry a tune in a Mack truck,' and I soon discovered he was correct; one of the very few tone-deaf people I have known. My task: to rehearse Sidney in the songs, helping him memorize all the lyrics. Once the recordings were made, he spent long hours in my office listening to the McFerrin performances—both of us on our knees 'Porgy-style' with me singing along with the records and him watching every movement of my body, arms, head, throat—where I took a breath, how the muscles moved."

The long familiar tale of *Porgy and Bess* unfolds along a waterfront ghetto in Charleston, South Carolina, known as Catfish Row. The year is 1912. Porgy, a crippled beggar, has secretly worshipped Bess, the town tramp, and when her

As Porgy.

lover, the swaggering Crown, kills a man during a crap game, Porgy lets Bess stay in his shack as the police search Catfish Row for the murderer. Bess finds love for the first time with Porgy and decides to forget Crown. Porgy has his woman, until the day of the annual picnic on nearby Kittiwah Island. Crown, who has been hiding there, grabs Bess, rapes her amid the thickets, and forces her back to her old way of life. Delirious, she returns to Porgy who nurses her back to health.

A hurricane hits Catfish Row and everyone takes refuge in the house of the God-fearing Serena, and at the height of the storm, Crown bursts in, boasting of his affinity with the Lord. To prove his courage, he sets out after young Clara who has gone in search of her lost fisherman husband. When the storm ends and neither Crown nor Clara returns, Porgy and Bess take Clara's infant as their own. Once again Crown reappears, demanding Bess. This time, Porgy kills him.

In the morning, the police come to investigate Crown's death and Porgy is carted away to identify the body. Superstitiously Porgy refuses to look at the body and he is jailed for contempt. Panic-stricken, Bess becomes easy prey for the evil dope-pusher, Sportin' Life, who convinces her that Porgy will never return, offers her "happy dust" and urges her to go with him to New York. Porgy is released from jail and returns to Catfish

With Dorothy Dandridge.

Row. Learning from Maria, the cook shop lady, that Bess is gone, Porgy vows to follow her and bring her back, leaving Catfish Row in his little goat cart in search of his lost happiness.

Assessing Poitier's acting of a singing role, Ken Darby feels: "His superb physical condition was as astonishing as his tone deafness. He adapted to the padded-board-on-roller-skates as

With Maurice Manson, Sammy Davis, Jr., Claude Akins and Dorothy Dandridge.

With Brock Peters.

though he had been pushing himself about on it all of his life! The muscular display was enormously effective . . . and when he sang to the playback, it was a weird experience to hear the voice of McFerrin coming from the giant speakers and to hear Sidney's voice bellowing along with it—word for word in a hoarse, semi-inflectional monotone."

Goldwyn's $7,000,000 budget on *Porgy and Bess* (including the extra $1.5 million he decided to spend by shooting it in the expensive Todd-AO process) showed in every foot. With advertising and promotion expenses, the breakeven gross was placed at $15 million, with all profits earmarked for Goldwyn's foundation charities. Unfortunately, it never recouped its original costs. And with *Porgy and Bess,* Goldwyn called it a career as an active moviemaker.

Poitier himself refuses to discuss *Porgy and Bess* beyond this admission: "I hated doing it but pressure was brought from a number of quarters and there was a threat of my career stopping dead. I toyed with the idea of being steadfast, but I weakened ultimately and I did it. I didn't enjoy doing it, and I have not yet completely forgiven myself."

Viewing *Porgy and Bess* for its entertainment values and for its matchless music, the majority of film critics were exceptionally kind. Arthur Knight wrote in *Saturday Review:* "Clearly, making Porgy into a movie was a labor of love for Mr. Goldwyn and he has spared none of his formidable resources to make it as impressive and popular as possible . . . The cast [he] has assembled is, almost without exception, flawless . . . Poitier, with his singular combination of

With Dorothy Dandridge.

gentleness and strength, manages to invest the crippled Porgy with a heart-rending dignity, even though he must play the entire role stumbling about on his knees." Bosley Crowther called *Porgy and Bess* "a truly magnificent motion picture," and decided that "Sidney Poitier's performance is as sensitive and strong as one could wish."

In the *New York Herald Tribune*, critic Paul V. Beckley said: "Deserves respect as one of the most ambitious and, frankly, one of the finest cinematic versions of an opera, and even its flaws ought to be seen in the light of the serious magnitude of the task its makers set themselves." And he felt that "Sidney Poitier does reasonably well with the role of Porgy."

And while Philip T. Hartung observed in *Commonweal* that "for all its glitter and perfection, *Porgy and Bess* is weakest in the heart department where, because of its stirring folk tale, it should excel," he found that "Sidney Poitier is excellent as the bighearted, strong-armed, crippled Porgy whose generosity and love for Bess are not enough to hold this weak willed woman."

Less enthusiastic was *Time*, which decided that "the worst thing about Goldwyn's *Porgy*, though, is its cinematic monotony . . . not so much a motion picture as a photographed opera . . . Sidney Poitier's Porgy is not the dirty, ragtag beggar of the [DuBose] Heyward script, but a well-scrubbed young romantic hero who is never seen taking a penny from anybody."

As Goldwyn's *Porgy and Bess* receded into screen history, more perspective can be viewed, and with it comes more unflattering commentary by black writers on film. Representative was the opinion of Donald Bogle, writing in his book *Toms, Coons, Mulattoes, Mammies, & Bucks:* "Here it was 1959. There was Martin Luther King, there were sit-ins, demonstrations, and boycotts. And what was America's black idol doing? There he stood singing, 'I got plenty of nothin,' and nothin's plenty for me.' "

Filming the Catfish Row picnic parade.

With James Darren and Alan Ladd.

# All the Young Men

Columbia Pictures                    1960

THE CAST:

*Kincaid,* ALAN LADD; *Towler,* SIDNEY POITIER; *Torgil,* Ingemar Johansson; *Cotton,* James Darren; *Wade,* Glenn Corbett; *Crane,* Mort Sahl; *Maya,* Ana St. Clair; *Bracken,* Paul Richards; *Dean,* Lee Kinsolving; *Jackson,* Joe Gallison; *Lazitech,* Paul Baxley; *Lieutenant,* Charles Quinlivan; *Cho,* Michael Davis; *Hunter,* Mario Alcalde; *Korean Woman,* Maria Tsien; *Marines,* Chris Seitz, Bill St. Johns, Jack McCall, Steve Drexel, Pat Colby, Morgan Roberts.

CREDITS:

A Hall Bartlett/Jaguar Production. *Producer/ director,* Hall Bartlett; *associate producer,* Newton Arnold; *screenplay,* Hall Bartlett; *photography,* Daniel L. Fapp; *music,* George Duning; *title song,* George Duning and Stanley Styne; *sung* by James Darren; *art director,* Carl Anderson; *technical advisor,* Lt. Col. C. J. Stadler (USMC); *assistant director,* Lee Lukather; *editor,* Al Clark. Running time: 86 minutes.

Fulfilling a commitment made before his stunning Broadway success in *A Raisin in the Sun,* Sidney Poitier took a leave of absence from the show to tramp around Glacier National Park, substituting for the rugged terrain around the 38th parallel in Korea of 1951. In Hall Bartlett's war movie, *All the Young Men,* Poitier once again did a lip service role, undoubtedly for the money. The film, into which was shoe-horned a racial prejudice diatribe, was cast with characters drafted from old war flicks and told, as one critic put it, in terms of soldier types instead of soldiers. There was the Poitier role, the black NCO who is forced to battle the North Koreans and fight his private racial war with the rest of his platoon; the hardboiled career soldier (Alan Ladd), who resents not being given the command which went to Poitier; the southern redneck (Paul Richards), who cannot bring himself to obey orders from a Negro and tosses racial epithets like "night fighter" at regular intervals; the wisecracking G.I. (Mort Sahl); the cocky, street-wise soldier (James Darren); the harried corpsman (Glenn Corbett); the nostalgic dreamer (Ingemar Johansson); even the obligatory, limited-scene love interest (Ana St. Clair).

Poitier's authoritative performance almost alone makes *All the Young Men* at all bearable. He has admitted, though: "I was unable to work in that movie, even on an elementary level, with any degree of imagination." He co-stars as Sergeant Towler, who survives a bloody ambush in the Korean hills during the winter of '51 with only a dozen of his Marine buddies. The dying C.O. puts him in charge, passing over the more experienced, recently demoted Kincaid (Ladd), and tells Towler to have the men occupy a nearby farmhouse to await help. The determined Towler ignores the disgruntled Kincaid's suggestion that they try to fight their way back to their lines instead of sitting tight, and, obeying orders, drives his men on to the desolate shack. There the platoon finds an old woman, her Eurasian daughter, Maya (Ana St. Clair), and the latter's nine-year-old son.

While the enemy threatens from without, Towler's men become embroiled in internal squabbles, instigated primarily by the bigoted Bracken (Richards). When one of the Marines tries to rape Maya, Towler's intervention increases the resentment of his command. Maya, though, becomes quite attracted to the sergeant, creating further hatred.

With Ingemar Johansson.

During the enemy siege of the strategic farmhouse, several of the men are picked off by snipers. The others manage to hold until their position is jeopardized by an enemy tank, which Towler and Kincaid struggle to put out of commission. Kincaid's leg is badly mangled by a tank tread, however, and when Wade (Corbett), the platoon's medic, is forced to amputate it without anesthetics, it is Towler who provides the blood for the lifesaving transfusion. As the enemy attacks intensify, Towler is forced to order his men and Maya and her family to higher ground. "You'll be able to see me real good up there against the snow," he cracks grimly. Then he returns to the farmhouse where the crippled Kincaid is manning a gun, and picking up a BAR, Towler joins him to stand off the final enemy assault as long as possible.

"It crashes the boldest boundary line ever stretched across the screen!" the ad copy read. Regardless, it emerged as a superficial study, jammed with well-worn situations and often repeated dialogue, altered only to reflect its Korean War milieu. It seemed suspiciously like a first

With Mario Alcalde.

With Alan Ladd and Paul Richards.

cousin to Poitier's earlier *Red Ball Express,* his only other war film. *All the Young Men* expertly blends two traditions rich in cinematic cliché—the big war movie and the fearless-denunciation-of-race-bigotry movie.

Wrote *Time:* "Sidney Poitier, an accomplished actor so discriminated against because of his color that he will probably never be allowed to play a character who is not strong, sensitive and noble, is a Marine sergeant whose unit is chopped to pieces during a Korean War skirmish."

Critic Bosley Crowther observed: "Racial tension in the United States Marines is sluggishly celebrated in a variation on a well used Western plot in the picture [and] all the clichés have been worked into it by Mr. Bartlett . . . Through it all, Mr. Poitier struggles with commendable patience and dignity, bearing the black man's burden of well-intended but specious patronage."

Arthur Knight's *Saturday Review* critique said: "To Bartlett's credit, and to that of Mr. Poitier, the Negro emerges not as a stereotype but as a *man*—strong but fearful, serious but with a grim humor, dedicated but human enough to recognize that he may be leading all his young men to their death. The other characters come off less well. It is not merely that the acting is one dimensional; so is the basic conception of the roles."

In the *New York Herald Tribune,* reviewer

Joseph Morgenstern felt that *"All the Young Men* tries to say some mordant things about racial prejudice among men whose lives depend upon mutual trust [and] skillful writing, in conjunction with Mr. Poitier's acting, could have made Sergeant Towler a memorable character. As it is, we are told little about Towler. The others at least have their stereotyped backgrounds and atti-

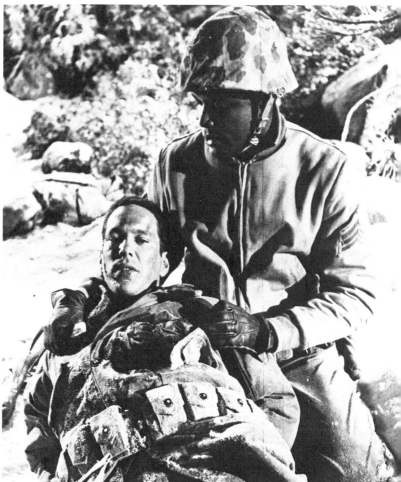

With Mario Alcalde.

As Sgt. Towler

tudes, but there is nothing to say about Towler except that he is courageous, and a Negro . . . We have encountered the same theme, with variations, in Stanley Kramer's *The Defiant Ones*. The difference is that this time Mr. Poitier is manacled to an inadequate script."

Writing about the film's exploration of racial prejudice at the front, *Variety* concluded: "The examination is neither dramatically plausible nor philosophically stimulating, at least one of which it ought to be . . . Of all the players, Poitier is the most convincing, but even he is not at his best under the circumstances."

Aside from the acting of Poitier and the waning marquee power of Ladd, the film's commercial appeal rested on the broad shoulders of the then recently deposed World Heavyweight Boxing Champion, Ingemar Johansson, who demonstrated that emoting was not his profession; comedian Mort Sahl, whose lines appeared to have been self-written; and good looking James Darren, who had his contract arranged to allow him to sing the easily forgettable title song.

With Alan Ladd, Ana St. Clair and Michael Davis.

[ 96 ]

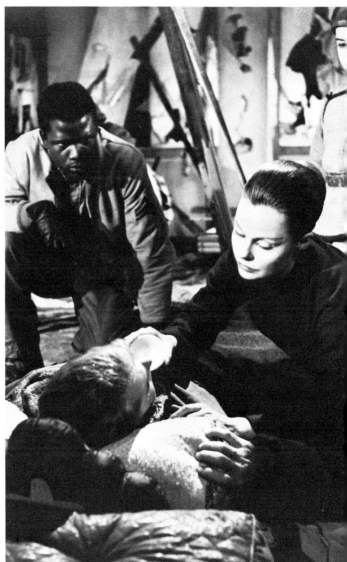

With Ruby Dee.

# A Raisin in the Sun

Columbia Pictures                    1961

THE CAST:

*Walter Lee Younger,* SIDNEY POITIER; *Lena Younger,* Claudia McNeil; *Ruth Younger,* Ruby Dee; *Beneatha Younger,* Diana Sands; *Asagai,* Ivan Dixon; *Mark Lindner,* John Fiedler; *George Murchison,* Louis Gossett; *Travis Younger,* Stephen Perry; *Bobo,* Joel Fluellen; *Willie Harris,* Roy Glenn; *Bartender,* Ray Stubbs; *Taxi Driver,* Rudolph Monroe; *Employer,* George DeNormand; *Herman,* Louis Terkel; *Chauffeur,* Thomas D. Jones; *Grocery Clerk,* Gene Collins.

CREDITS:

A Paman-Doris Production. *Producers,* David Susskind and Philip Rose; *director,* Daniel Petrie; *screenplay,* Lorraine Hansberry; based on her 1959 play; *photography,* Charles Lawton, Jr.; *music,* Laurence Rosenthal; *art director,* Carl Anderson; *assistant director,* Sam Nelson; *editors,* William A. Lyon and Paul Weatherwax. Running time: 127 minutes.

The screen version of Lorraine Hansberry's stirring, prize winning play (New York Drama Critics Circle Award as Best Play of 1959) preserves on film the electrifying stage performances of Sidney Poitier and six other members of the original Broadway production. Perhaps because it had been transferred literally to the screen, there is the perennial contention that *A Raisin in the Sun* is less a movie than a filmed stage play, but the criticism takes nothing away from Poitier's towering portrayal of Walter Lee Younger, a frustrated panther of a man seeking dignity for himself and the family he has been forced to squeeze into a tiny Chicago ghetto flat. "Man! I'm a volcano," he snarls, "a giant surrounded by ants!" Equally as powerful is the acting of Claudia McNeil as his mother, Ruby Dee as his wife, and Diana Sands (in her film debut) as his sister—all from the Broadway version.

*A Raisin in the Sun*—the title is taken from a Langston Hughes poem—was the most distinguished all-Negro movie to that time and was the official U.S. entry in the 1961 Cannes Film Festival. It also marked a new screen plateau for Poitier: sole above-the-title billing (as he was accorded for the Broadway version), demonstrating producers' faith in his ability to carry a vehicle to box-office success. The major concession to the film industry's money men (some still insist that pressure from the Directors Guild was a deciding factor) was giving the directorial chores to Daniel Petrie rather than allowing Lloyd Richards, a black director, to restage his original Broadway production.

The film tells touchingly of a frustrated but indestructible Negro family which is given the opportunity to rechart its future with the arrival of a $10,000 life insurance payment. The Young-

With Diana Sands and Ruby Dee.

ers, five people crowded into three sunless rooms on Chicago's South Side, soon find themselves clawing at each other over the money. Lena Younger (Claudia McNeil), the proud matriarch, wants to use her dead husband's insurance to buy a house and help her daughter, Beneatha (Diana Sands), finish medical school. Her son, Walter Lee (Poitier), wants the money to help him rise above his hated job as a chauffeur to a wealthy white man, and has the opportunity to invest in a liquor store. Walter's wife, Ruth (Ruby Dee),

With Claudia McNeil.

With Ruby Dee.

distressed at what he is doing to himself in his anguish, sees her marriage breaking up.

When Lena, stubbornly determined not to be influenced by her family, makes a down payment of $3500 on a small house in a white neighborhood, her enraged son quarrels bitterly with her and with Ruth, and then storms out of the flat. After he stays away from work for three days, Lena goes in search of him and locates him in a bar, where she gives him the remaining money which she had planned to set aside for Beneatha's schooling. Lena hopes that the responsibility will make a man of Walter Lee, but he immediately squanders it in a get-rich-quick scheme, and his dream is destroyed when one of his "partners" absconds with the money.

As Walter Lee's world is collapsing, Lena is receiving a visit from Mark Lindner (John Fiedler), a representative of an "improvement association" that wants to buy back the house she had just purchased, in order to preserve the community's all-white character. Realizing he has betrayed his mother's trust, threatened his sister's future (she has decided to run off with an African student in search of her heritage), and thrown away his father's life savings, Walter Lee desperately decides to accept the association's offer. Under the eyes of the three women and his young son, however, he determines that such a move is only a step backward and he once again rejects the offer. Knowing that it means hard work and years of sacrifice, he vows to move his family into their new home and see that Beneatha gets to be a doctor.

Nearly without exception, *A Raisin in the Sun* was well-received critically. *The New York*

With Joel Fluellen.

*Times* named it one of the year's Ten Best; the *New York Herald Tribune* urged: "If you see no other picture this year, this is the one you ought to see. Few films put so much humor and such fierce drama together so successfully"; *Saturday Review* referred to it as "an important and memorable movie"; *Cue* raved: "An utterly magnificent motion picture!" And *Variety* called it "stirring film . . . an important, worthwhile, timely document . . . a powerful and moving drama."

Sidney Poitier, too, received hosannas. Bosley Crowther wrote: "Mr. Poitier, lithe and electric, emits the lightning of an angry, violent man who dreams of smashing the chains of his economic enslavement." Jesse Zunser said in *Cue:* "Poitier gives one of the finest performances of the year." Wanda Hale, critic for the New York *Daily News,* hailed: "Sidney Poitier is one of the true artists of our time." Arthur Knight observed in *Saturday Review:* "Poitier, always a splendid actor, rises to new heights . . . His is one of the few truly realized character portraits ever to come onto celluloid, and one of the most moving."

In *Variety,* these words: "Poitier gives a striking, commanding performance. There is poetry in the very expression of his body movements—wild, desperate gestures and thrusts of arms and restless, almost choreographic floor pacing gyrations that convey physically but clearly the inner turmoil, the years of denial that the character has had to seal within himself." And in *The Cleveland Press,* critic Paul Mooney felt: "Poitier achieves awesome heights as he strug-

With Louis Gossett.

[ 99 ]

With Diana Sands, Ruby Dee and Claudia McNeil.

gles with himself and the people around him to break the chains of poverty. He never slips in etching out one of the most pathetic yet noble characters ever filmed."

Poitier, who had portrayed Walter Lee Younger 198 times on Broadway, and previously in the New Haven and Chicago tryouts, subsequently has said: "There is that about Walter Lee . . . that is hard to find in terms of character structure. There is a central kernel from which all of Walter Lee blossoms. He has an obsession—he wants to and has not been able to carve for himself a badge of distinction. The only acceptable one, the only one he recognizes, would be some material symbol of his life's worth. This is a guy who has no sense of direction; his wherewithal is that failure rather than success would be his lot. Nevertheless, he has gigantic needs—kookie though they may be—and the consequences of not filling them would be gigantic."

In 1968, following the extraordinary success of *Guess Who's Coming To Dinner,* Columbia re-issued *A Raisin in the Sun* with an all new ad campaign highlighted by a full length photo of a remarkably relaxed Sidney Poitier (in contrast to the explosive shot of the original), together with simple headline: "Guess Who's Moving Next Door!"

Fourteen years after *A Raisin in the Sun* first opened on Broadway, a musical version of Lorraine Hansberry's unforgettable play brought the Younger family to a new generation of theatregoers. Now entitled simply *Raisin,* it featured Joe Morton in the original Poitier role of Walter Lee Younger, with Morton, consciously or not, adopting many of the familiar Poitier physical movements as well as the gracefully characteristic "Poitier glide," a distinctive walk-dance step which has become an integral part of Poitier's acting style.

With Stephen Perry, Ruby Dee, Claudia McNeil and Diana Sands.

With Diahann Carroll, Joanne Woodward and Paul Newman.

# Paris Blues

United Artists                    1961

THE CAST:

*Ram Bowen*, PAUL NEWMAN; *Lillian Corning*, JOANNE WOODWARD; *Eddie Cook*, SIDNEY POITIER; *Wild Man Moore*, Louis Armstrong; *Connie Lampson*, Diahann Carroll; *Michel Duvigne*, Serge Reggiani; *Marie Seoul*, Barbara Laage; *Rene Bernard*, Andre Luguet; *Nicole*, Marie Versini; *Gypsy Guitarist*, Roger Blin; *Pusher*, Helene Dieudonne; *Ricardo*, Niko; *Pianist*, Maria Velasco; *Ram's Drummer*, Moustache; *Ram's Pianist*, Aaron Bridges; *Ram's Bass Player*, Guy Pederson.

CREDITS:

A Pennebaker Production. *Executive producers,* George Glass and Walter Seltzer; *producer,* Sam Shaw; *director,* Martin Ritt; *screenplay,* Jack Sher, Irene Kamp and Walter Bernstein; based on a novel by Harold Flender; *adaptation* by Lulla Adler; *photography,* Christian Matros; *music,* Duke Ellington; *second unit director,* Andre Smagghe; *assistant director,* Bernard Farrel; *art director,* Alexander Trauner; *editor,* Roger Dwyre. Running time: 98 minutes.

Martin Ritt's *Paris Blues* is best summarized as two weeks in Paris with a couple of expatriate jazz musicians—one white, one black—and two American tourists—one white, one black—plus some knockout jazz by Louis Armstrong and Duke Ellington's band. Sidney Poitier took third billing to Paul Newman and Joanne Woodward in this lightweight tale that one critic described as basically two beautiful couples in raincoats running around the streets of Paris and into its jazz cellars.

The film seems to have been an American attempt at turning out a New Wave-type movie reflecting the restlessness of the day's French cinema, with director Ritt working on location with a completely French crew and—except for the four leads and Louis Armstrong—French cast. The emphasis of the script, slaved over by what seems to have been a platoon of writers, appears misplaced, focusing on the steamy affair between the Newmans rather than on racial injustice in the States.

Poitier has said of *Paris Blues:* "The novel on which it ostensibly was based really went into the lives of the jazz musicians in Paris, but what we did was not that . . . By the time we were finished, five other writers had been called in, one after the other, to change the script according to some idea that one or another of a dozen people connected with the movie had for making it a success. Instead it was a shambles."

The film concerns Eddie Cook (Poitier) and Ram Bowen (Newman), a couple of musicians from the States working in a jazz club on the Left Bank. Each feels he is protected—Eddie from the racial prejudices at home, Ram from distractions that will interfere with a jazz concerto he is writing. The legendary trumpet star, Wild Man Moore (Louis Armstrong), has promised to pass Ram's concerto on to Rene Bernard (Andre Luguet), an impresario, and Ram expects jazz immortality to follow.

When black-and-beautiful Connie Lampson (Diahann Carroll) and her white friend, Lillian Corning (Joanne Woodward), come into Ram's life, he immediately makes a beeline for Connie, oblivious to Lillian's charms. He tells Connie, "All white girls look alike to me," as he invites her to join him at the club. Both girls show up, however, and Eddie makes it a foursome. Lillian, man-hungry and on the prowl, snatches up Ram after learning that Connie had been cool on him anyway. The foursome not long afterwards divides into two couples, and Eddie and Connie soon are in love. When she tries to convince him that he should be back in America helping knock down racial barriers, he argues that in Paris he has the freedom and dignity denied him at home. Ram, too, is reluctant to give up his independence

With Paul Newman.

and become merely another second-rate trombone player making a meager living in the States.

When Ram learns that Bernard has turned down his concerto as too trivial, he dejectedly agrees to accompany Lillian home to America. By this time, Eddie, too, has decided to go back, but on the morning of their departure, the girls learn that both men have changed their minds. Eddie may follow within a few weeks, but Ram says goodbye to Lillian and then returns to his music.

With Paul Newman, Diahann Carroll and Joanne Woodward.

With Diahann Carroll.

"By and large, the film is a sightseeing tour of Paris with minor sermons advising against the use of narcotics and the like," critic Paul V. Beckley wrote in the *New York Herald Tribune.* "The principal characters are no more than attitudes, so it is by no means the fault of Miss Woodward, Miss Carroll, Newman and Poitier that they come off so poorly . . . Actually the best thing in the film is the Duke Ellington score—you might say that it is one of the few pictures that is a distraction from its own soundtrack."

Stanley Kauffmann concluded in *The New Republic* that *"Paris Blues* has a rewarding idea buried in it, but it does not involve Newman's part . . . Sidney Poitier, whose story this ought to be, is superb. What this magnificently endowed man does with this tritely written role deserves more attention than present space allows." And reviewer Philip T. Hartung of *Commonweal* said: "The Negroes behave so much better than the whites throughout the film one wonders if *Paris Blues* means to be or is only accidentally anti-white. In any case, the poorly conceived story is only a starting point for all the attractive decoration."

*"Paris Blues* reaches for a contemporary

With Paul Newman.

significance, but also in a curiously halfhearted way," observed Arthur Knight in *Saturday Review.* "It has Sidney Poitier as an expatriate jazz musician uttering some strong lines about racial inequality in the United States. But they simply hang there. Instead of following through on Poitier's dilemma . . . the producers nimbly dodge into a steamy affair between Paul Newman and Joanne Woodward . . . The fundamental weakness of *Paris Blues,* however, is that one couldn't care less what happens to its central characters."

The critic for *Variety* felt that "incongruously conspicuous within its snappy, flashy veneer is an undernourished romantic drama of a rather traditional screen school. The upshot is a choppy, shallow, and discordant picture in which story runs a poor and distant second to style . . . especially disappointing in view of the acknowledged caliber of performers such as Newman, Poitier and Miss Woodward."

Brendan Gill's comments in *The New Yorker:* "What could be more agreeable, after all, than to sit and watch for an hour or so while Paul Newman, Joanne Woodward, Sidney Poitier and Diahann Carroll meet, pair off, quarrel, make up, and ruefully part? I don't mean to diminish them as actors . . . but their attractiveness as human beings *is* a crucial factor in the success of the picture, and it would be silly to pretend it isn't

... *Paris Blues* is something of a novelty in handling the color question on a comparatively free and easy basis; we're encouraged to perceive that Miss Carroll is every bit as cute a chick as Miss Woodward, and only now and then does the natural course of action grind to a stop in order to let Mr. Poitier utter some worthy but conspicuously NAACP-like sentiment."

The final word came from *Time:* "The only general truth that *Paris Blues* propounds is one that might have prevented this production: expatriates are a pretty dull bunch."

With Paul Newman and Diahann Carroll.

With Diahann Carroll.

With Joanne Woodward.

With Bobby Darin.

# Pressure Points

Stanley Kramer-United Artists          1962

THE CAST:

*Doctor*, SIDNEY POITIER; *Patient*, BOBBY DARIN; *Psychiatrist*, Peter Falk; *Chief Medical Officer*, Carl Benton Reid; *Bar Hostess*, Mary Munday; *Boy*, Barry Gordon; *Tavern Owner*, Howard Caine; *Mother*, Anne Barton; *Father*, James Anderson; *Drunken Woman*, Yvette Vickers; *Pete*, Clegg Hoyt; *Jimmy*, Richard Bakalyan; *Playmate*, Butch Patrick.

CREDITS:

A Stanley Kramer Production. *Producer*, Stanley Kramer; *director*, Hubert Cornfield; *screenplay*, Hubert Cornfield and S. Lee Pogostin; based on *"The Fifty Minute Hour"* by Dr. Robert Lindner; *photography*, Ernest Haller; *music*, Ernest Gold; *assistant director*, Philip Bowles; *art direc-*tor, Rudolph Sternad; *editor*, Fred Knudtson. Running time: 91 minutes.

Poitier's second film for Stanley Kramer (this time as producer only) teamed him with Bobby Darin for a provocative if decidedly downbeat and overly arty study in prejudice. As in Kramer's *The Defiant Ones*, the focus in *Pressure Point* is the counterpoint relationship between the black man and the white man, with all other roles subsidiary, told through the black-white psychiatrist-patient dealings.

Taken from a composite of case histories that Dr. Robert Lindner had written into his book, *The Fifty-Minute Hour* (in which the psychiatrist was white and Jewish), the film is a

With Bobby Darin.

carefully molded, melodramatic attack on bigotry, told mainly in flashback and, often, surrealistically. Poitier is cast as a coolly articulate prison psychiatrist and Darin is a paranoid American-Nazi bundist and race-hater, imprisoned for sedition during the early days of World War II. The psychiatrist tries to learn the reasons for the young man's chronic insomnia and inadvertently uncovers his political philosophy. Woven into all of this is the point about the insidious intellectual enslavement of the black man in a white society after physical enslavement has been overcome.

Framing the body of the film is a situation involving a young psychiatrist (Peter Falk), facing a similar situation in reverse. Admitting failure with a Negro patient, who hates whites, the doctor asks his superior (Poitier) to remove him from the case. The older doctor dissuades him from giving up and then proceeds to describe a similar case early in his own career. As a prison doctor serving on the staff of a federal penitentiary in 1942, he had been asked to undertake the treatment of a young Fascist, who, despite his hatred of Negroes, submits to therapy in hopes of ending his recurrent nightmares and blackouts preceded by hallucinations in which he saw himself—and later his father—being washed down a sink drain.

With Barry Gordon.

With Bobby Darin.

The doctor discovers that the young man's father was a drunken sadist and his mother a whining invalid, and that, cut off from other children, the boy had invented an imaginary playmate whom he bullied, had drifted into delinquency and left home at fifteen. He first had exhibited overt sadistic tendencies in a drunken orgy at a small town saloon, and later was rebuffed by the father of a well-bred Jewish girl who had taken a liking to him. He soon found an outlet for his mounting hatreds and prejudices by joining the Nazi party.

When the psychiatrist explains the causes of the patient's nightmares, the young man finds relief and, once able to sleep, refuses to continue the therapy. The prison authorities then ignore the doctor's warning (simply, it seems, since they would rather accept the patient's word about being cured over that of a black psychiatrist), despite the fact that the psychiatrist is convinced that the young man is a dangerous paranoid. The psychiatrist threatens to resign, but then swallows his pride and decides to remain after the patient is paroled and, subsequently, is hanged for the brutal murder of an old man.

After listening to the story, the young psychiatrist now chooses to profit from the elder's experience and remain on his own case.

With Bobby Darin.

With Bobby Darin.

"That excellent actor, Sidney Poitier, makes the psychiatrist a believable figure of strength and humanness, and gives much conviction to the film, which suffers now and then from a failure to relate all its strands . . . Too bad this film could not have been shown at recent international festivals. It would have demonstrated a fresh current in Hollywood." George Bourke, reviewing in *The Miami Herald,* hailed "fine performances by Sidney Poitier and Bobby Darin . . . and imaginative production by director Hubert Cornfield." These were among the best of the reviews.

With Peter Falk.

A flawed film, brilliantly directed by newcomer Hubert Cornfield (with only one previous movie, *The Third Voice,* to his credit), *Pressure Point* disappointed many despite its powerful performances and its tackling of race prejudice, psychoanalysis, and the psychoneurotic bases of Fascism. The characters in it remain nameless, and of the psychiatrist, there is little personal information, only what is revealed by satellite figures. In keeping with his professional tradition, he speaks little, listens a great deal, and exercises extreme patience when racially baited. He is, though, greatly frightened by his vulnerability in this graphic indictment of American racial injustice.

Hollis Alpert wrote in *Saturday Review:*

Howard Thompson, critiquing the movie for *The New York Times,* gave it a thumbs-down notice, but observed "Even though we're never told what makes Mr. Poitier tick, his is a coolly forceful performance, ticking steadily—and superbly—in his climactic flareup."

In another negative review, Stanley Kauffmann said in *The New Republic:* "The cleverness of the idea makes the heart sink and the film does little to raise it . . . To no one's surprise, the producer is Stanley Kramer [who] believes that a serious subject makes a serious film and that the choice of such a subject excuses what would be arrant show-biz commercialism in another context." Critic Kauffmann further commented: "The psychiatrist is played by Sidney Poitier, a re-

As the Doctor.

strained panther of an actor. Having burst the seams of *A Raisin in the Sun* and *Paris Blues,* he is here only marking time until he gets parts worthy of his powers."

Of Poitier, *Variety* wrote: "[He] is careful as the psychiatrist, acting with intense, planned response at all times. He is strong and clinical, perhaps too much so at times."And from Britain's *Monthly Film Bulletin:* "Sidney Poitier, obliged to voice some absurdly pat pieces of psychoanalysis, gives a performance so hypnotically wholesome that one temporarily forgets the grinding mechanics of the plot."

Producer Stanley Kramer wrote of *Pressure Point:* "The film was directed by Hubert Cornfield and I think there were some extremely creative moments, although it was not very successful. Poitier and Bobby Darin seemed to make the necessary sparks—the black doctor vs. the Nazi sympathizer. I think this film helped to add to the imagery of the black man in film: he came on as a psychiatrist with no comment except from the racially oriented and bigoted prisoner."

With Lilia Skala.

# Lilies of the Field

United Artists                1963

## THE CAST:

*Homer Smith,* SIDNEY POITIER; *Mother Maria,* Lilia Skala; *Sister Gertrude,* Lisa Mann; *Sister Agnes,* Iso Crino; *Sister Albertine,* Francesca Jarvis; *Sister Elizabeth,* Pamela Branch; *Juan,* Stanley Adams; *Father Murphy,* Dan Frazer; *Mr. Ashton,* Ralph Nelson.

## CREDITS:

*Producer/director,* Ralph Nelson; *screenplay,* James Poe; based on the novel by William E. Barrett; *photography,* Ernest Haller; *music,* Jerry Goldsmith; *editor,* John McCafferty. Running time: 94 minutes.

The role of Homer Smith in *Lilies of the Field* made Sidney Poitier an international star. As the single known name in a small cast, he carried this movie sleeper of 1963 to its subsequent, well-earned renown, won the Silver Bear as Best Actor at the Berlin Film Festival for the second time, and became the first (and to date only) member of his race to be given the top acting award from the Academy of Motion Picture Arts and Sciences.

Poitier had laid his reputation on the line for a film budgeted at only $247,000, receiving for the first time in his career a percentage of the

As Homer Smith.

profits. Ralph Nelson, whose only previous film credit had been *Requiem for a Heavyweight,* persuaded Poitier to star in the lead, a role calling simply for an actor without regard to race (another first for Poitier), and permitting him to carry the picture by his presence alone.

The James Poe screenplay, from William E. Barrett's 92-page novel, offered Poitier a complete change of pace as well as a chance to demonstrate his flair for comedy, in the meaty role of an ex-G.I. who, touring the southwest in his campout station wagon, encounters a group of German nuns in the desert country of Arizona, struggling to farm the dust-laden earth. He accepts a day's work from them, but when night falls, there is no pay, only a warm meal and a proffer of friendship from the strong-minded Mother Superior, Sister Maria (Lilia Skala). The nuns' zeal and faith ignite in Homer and he decides to stick around and be helpful. "Schmidt," the Mother Superior tells him, "you are going to build us a 'shapel.'" And Homer, himself a Bap-

With Stanley Adams, Dan Frazer and Lilia Skala.

[ 112 ]

With Ralph Nelson, who directed as well as acted in the film.

tist, finds himself building it for them, taking an outside job and buying supplies out of his earnings. When he discovers, though, that even the townspeople, poor Mexican-Americans with no church of their own, think he is crazy, he packs up and prepares to leave in disillusionment. Convinced to stay, he accepts a part time job from a local, wealthy contractor, Harold Ashton (director Ralph Nelson), and resumes buying bricks to finish the chapel. Impressed, the poor neighbors

and the wary Mexican-American roadside cafe owner (Stanley Adams) soon are pitching in. Even circuit-riding Father Murphy (Dan Frazer), who brings mass to his people from the back of an automobile and has little hope of realizing his early dreams of a church of his own, offers encouragement.

As the chapel rises, so do the spirits of the townspeople. Its completion awaits only the bishop for its consecration. But early on the

With Lilia Skala.

[ 113 ]

As Homer Smith.

As Homer Smith.

morning of the big day, Homer creeps back into his station wagon and takes off for nowhere again, his mission completed. He has fulfilled an ambition to build something and has derived the deep inner satisfaction which comes from having been of service selflessly.

"A joyous film," Judith Crist raved in the *New York Herald Tribune.* "Sidney Poitier is one of the finest actors of our time, and if you have any doubts about his stature, consider *Lilies of the Field,* a film that provides an ideal showcase for his talents as well as many pleasures of its own ... The film is not without its sticky moments [but] a joyousness, a sense of decency and an appreciation of the human spirit pervade *Lilies of the Field* and Sidney Poitier makes it a movie worth seeing."

Philip T. Hartung felt in *Commonweal* that "what makes [it] such a delightfully engrossing film are its trimmings, its true characteriza-

With Stanley Adams and Ralph Nelson.

tions, its good acting, its warm spirit and good will that convey a lesson in integration of race and creed far more valuable than many elaborate religious spectacles . . . Sidney Poitier is superb as Homer. He makes a blithe spirit who is also human . . . *Lilies of the Field* may be over simplified and overly sentimental at times, but it is a thoughtful, unpretentious picture that gives a great deal of pleasure."

*The New York Times* critic Bosley Crowther found it "a bright little film that is so gentle and ingenious in constructing a modern parable that it fairly disarms the stubborn critic who would apply the yardstick of logic to it. And it is played so sincerely and with such charm by Sidney Poitier and a pre-Hitler Viennese star, Lilia Skala, that it captivates the heart, if not the brain." Crowther admired "a quiet but persistent intensity in Mr. Poitier's performance" and concluded: "It is idealistic and sentimental, but it is warm [and] we can do with a nice chunk of sweetness and optimism in a movie for a change."

*Variety* caught the film originally at the Berlin Film Festival in June of 1963 and noted appreciatively: "*Lilies* reveals Sidney Poitier as an actor with a sharp sense of humor. His performance is in striking contrast to many of his earlier roles . . . Many factors combine in the overall success of the film, notably . . . Poitier's own standout performance."

"Poitier's infectious enthusiasm," Arthur Knight wrote in *Saturday Review,* "is merely the most visible manifestation of rare *esprit de corps* that sustained the entire production . . . Poitier, of course, is a joy throughout . . . Not that [it] represents the ultimate in interracial films: until Sidney Poitier can play a character like *Hud* and be recognized as an evil man, not a bad Negro, we still have a long way to go. But *Lilies* does take a giant stride in the right direction."

Not all the reviewers were enchanted. In *Newsweek,* a fast single paragraph critique noted: "The screen soon overflows with enough brotherhood, piety, and honest labor to make even the kindliest spectator retch. One begins to wish that Poitier would belt one of the nuns in the chops, and that the rest would set upon him and toss him bodily out of the convent." And in Britain's *Monthly Film Bulletin:* "The sentimental pitfalls of such a subject are only too apparent and producer-director Ralph Nelson has marched boldly into every one of them . . . Sidney Poitier's rather self-conscious charm works overtime."

With Lilia Skala.

With Richard Widmark.

# The Long Ships

Columbia Pictures                    1964

THE CAST:

*Rolfe*, RICHARD WIDMARK; *El Mansuh*, SIDNEY POITIER; *Orm*, RUSS TAMBLYN; *Aminah*, ROSANNA SCHIAFFINO; *Krok*, Oscar Homolka; *Aziz*, Lionel Jeffries; *Sven*, Edward Judd; *Princess Gerda*, Beba Loncar; *King Harald*, Clifton Evans; *Rykka*, Colin Blakely; *Vahlin*, Gordon Jackson; *Olla*, David Lodge; *Auctioneer*, Henry Oscar; *Raschid*, Paul Stassino; *Ylva*, Jeanne Moody.

CREDITS:

A Warwick/Avala Production. *Producer*, Irving Allen; *associate producer*, Denis O'Dell; *director*, Jack Cardiff; *screenplay*, Berkely Mather and Beverley Cross; based on the novel by Frans Bengtsson; *photography*, Christopher Challis; *music*, Doran Radic; *second unit director*, Cliff Lyons; *art director*, John Hoesli; *technical advisor*, Erik Kiersgaard; *assistant director*, Bluey Hill; *editor*, Geoffrey Foot. Technirama and Technicolor. Running time: 124 minutes.

Following his splendid performance as Homer Smith in *Lilies of the Field*, Poitier turned to the role of El Mansuh, the Moorish sheik, in *The Long Ships*. "To say it was disastrous is a compliment," was Poitier's own conclusion.

*Time* Magazine described the film as "a riotous sea saga [with] impossible acting, a preposterous script, some eminently see-worthy ship reconstructions, and more enjoyable bloody foolishness than many an epic costing three times as much."

*The Long Ships* is a boisterous adventure yarn, made by British director, Jack Cardiff, for an English/Yugoslav film combine. It concerns the rivalry of the Vikings (under Richard Widmark) and the Moors (headed by Poitier) in search of a legendary Golden Bell, framed in a conglomeration of pitched battles, seastorms, floggings, double-crosses, unarmed combat and winking views of sexy maidens. *Time* called it "a thing of booty."

With Beba Loncar.

Mansuh (Poitier), after learning of the whereabouts of the legendary Golden Bell of St. James, fashioned from the gold that crusaders had looted in Byzantium.

Determined to mount an expedition to retrieve the bell, Rolfe recruits his brother, Orm (Russ Tamblyn), kidnaps Orm's girlfriend, Princess Gerda (Beba Loncar), and holds her hostage on a new Long Ship, the magnificent funeral ship Krok had just made for Gerda's father, King Harald (Clifford Evans). Rolfe and crew set sail southward with Harald and his nobles in desperate pursuit. When a whirlpool wrecks their ship off the Moorish coast, Rolfe and his men fall into the hands of El Mansuh, who forces them to use their superior seamanship to lead him to the bell.

Aside from being Poitier's first film after winning his Oscar, it allowed him to read some of the most ridiculous dialogue in decades and, for the first time, permitted him to have a white wife (Rosanna Schiaffino), although she ultimately betrays him to blue-eyed, blond Richard Widmark. In the movie, Rolfe (Widmark), the Viking adventurer son of Norse shipbuilder, Krok (Oscar Homolka), returns from a voyage in which he ran afoul of the Moorish prince, El

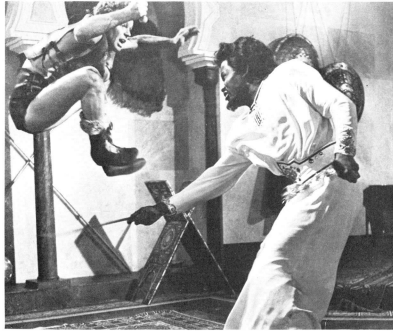

With Russ Tamblyn.

While another ship is being built, the Vikings are imprisoned and Gerda is taken to El Mansuh's harem, to the annoyance of his chief wife, Aminah.

Rolfe engineers an escape and, with his men, wrecks the harem, before being recaptured, and El Mansuh orders Rolfe to ride the Mare of Steel—a torture device that slits its riders length-

With Rosanna Schiaffino.

As El Mansuh.

wise, from the groin up. Aminah, though, persuades El Mansuh that the only way to get the Golden Bell is for Rolfe and his men to guide the Moors past the treacherous whirlpool. The sheik agrees, but while the Moors and the Vikings are recovering the treasure in a delicate operation, King Harald is capturing El Mansuh's stronghold.

El Mansuh and Aminah are among those who die in the subsequent fighting. Orm and Gerda are reunited, and King Harald, delighted to have the Golden Bell, pardons Rolfe, who then interests Harald in the long lost Three Crowns of the Saxon Kings, one of which reportedly holds a diamond as big as the egg of a seagull.

In a piece on Poitier in the *Sunday New York Times,* playwright Clifford Mason observed: "At least the villain he played in *The Long Ships*

was a fighter—on his own mission in his own world . . . He was not killed as a mean, despicable villain, but rather as a noble enemy. Even more important, he was nobody's eunuch or black mammy busting his gut for white folks as if their problems were all that's important in the world."

Generally, however, Poitier received his worst screen notices for *The Long Ships.* Judith Crist, reviewing for the *New York Herald Tribune,* called the film "one of the best awful spectacular adventure movies around," and then noted: "Widmark out-Fairbanks them all, with eye aglint and tongue not quite visibly in cheek, while Poitier, a fairy tale ebony figure in cloth-of-gold splendor, plays it dedicated-straight." Howard Thompson wrote in *The New York Times:* "As the two wily, warring leaders, Messrs. Wid-

With Richard Widmark.

mark and Poitier glare at each other reasonably in surface characterizations laconically returned to the writers (and the audience)."

In *The Cleveland Press,* critic Stan Anderson found that: "Poitier, who ought to play Othello on the stage, here puts on some fancy raiment to act a Moorish sheik whose greatest passion in life is to find the legendary bell." George Bourke, in *The Miami Herald,* said: "Poitier, as the Moor, is called upon to play a subdued, smoldering personality, and is thus eclipsed by the vigor of Widmark, who seems to be having an actor's lark."

The judgement in *Variety:* "Leaders of the rival factions are Richard Widmark, an adventurous Viking con man, who plays strictly tongue-in-cheek, and Sidney Poitier, dignified, ruthless top man of the Moors. In contrast to Widmark, he seeks to take the film seriously. The clash in styles between these two is a minor disaster [and] Poitier's less robust, more subtle performance is often lost in the surrounding babel."

Critic Robin Bean of *Films and Filming* felt that *"The Long Ships* is a celluloid fish that has rather missed the tide by about five years [and] in comparison with Richard Fleischer's *The Vikings,* it is comic book stuff . . . Poitier seems quite lost as a bell-obsessed sheik and contents himself with an interpretation of what seems nearer Othello . . . Still, there is a thoroughly entertaining performance from Richard Widmark as the 'fearless' Rolfe, who turns out more of a Viking Billy Liar." Dennis John Hall, also writing in *Films and Filming,* later said: "Action is the film's *raison d'être* and along with the rest of the cast, Poitier hams it up with great gusto—a welcome change from the sombre didactics of his more serious roles. Technically substandard for an epic, it has an endearing archness typified by Poitier's portrayal of the sheik as a sort of cut-price Othello."

With Eric Portman.

# The Bedford Incident

Columbia Pictures                    1965

THE CAST:

*Capt. Eric Finlander,* RICHARD WIDMARK; *Ben Munceford,* SIDNEY POITIER; *Ensign Ralston,* James MacArthur; *Lt. Cmdr. Chester Potter, M.D.,* Martin Balsam; *Seaman Merlin Queffle,* Wally Cox; *Commodore Wolfgang Schrepke,* Eric Portman; *Commander Allison,* Michael Kane; *Seaman Jones,* Colin Maitland; *Lt. Krindlemeyer,* Michael Graham; *Lt. Hazelwood,* Bill Edwards; *Lt. Bascombe,* Gary Cockrell; *Lt. Berger,* George Roubieck; *Lt. Beckman,* Brian Davies; *Lt. Hacker,* Edward Bishop; *Chief Hospitalman McKinley,* Phil Brown; *Hospitalman Nerney,* Donald Sutherland; *Hospitalman Strauss,* Warren Stanhope; *Communications Petty Officer,* Laurence Herder; *Sailors on Bridge,* Paul Tamarin, Frank Lieberman, James Caffrey, Burnell Tucker, Stephen Von Schreiber, Ronald Rubin and Eugene Leonard; *Sailors in C.I.C.,* Roy Stephens, John McCarthy, Shane Rimmer and Glen Beck.

CREDITS:

*Producers,* James B. Harris and Richard Widmark; *associate producer,* Denis O'Dell; *director,* James B. Harris; *screenplay,* James Poe; *based on* the novel by Mark Rascovich; *photography,* Gilbert Taylor; *music,* Gerard Schurmann; *assistant director,* Clive Reed; *art director,* Arthur Lawson; *editor,* John Jympson. Running time: 102 minutes.

In *The Bedford Incident,* a first-rate contemporary sea drama, Sidney Poitier and Richard Widmark were the adversaries for the third time on the screen. Unfortunately, Poitier had little to do as the journalist aboard a nuclear destroyer commanded by a psychopathic martinet, a role which allowed Widmark to chew the scenery. Poitier later described *The Bedford Incident* as "a bad movie, but it didn't start out to be a bad movie." His cryptic remark never was elaborated on further, and it remains for others to judge the reasons for the failure of the film, which closely parallels in characters and events Columbia's earlier release, Sidney Lumet's *Fail Safe.*

*The Bedford Incident,* the directorial debut of James B. Harris (who co-produced the film with Richard Widmark), deals with an encounter between an American destroyer on NATO duty in the North Atlantic and a Russian submarine that escalates into a nuclear disaster. Sidney Poitier is Ben Munceford, a correspondent-photographer who is on board the U.S.S. *Bedford* looking for a promising story. He is greeted coldly by Captain Eric Finlander (Widmark), known at the Pentagon as "the most aggressive, result-getting officer in the U.S. Navy," a by-the-book commander. Also on the cruise is Commodore Wolfgang Schrepke (Eric Portman), veteran German submarine commander assigned to the *Bedford* as a NATO observer. Both discover that Finlander has turned his crew into hero-worshippers although he drives his men almost to the point of breakdown in his phobia about the Communists' edge in the military balance of power.

Although Munceford and Schrepke conclude that Finlander is a dangerous man, they are powerless to report their feelings. When Seaman Merlin Queffle (Wally Cox), the ship's sonar operator, picks up an unidentified submarine on his multiplicity of electronic devices, Finlander comes alive and initiates a relentless pursuit of the lurking sub, under the pretense that it is a training exercise for his crew. As such, he keeps the men at battle readiness for nerve tense hours. Schrepke warns Finlander that the harassed sub will strike back; that its crew is as worn down by this war of nerves as is the *Bedford*'s.

Munceford accuses Finlander of being prepared for a "kill" and actually hoping for it. Even the ship's medical officer, Lt. Commander Potter (Martin Balsam), warns against driving the crew too far, after Queffle collapses at his sonar board. The situation suddenly explodes when Ensign Ralston (James MacArthur), a new officer earning his stripes under Finlander's relentless prodding,

With Richard Widmark.

misinterprets an order and nervously fires an atomic weapon at the submarine. Its own dying action is to fire its torpedoes in response, and the *Bedford* and her victim sink together under a mushroom cloud, signalling a possible new holocaust.

"Sidney Poitier and Eric Portman are little more than straight men for Widmark," Arthur

With Richard Widmark and
Eric Portman.

With Eric Portman.

Knight observed in *Saturday Review,* and then went on to rave about the latter: "Not in years has [he] had a role so completely suited to his talents, combining cynicism, self-assurance and refined sadism." Robert Salmaggi wrote in the *New York Herald Tribune:* "Poitier's role appears to have been enlarged from the book, and perhaps because of this doesn't ring true. It is, save for one or two scenes, a static, thankless role."

In *The New York Times,* Bosley Crowther called the film an "austerely masculine picture of a maritime episode in the cold war, a grimly absorbing speculation of how wrong one ship's captain might be . . . but the whole thing transcends plausibility." Crowther also noted: "Sidney Poitier plays the reporter with a casual and cocky air that any self-respecting skipper would not long tolerate. Certainly no reasonable captain would give this fellow the run of his ship and allow him to snap candid pictures on such a sensitive cruise as this."

*Variety* commented: "Poitier does an excellent job in the light and serious aspects of his role, and manages to leave a personal stamp on his scenes. The part provides vital identity to civilian audiences since it lends exposition to certain aspects of Naval life." And Kathleen Carroll wrote in her New York *Daily News* review: "Poitier has to buck a sketchy part, which he does with his customary finesse."

As photo-journalist Ben Munceford.

Most critics, however, either sloughed off Poitier—Brendan Gill, in *The New Yorker,* called him "distressingly inept as a journalist"—or mentioned him only in passing (as did *Time)* or not at all *(Newsweek).*

Playwright Clifford Mason, in his later piece on Poitier in *The New York Times,* complained: "Poitier is a black correspondent who went around calling everyone sir. . . . And after Widmark barks at him and pushes him around all over the ship for almost two hours, the only thing he gets to do at the end is shout at bad Dickey Widmark . . . For [Widmark's] kind of mistake, Poitier should at least have been allowed to bust him one in the jaw."

With Telly Savalas, Indus Arthur and Paul Newlan.

# The Slender Thread

Paramount                                     1965

THE CAST:

*Alan Newell,* SIDNEY POITIER; *Inga Dyson,* ANNE BANCROFT; *Dr. Joe Coburn,* Telly Savalas; *Mark Dyson,* Steven Hill; *Marion,* Indus Arthur; *Chris Dyson,* Greg Jarvis; *Patrolman Steve Peters,* Robert Hoy; *Patrolman Bert Enyard,* John Benson; *Sgt. Harry Ward,* Paul Newlan; *Det. Judd Ridley,* Edward Asner; *Medical Technician,* Jason Wingreen; *Charlie,* Dabney Coleman; *Edna,* Janet Dudley; *Al McCardle,* Lane Bradford; *Dr. Alden Van,* John Napier; *Mrs. Thomas,* Marjorie Nelson; *Doctor,* H. M. Wynant; *Arthur Foss,* Steven Marlo; *Liquor Salesman,* Thomas Hall.

CREDITS:

*Producer,* Stephen Alexander; *director,* Sydney Pollack; *screenplay,* Stirling Silliphant; based on a *Life* Magazine article "Decision to Die" by Shana Alexander; *photography,* Loyal Griggs; *music,* Quincy Jones; *assistant director,* Don

Roberts; *art directors,* Hal Pereira and Jack Poplin; *costumes,* Edith Head; *editor,* Thomas Stanford. Running time: 98 minutes.

Except for its two recent Academy Award winners in the leads, *The Slender Thread* might well have been a made-for-TV movie—and worked better as one. Sidney Poitier and Anne Bancroft co-starred in this one in only the figurative sense. They had no scenes together, and Miss Bancroft could just as well have phoned in her part of a would-be suicide calling a crisis clinic for help. Each turned in the type of convincing, tour-de-force performance to be expected of these fine artists, but as a thriller with psychological pretensions, *The Slender Thread* never caught fire.

The film, which, like *The Bedford Incident,* used Poitier's talents as an actor without regard to race, marked the feature film directorial debut of Sydney Pollack (late of television) and was

As Alan Newell.

based on journalist Shana Alexander's series of 1964 articles describing the psychological crisis that led one anonymous Seattle housewife to attempt suicide. The movie itself, originally entitled *Call Me Back*, was filmed on location in Seattle.

In *The Slender Thread*, as in his later *A Patch of Blue*, Poitier is bent on saving the life of a girl, playing a sort of "suicides anonymous" volunteer who battles to maintain a telephone connection with the would-be suicide until the police can locate her. He plays Alan Newell, a University of Washington anthropology student, who is on duty at the Seattle Crisis Clinic when the call comes in. The head of the staff, Dr. Joe Coburn (Telly Savalas) has left for home, and Newell is alone.

Talking to the phantom caller who has told him she has swallowed an overdose of sleeping pills, Newell tries frantically to get some clue to her identity and location, realizing that the telephone line has become the slender thread with which he must try to save her life against her will. He manages to start an emergency trace on the call and to dispatch an urgent summons to Dr. Coburn. Meanwhile, the woman gives a confused account of herself, during which Newell learns that her name is Inga (Anne Bancroft), she is married, and that she has attempted suicide before.

Gradually, he draws from her the background of her life and her reasons for trying to end it. Her husband (Steven Hill), the skipper of a commercial fishing boat, has discovered that he is not the father of her son and cannot forgive her for deceiving him. She describes her first suicide attempt and resulting hospitalization, but stubbornly refuses to give Newell any information that might save her. She now has less than thirty minutes to live, and when two police officers reach her house, they find her gone, but, from the babysitter, learn where she works, the kind of car she drives, and the whereabouts of her husband, who is quickly contacted by the Coast Guard.

Newell, though, desperately refuses to give up and persuades her to keep talking. Wild with frustration, he pours forth an impassioned argu-

As Alan Newell.

ment for life and love, but her voice gradually grows faint, her words incoherent. The police finally break into her motel room, and find her still breathing. She can be saved, Newell is told. With mingled relief and elation, he then returns to his phones and takes the next call.

"For Poitier the portrayal is a tour-de-force," critic Tony Mastroianni wrote in *The Cleveland Press*, "an exercise in how to act under limited conditions. He is confined to one room and the phone is his only prop. He pleads with it, laughs at it, screams into it, scorns it. Every emotion registers on his face, in the movements of his body, the sag of his shoulders, his gestures."

A. H. Weiler, reviewing *The Slender Thread*

With Telly Savalas.

for *The New York Times,* thought: "The role of the student who tenaciously and selflessly clings to the slender thread in her behalf is portrayed by Mr. Poitier with rewarding naturalness. The fact that Mr. Poitier is a Negro has no bearing on the drama unfolded. Except for a lapse or two into flamboyance, he does ample justice in wonderfully restrained style, to an exacting assignment."

In the *New York World Telegram,* Alton Cook viewed: "Sidney Poitier roars, wheedles, jeers, even tries a whispered word of love as he pleads for the woman's name and whereabouts so help can be rushed. Most important, he conveys a spirit of deep concern that is readily shared . . . Even if you begin with condemnation [about Anne Bancroft's self-created dilemma], chances are that Poitier will win you over to his attitude that life, not retribution, is the key factor here."

W. Ward Marsh raved in the *Cleveland Plain-Dealer:* "Poitier, Oscar winner for *Lilies of the Field,* gives a brilliant performance. He also merits another nomination." A similar notice came from Charles Aaronson in *Motion Picture Herald:* "The woman attempting suicide and the man who seeks to save her are Anne Bancroft and Sidney Poitier, both Academy Award winners, both clearly indicating why they have been accorded these high honors. They may yet be nominated again."

Less enthusiastic was the review given the film by Arthur Knight in *Saturday Review,* who decided that "neither Stirling Silliphant's talk-clogged script nor director Sydney Pollack's restless camera ever penetrates the surface of the characters involved. We see what they are doing, we hear what they are saying, but neither is sufficient to make us share Poitier's urgency to keep the would-be suicide alive."

*Time* wrote: "The movie is a routine, sometimes mawkish melodrama and a sorry misuse of talent . . . Poitier behaves precisely like an Oscar winning actor who has to work up an hour or more of excitement with a hot line as his only prop." And *Newsweek* said: "They carry on, these two talented Academy Award winners, as if they had never made a movie. Pollack allows or encourages Poitier to wave his arms like a windmill trying to dodge Sancho Panza, and allows or encourages Miss Bancroft to luxuriate in the bathos of Stirling Silliphant's dialogue."

Shorter notices included *Commonweal* critic Philip T. Hartung's observation that "there is little to say about Poitier's performance except that he registers concern and elation, and uses the telephone well;" Robert Salmaggi's comment in the *New York Herald Tribune* that "Poitier, although admittedly in a difficult role, chained as he is to a telephone in a single room, seems to overplay it, bearing too heavily on an assortment of Pollyanna and who-do-you-think-you-are? lines"; and the conclusion of Britain's *Monthly Film Bulletin* that "Poitier . . . brings to his role almost more enthusiasm than it can comfortably bear."

As Alan Newell.

With Max Von Sydow.

# The Greatest Story Ever Told

United Artists                     1965

THE CAST:

*Jesus Christ*, Max Von Sydow; *Mary*, Dorothy McGuire; *Joseph*, Robert Loggia; *John the Baptist*, Charlton Heston; *James the Younger*, Michael Anderson, Jr.; *Simon the Zealot*, Robert Blake; *Andrew*, Burt Brinckerhoff; *John*, John Considine; *Thaddeus*, Jamie Farr; *Philip*, David Hedison; *Nathanael*, Peter Mann; *Judas Iscariot*, David McCallum; *Matthew*, Roddy McDowall; *Peter*, Gary Raymond; *Thomas*, Tom Reese; *James the Elder*, David Sheiner; *Martha of Bethany*, Ina Balin; *Mary of Bethany*, Janet Margolin; *Lazarus*, Michael Tolan; *Simon of Cyrene*, Sidney Poitier; *Mary Magdalene*, Joanna Dunham; *Veronica*, Carroll Baker; *Young Man at the Tomb*, Pat Boone; *Bar Amand*, Van Heflin; *Uriah*, Sal Mineo; *Woman of No Name*, Shelley Winters; *Old Aram*, Ed Wynn; *The Centurion*, John Wayne; *Pontius Pilate*, Telly Savalas; *Claudia*, Angela Lansbury; *Pilate's Aide*, Johnny Seven; *Questor*, Paul Stewart; *General Varus*, Harold J. Stone; *Caiaphas*, Martin Landau; *Shemiah*, Nehemiah Persoff; *Nicodemus*, Joseph Schildkraut; *Sorak*, Victor Buono; *Emissary*, Robert Busch; *Alexander*, John Crawford; *Scribe*, Russell Johnson; *Speaker of Capernaum*, John Lupton; *Joseph of Arimathaea*, Abraham Sofaer; *Theophilus*, Chet Stratton; *Annas*, Ron Whelan; *Herod Antipas*, Jose Ferrer; *Herod the Great*, Claude Rains; *Aben*, John Abbott; *Captain of Lancers*, Rodolfo Acosta; *Herod's Commander*, Michael Ansara; *Chuza*, Philip Coolidge; *Philip*, Dal Jenkins; *Archelaus*, Joe Perry; *Herodias*, Marian Seldes; *The Dark Hermit*, Donald Pleasance; *Barabbas*, Richard Conte; *The Tormentor*,

Frank De Kova; *Dumah,* Joseph Sirola; *Melchior,* Cyril Delevanti; *Balthazar,* Mark Lenard; *Caspar,* Frank Silvera.

CREDITS:

A George Stevens Production. *Executive producer,* Frank I. Davis; *producer/director,* George Stevens; *associate producers,* George Stevens, Jr., and Antonio Vellani; *screenplay,* James Lee Barrett and George Stevens; based on *Books of the Old and New Testaments* and other ancient writings, the book by Fulton Oursler, and writings by Henry Denker; *photography,* William C. Mellor and Loyal Griggs; *music,* Alfred Newman; *choral supervision,* Ken Darby; *art directors,* Richard Day and William Creber; *special effects,* J. McMillan Johnson, Clarence Slifer, A. Arnold Gillespie and Robert R. Hoag; *costumes,* Vittorio Nino Novarese; *editors,* Argyle Nelson, Jr., and Frank O'Neill. Filmed in Ultra Panavision and Technicolor. Running time: 222 minutes.

Befitting his major star screen status—the type which allows the best known and most recognizable film personalities to do nothing more than walk-ons (or, as they prefer to call them, cameos), Sidney Poitier was asked by producer/director George Stevens to do a guest appearance in *The Greatest Story Ever Told.* He appears fleetingly as Simon of Cyrene and has a line or two of dialogue as he helps Jesus (played with strength and dignity by Max Von Sydow) arrange the wooden cross on his shoulder as he drags it through the streets of Bethlehem to the Crucifixion.

The film, made with grandeur and reverence in the well-established epic screen style, was the realization of a lifelong dream for Stevens, and a bitter disappointment subsequently because of its generally indifferent reception. He apparently had counted on his spectacular cast of primarily Hollywood superstars and second magnitude film personages portraying the important and peripheral Biblical figures to help attract audiences which historically avoid religious (non-Cecil B. De Mille) screen pageants. In this instance, Poitier was joined by fellow "guests" ranging from the virtually obligatory Charlton Heston as John the Baptist to Telly Savalas as Pontius Pilate to David McCallum as Judas to Claude Rains as Herod the

Great to John Wayne as a centurion to the entire Inbal Dance Theatre of Israel.

*The Greatest Story Ever Told,* made over a period of nearly three years (it was filmed in northern Arizona and Utah, in the vicinity of the now-submerged Glen Canyon Valley, along the buttes and washes of the Colorado River, on Pyramid Lake outside of Reno, and at the Desilu Studios in Hollywood), is generally considered among the finest Biblical epics produced for the screen. Unfortunately, critical reviews were tepid at best and United Artists, the distributor, frantically began slashing away at it shortly after its premiere engagement. Its original running time of 222 minutes was pared to 141 minutes during its several "initial release" runs and it never was given a full blown reissue prior to being sold to television. During its various "shearings," *The Greatest Story Ever Told* lost the entire 40 Days in the Wilderness sequence with Donald Pleasance as the apocryphal Dark Hermit (according to *Variety),* as well as, among others, several bits which reportedly had annoyed reviewers: Shelley Winters' leper, John Wayne's centurion, etc.

In reviewing the film, which is listed among the all-time boxoffice champs as computed by *Variety* (grossing $7,000,000), most critics made disparaging remarks about the unending parade of movie stars crossing Christ's path. One or two made note of Sidney Poitier's appearance. Bosley Crowther admired the film itself, calling it "surely the world's most conglomerate Biblical picture with things of supreme and solemn beauty . . . scenes in which the grandeur of nature is brilliantly used to suggest the surge of the human spirit in waves of exaltation and awe . . . glimpses of Max Von Sydow that light the huge screen with revelation of the raptures and torments of the soul." *The New York Times* critic then regretted: ". . . most distracting are the frequent pop-ups of familiar faces in so-called cameo roles, jarring the illusion of the moment with the diversion of the mind to the business of discovery . . . Sidney Poitier's Simon of Cyrene is the only Negro conspicuous in the picture and seems a last minute symbolization of racial brotherhood."

In the *New York Herald Tribune,* Judith Crist wrote: "[It] succeeds in a number of areas where other Hollywood spectaculars have failed in detailing the life of Christ [but] Mr. Stevens has vitiated the power of his 'unknown' Christ and disciples by casting any number of too well known players in less-than-bit barely-flash-in-the-pan parts . . . and before you know it you're caught in a game of spot-the-stars."

*Time* concluded that Stevens' film was "3 hours and 41 minutes worth of impeccable boredom . . . Its sole distinction lies in its contrast to those rambunctiously zealous camp meetings that Cecil B. DeMille used to patch together out of breastplates, flexed muscles and Persian rugs . . . The long, long road to Calvary is lined with the usual yea-verily types plus, it would seem, any other celebrity ready to trade top billing for a chance to play holy charades."

Britain's *Monthly Film Bulletin* felt that "this film, for all its sincere piety and anxious good taste, for all the immense time and effort lavished on it, and for all the technical expertise and resources at the command of its maker, enshrines a minimum of spiritual and intellectual content [but] what finally undermines the film's pretensions to be taken seriously is the use of stars in bit parts, producing such incongruities as . . . Sidney Poitier's succoring Simon of Cyrene (a liberal gesture as gratuitous as that final, banal image of [Stevens'] *Giant)."*

With Max Von Sydow.

With Elizabeth Hartman.

# A Patch of Blue

Metro-Goldwyn-Mayer                    1965

THE CAST:

*Gordon Ralfe*, SIDNEY POITIER; *Rose-Ann D'Arcey*, SHELLEY WINTERS; *Selina D'Arcey*, ELIZABETH HARTMAN; *Ole Pa*, Wallace Ford; *Mark Ralfe*, Ivan Dixon; *Sadie*, Elizabeth Fraser; *Mr. Faber*, John Qualen; *Yanek Faber*, Kelly Flynn; *Selina at age 5*, Debi Storm; *Mrs. Favalore*, Renata Vanni; *Mr. Favalore*, Saverio LoMedico; and David Richards, Fred Holliday, Vincent Chase, Gregg Martell, Dorothy Lovett, Robert B. Williams, Tom Curtis.

CREDITS:

*Producer*, Pandro S. Berman; *associate producer*, Kathryn Hereford; *director*, Guy Green; *screenplay*, Guy Green; based on the novel *Be Ready with Bells and Drums by* Elizabeth Kata; *photography*, Robert Burks; *music*, Jerry Goldsmith; *assistant director*, Hank Moonjean; *art directors*, George W. Davis and Urie McCleary; *editor*, Rita Roland. Panavision. Running time: 105 minutes.

In the film version of Elizabeth Kata's novel, *Be*

*Ready with Bells and Drums*, Sidney Poitier again donned his predictable good guy persona to star opposite Elizabeth Hartman (in her film debut), to play Prince Charming to her Cinderella. The twist here is that the Cinderella is a blind white girl and the Prince Charming who helps rehabilitate her from her shabby tenement is black. Several critics alluded to the film's basic similarities to early D. W. Griffith melodramas and to Chaplin's *City Lights* in its concept (focusing on the afflicted girl) while flirting openly—and rather startlingly by contemporary Hollywood standards —with the issue of interracial love. Poitier himself has been less than enthusiastic when recalling the film, however. "I had never worked in a man-woman relationship that was not symbolic," he chafed. "Either there were no women, or there was a woman but she was blind, or the relationship was of a nature that satisfied the taboos. I was at my wits' end when I finished *A Patch of Blue.*"

In the film, Selina D'Arcey (Elizabeth Hartman), a blind teenager who shares a dreary apart-

With Elizabeth Hartman.

ment with her sluttish mother Rose-Ann (Shelley Winters), and her drunken grandfather, Ole Pa (Wallace Ford), drudges her days away stringing beads when she's not cooking and cleaning up after her mother. Selina had been blinded at the age of five during a family quarrel and later was raped by one of her mother's clients, and thereafter was kept as an illiterate chattel whose only joy comes from the few hours she has in a nearby park, accompanied by Mr. Faber (John Qualen), the man who supplies her with beads.

Despite Rose-Ann's disapproval, Selina persuades Ole Pa to take her to the park again on his way to the nearest bar, and there she strikes up a friendship with Gordon Ralfe (Poitier), a courteous, well-spoken clerk in a nearby store. The two meet whenever Selina can get Ole Pa or Mr. Faber to escort her to the park, and through Gordon she blossoms, receiving from him selfless love, sympathy and understanding, the beginnings of a formal education, an introduction to life, and the ability to laugh for the first time.

Gordon is reluctant to confess that he is a Negro despite the fact that Selina is falling in love with him, and she remains unshaken in her adoration even when Rose-Ann maliciously reveals the truth, humiliating her daughter publicly and screaming, "I seen you with that nigger, that black buck." And Gordon's own doctor brother, Mark (Ivan Dixon), berates him about his growing relationship with a white girl. Gordon, though, goes through with his plans to get Selina into a school for the blind, and succeeds in wresting her from Rose-Ann who, with her friend and ex-hooker Sadie (Elizabeth Fraser), had hoped to turn Selina into a prostitute. Despite Selina's appeal that he should marry her, Gordon decides that school is the best course for her at the present time, relegating their future relationship to limbo.

"*A Patch of Blue* is an arrantly sentimental film that batters the emotions mercilessly and strikes cruelly at the sensibilities," Judith Crist wrote in the *New York Herald Tribune*. "Its triumph is that through four excellent performances it holds the attention and touches the heart and even attains credibility . . . Sidney Poitier, so thoroughly the embodiment of a man secure within himself, is remarkable as the outgoing and dignified man on the tightrope of interracial relations." In *Commonweal*, Philip T. Hartung said: "Guy

With Elizabeth Hartman and Shelley Winters.

Green . . . was successful in keeping this tender tale from becoming soupy. His cast is also helpful in this direction, especially Sidney Poitier, superb as the soft-voiced, thoughtful Negro." And Kathleen Carroll, in her rave review in the New York *Daily News,* spoke of Poitier's "glowing performance," and noted: "In a soft, pliant manner, it seems that Poitier can say more than any other actor."

Less ecstatic was Bosley Crowther, who commented: "It is obvious that this mild and modest film about the surge of gratitude and devotion in the heart of a white girl, who is blind, toward a Negro man who befriends her, is meant to convey a moving sense of the absence of racial prejudice where an exchange of true humanity is concerned . . . The action is too patly formulated, and Mr. Poitier, who is an honest performer, has to act too much like a saint."

In *Time,* these words: *"A Patch of Blue* takes some getting used to. It starts as a pointless little tearjerker, then turns abruptly into contemporary hope opera. To save it from itself requires extraordinary skill, and the movie is fortunate in having miracle workers at hand . . . In their quiet, tender scenes together, Hartman and Poitier conquer the insipidity of a plot that reduces tangled human problems to a case of the black leading the blind."

With Elizabeth Hartman.

More virulent was the critic for *Newsweek,* who referred to Poitier simply as "part Romeo and part Annie Sullivan," and wrote that "no other film has managed to simultaneously insult the Negroes and the blind. Neither of these Firsts

With director Guy Green and Elizabeth Hartman.

With Elizabeth Hartman.

came easily. It took a master of the maudlin, a thoroughly eclectic vulgarian, to get such results from the simple story of a blind white girl falling in love with a Negro . . . but this monument to bad taste is bigger than both its makers." And Brendan Gill, in his review in *The New Yorker,* never bothered mentioning Poitier while complaining: ". . . a terrible movie [that] comes close to being literally sickening in its sentimentality . . . a more accurate title for the movie would have been 'A Pot of Glue' or even 'A Pat of Goo.' "

Britain's *Monthly Film Bulletin* also gave it a negative notice, while conceding that "considering the parlous nature of his material, Sidney Poitier manages to turn in a remarkably tactful performance, so that most of his scenes are agreeably touching."

Elizabeth Hartman received a Best Actress nomination at Oscar time for her role in the film, but lost the award to Julie Christie. For her performance as the slatternly mother, though, Shelley Winters was selected Best Supporting Actress of 1965.

As Toller.

# Duel at Diablo

United Artists                    1966

THE CAST:

*Jess Remsberg*, JAMES GARNER; *Toller*, SIDNEY POITIER; *Ellen Grange*, Bibi Andersson; *Willard Grange*, Dennis Weaver; *Lt. Scotty McAllister*, Bill Travers; *Sgt. Ferguson*, William Redfield; *Chata*, John Hoyt; *Clay Dean*, John Crawford; *Major Novak*, John Hubbard; *Norton*, Kevin Coughlin; *Tech*, Jay Ripley; *Casey*, Jeff Cooper; *Nyles*, Ralph Bahnsen; *Swenson*, Bobby Crawford; *Forbes*, Richard Lapp; *Ramirez*, Armand Alzamora; *Col. Foster*, Alf Elson; *Chata's Wife*, Dawn Little Sky; *Alchise*, Eddie Little Sky; *Miner*, Al Wyatt; *Cpl. Harrington*, Bill Hart; *Crowley*, J. R. Randall; *Stableman*, John Daheim; *Burly Soldier*, Phil Schumacker; *Wagon Drivers*, Richard Farnsworth and Joe Finnegan.

CREDITS:

A Nelson/Engel/Cherokee Production. *Producers*, Ralph Nelson and Fred Engel; *director*, Ralph Nelson; *screenplay*, Marvin H. Albert and Michel M. Grilikhes; based on the novel *Apache Rising* by Marvin H. Albert; *photography*, Charles F. Wheeler; *music*, Neal Hefti; *assistant directors*, Emmett Emerson and Philip N. Cook; *art director*, Alfred Ybarra; *special effects*, Roscoe Cline, Larry Hampton and George Peckham; *editor*, Fredric Steinkamp. Color by DeLuxe. Running time: 103 minutes.

In his first Western, Sidney Poitier was reunited with *Lilies of the Field* director, Ralph Nelson. The film, a grim, taut melodrama set in the old

With James Garner.

West, blended mystery, suspense and an endless flow of violence with the magnificent sweep of Utah scenery, as it explored, among other things, the subject of miscegenation. Refreshingly, Sidney Poitier was not involved in this theme, but rather in a running antagonism with Bill Travers, playing an overambitious Scottish cavalryman, not over the color issue (never mentioned in the film) but because of Poitier's civilian dealings with the Army as a bronco busting ex-soldier selling horses.

Dressed in fancy gambler duds, Poitier turns a striking figure among the mud-caked, weather-beaten characters who help people *Duel at Diablo,* which has James Garner as a stubble-chinned frontier scout hunting the man who had scalped his Comanche wife; Bibi Andersson (of the Ingmar Bergman stock company in her American film debut) as the outcast bride of an Army muleskinner who, as a former captive of the Apaches, had given birth to a child; Bill Travers as a staunch cavalry officer in charge of a company of green recruits.

On his way to Fort Creel, Jess Remsberg (Garner) rescues Ellen Grange (Bibi Andersson), a white woman, from marauding Apaches and learns that she had been their captive for more than a year. When her husband, Willard (Dennis Weaver), a freighter at the fort, denounces her for not killing herself after Apache Chief Chata (John Hoyt) had kidnapped her, she attempts to steal some horses and make her way back to the Apache settlement.

Mrs. Grange is surprised by three men who attempt to rape her but is saved by Jess and his buddy, Toller (Poitier), an Army horse wrangler. The two had just battled over an Indian woman's scalp which Jess' friend, Lt. Scotty McAllister (Travers), had gotten from Clay Dean (John Crawford), the marshal at Fort Concho. The scalp, which Toller had tried to price, turns out to be that of Jess' Indian wife.

Jess and Toller escort Ellen Grange back to the fort, but during the night, she manages to make good her escape. The next morning, McAllister leads a detachment of raw recruits and heads the Army supply train for Fort Concho,

With Bill Travers and James Garner.

with Jess scouting for the troop. He rides ahead into Apache country and once again rescues Ellen, noticing this time a child under her cloak as they ride back. She tells Jess it is hers by Chata's son. Rejoining the supply train, Jess and Ellen find that the outfit has suffered heavy losses in an Indian ambush and that the water supply has been destroyed. After outwitting the Apaches at Diablo Canyon, where there is fresh water,

Jess rides off to Fort Concho for reinforcements.

There Jess learns from Clay Dean that he had won the Indian scalp in a poker game with Willard Grange. Angered, he returns to Diablo where the remnants of the troop are under another attack by Chata and his braves. During the savage fighting, McAllister is killed and Grange is taken hostage. Soon, only Jess, Toller and Ellen and four troopers are left alive in the duel at

With Bill Travers and Dennis Weaver.

[ 139 ]

With Armand Alzamora, Jeff Cooper (partially hidden), Ralph Bahnsen and James Garner.

Diablo, but as Chata leads his remaining braves for the final assault, the cavalry reinforcements appear on the rim of the canyon. Jess then goes in search of Grange and finds him strapped to a wagon wheel hung over hot coals. He is barely alive and begs Jess to shoot him. Instead, Jess hands him a pistol, and, as the survivors ride off with the troops, a shot rings out. Jess and Toller patch up their differences and Ellen is free to ride back to the Apache camp and to the father of her child.

"*Duel at Diablo* is a brutal film and a brilliant one," reviewer Robert Alden wrote in *The New York Times*. "It is a vicious film—grim, tough and taut. There is barely a moment in it that is not a moment of violence or a moment of tension . . . Sidney Poitier is cast in the not-quite-believable role of a dandified but courageous ex-cavalry sergeant."

"*Duel at Diablo* packs enough fast action in its cavalry-Indians narrative to satisfy the most avid follower of this type of entertainment," said the critic for *Variety*. "Poitier tackles a new type of characterization here, far afield from anything he has essayed in the past."

"*Duel at Diablo* has a plot that is more com-

With Bill Travers (with saber).

As Toller.

plicated than usual. And two of its complications have to do with miscegenation," Philip T. Hartung observed in *Commonweal*. "But more startling than the miscegenation themes is the presence of Sidney Poitier in the second-leading role. He gives another of his fine performances, and his color is never mentioned."

In *Cue,* William Wolf decided: "Sidney Poitier is the only one who manages to stylishly survive the implausible doings in this mixed up action stew. He still looks dapper after grueling battles with rampaging cigar store Indians . . . that Poitier! Playing a horse dealer, he goes through it all looking real cool, fancy shirt and all. It is highly doubtful whether audiences can survive as well." Another negative review was supplied by critic Kathleen Carroll in the New York *Daily News,* who called the film "better than the average disaster. True to Western movie tradition, it hits hard in the action department. The fights are really fights [but] the characters are left half-baked. The actors appear grimly determined to get away with the script as written, except for Poitier who tags each line with a smirk."

*Duel at Diablo* garnered more of a following in Great Britain, especially among Ralph Nelson cultists, and *Monthly Film Bulletin* concluded: "Nothing if not versatile, Ralph Nelson has here produced a tough, action-packed Western of the old school . . . The acting is uniformly good [and] Sidney Poitier is amusingly sardonic as the horse breaker whose only concern is the pay chit he gets for each horse he breaks in."

In his view of the film (originally called *29 to Duel),* Clifford Mason complained in *The New York Times* about Poitier's secondary role, with a star of his magnitude stooging for James Garner. Despite the fact that the film marked a departure from previous attempts to portray the Negro as part of the Western scene, playwright Mason argued: "In *Duel at Diablo,* [Poitier] did little more than hold Garner's hat, and this after he had won the Academy Award. What white romantic actor would take a part like that? He gets to kill a few Indians, but Garner gets the girl and does all the fighting. Poitier was simply dressed up in a fancy suit, wth a cigar stuck in his mouth and a new felt hat on his head."

With Suzy Kendall.

# To Sir, With Love

Columbia Pictures          1967

THE CAST:

*Mark Thackeray,* SIDNEY POITIER; *Pamela Dare,* Judy Geeson; *Denham,* Christian Roberts; *Gillian Blanchard,* Suzy Kendall; *Barbara Pegg,* Lulu (Marie Lawrie); *Mrs. Evans,* Faith Brook; *Potter,* Christopher Chittell; *Mr. Weston,* Geoffrey Bayldon; *Clinty,* Patricia Routledge; *Moira Jackson,* Adrienne Posta; *Mr. Florian,* Edward Burnham; *Mrs. Joseph,* Rita Webb; *Miss Phillips,* Fiona Duncan; *Seales,* Anthony Villaroel; *Fernman,* Grahame Charles; *Buckley,* Roger Shepherd; *Tich,* Gareth Robinson; *Jose Dawes,* Mona Bruce; *Mrs. Dare,* Ann Bell; *Mr. Pinkus,* Cyril Shaps; *Ingham,* Peter Attard; *Rock Group,* The Mindbenders; and Fred Griffiths, Dervis Ward, Sally Cann, Albert Lampert, Chitra Neogy, Elna Pearl, Stewart Bevan, Carla Challoner, Joseph Cuby, Lynn Sue Moon, Jane Peach, Michael Des Barres, Margaret Heald, Ellison Kemp, Donita Shaw, Richard Wilson, Sally Gosselin, Kevin Hubbard, Howard Knight, Stephen Whittaker.

CREDITS:

*Executive producer,* John R. Sloan; *producer/ director,* James Clavell; *screenplay,* James Clavell; based on the novel by E. R. Braithwaite; *photography,* Paul Beeson; *music,* Ron Grainger; *conducted* by Philip Martell; *title song,* Don Black and Marc London; songs *sung* by Lulu and The Mindbenders; *assistant director,* Ted Sturgis; *art director,* Tony Woollard; *editor,* Peter Thornton. Technicolor. Running time: 105 minutes.

The role of Mark Thackeray, the teacher whose first job is in a school in London's tough East End, amply demonstrates how far Sidney Poitier had come in the decade since *Blackboard Jungle.* In just ten years, he was doing the Glenn Ford part and the angry classroom toughs (here aggressive, insolent girls are among the rebellious hoods) were speaking with Cockney accents. As in *Lilies of the Field,* Poitier was the only recognizable name connected with the film, and it is his splendid performance as the stiff-necked, starched-shirt engineer from British Guiana who is forced to take an interim teaching position until something opens up in his chosen profession that completely dominates this film version of Edward Ricardo Braithwaite's 1959 autobiographical novel. (Braithwaite at the time the movie was made was British Guiana's ambassador to the United Nations.)

*To Sir, With Love* was released on the heels of the similar-themed *Up the Down Staircase,* and both deal with idealistic novice instructors who get their classroom indoctrination from surly, unsupervised students who pass the day baiting the teachers, reading nudie magazines in class, and rock 'n' rolling during recess. Poitier's students, though, are less hard-boiled or incorrigible than his own Gregory Miller of *Blackboard Jungle* than, it has been noted, simply lower middle-class teenagers brought up in a sordid environment or by neglectful parents. His sensitive portrayal and a demonstration of Job-like patience make credible the teacher's tenacity and his ability in exercising what he calls "survival training" to win over his class. Some, however, questioned the character's power to not only probe the veneer of his students' toughness and overcome their ignorance and contempt for him (to them, Thackeray is "Sir"—at first sarcastically, later respectfully) but also develop a rapport with them, change them from immature, apathetic adolescents into well-groomed, polite, curious young adults, and turn about an entire class in a single term. (A slightly altered twist to this plot development found its way, intentionally or not, into Poitier's *A Piece of the Action* a decade later.)

Poitier—here simply a teacher who incidentally is black—used a personal magnetism to make this frankly sentimental, though warm, humorous and moving, yarn as the veteran around whom director James Clavell (his first directing job) positioned a company of relative unknowns—at least to American audiences: Christian Roberts, the hard-to-reach class leader (Poitier's Gregory Miller of *Blackboard Jungle*); Christopher Chittell as the unredeemable punk (the Vic Morrow role of the Richard Brooks film); Judy Geeson as the blonde teenybopper who has a crush on Poitier and tries to seduce him; Suzy Kendall, another teacher on her first job who, for a while, is Poitier's only friend in the school (in the book, there was a mature inter-racial romance between them); Geoffrey Bayldon as the cynical veteran instructor; Edward Burnham, the remote principal.

Race is virtually ignored in *To Sir, With Love,* although one or two color-oriented quips are hurled at Thackeray—by the cynical teacher, not the students, and the only black student (Anthony Villaroel) is just "the unhappy non-white,"

With Judy Geeson.

With Faith Brook.

With Christian Roberts, Adrienne Posta, Richard Wilson, Christopher Chittell, Lulu, Peter Attard and Sally Cann.

the offspring of a black mother and a white father. The entire action of the story covers a single term at an East London secondary school, where Mark Thackeray finds himself facing a rough, unruly bunch of teenagers and soon discovers that his colleagues are either incompetent or uninterested in their students. The one exception, he finds, is the new music teacher, Gillian Blanchard (Suzy Kendall). Realizing that his class is basically decent and that his students' crude behavior and language simply reflect an indifferent upbringing, Thackeray decides to abandon the prescribed curriculum and deal with the kids on an adult level. He throws away the class textbooks and talks to them about marriage, rebellion, sex and the society that they will be entering. Shocked by suddenly being treated as equals, the confused students, led by Denham (Christian Roberts), Pamela Dare (Judy Geeson) and Barbara Pegg (pop singer Lulu) drop their plans to destroy Thackeray as they did his predecessor, and soon find themselves trying to meet the standards of conduct and decency he has set before them.

Inevitably, Thackeray suffers a few setbacks, despite his teaching plan of classroom discussions and excursions to London museums: Pamela imagines herself in love with him; Seals, an embittered half-caste, is forced to overcome his initial resentment and turns to Thackeray when his mother dies; Denham, the most recalcitrant of the boys, must be outboxed in gym class before there can be a mutual respect with Thackeray; the faculty itself has to be convinced by Thackeray of the value of his unorthodox teaching methods. So strong is Thackeray's influence, though, that his class defies local convention by attending the funeral of Seals' black mother.

Eventually, Thackeray is offered a post with a prestigious engineering firm, but when his students, at their senior dance, express their admiration by presenting him with a gift, labeled "To Sir, With Love," he tears up his acceptance of the job and decides to continue in the teaching profession.

In his review of the film in *Saturday Review,* Hollis Alpert wrote a lengthy piece on Poitier, likening him to Gary Cooper with his "vaguely shy dignity, a taciturnity that denotes inner strength, and a sensitivity that tells us he has gone through pain and suffering." Critic Alpert then considered: "Poitier is also a splendid responsive actor, and now and then his pictures have a way of seeming better than they actually are, made so by the conviction he establishes . . . But unlike Cooper, Poitier isn't allowed to get the girl (or even *a* girl) in the end, and all the handsome masculinity he represents must wait for the day when mores and attitudes change sufficiently to allow him to respond to the love signals sent his way by white females who aren't particularly concerned about color barriers. The suggestion of a breaching of those barriers is present in *To Sir, With Love.*"

Alpert continued: "But Poitier, while insisting on all his elemental rights as a human being, draws a firm line in matters of romance. This renunciation is meant as one more example of his dedication to righteousness, as a reinforcement of his essential dignity, and perhaps also to demonstrate his awareness of realities. But it's an easy way out, too, for his screenwriters, who become curiously race conscious while seeming to promote both tolerance and idealism [and] it does seem a shame that Poitier is being consistently de-sexualized in his films. So, with each passing film, he becomes an even more solid symbol, a

With Christian Roberts (extreme left), Lulu (white skirt), Judy Geeson and the class.

As Mark Thackeray with his class.

minority figure who must eventually triumph over the majority types, while making prejudice seem lowly and nasty."

In the New York *Daily News,* Wanda Hale awarded three-and-one-half stars to *To Sir, With Love* and observed that Poitier "rewards viewers with a forceful characterization of a high-minded human being who is determined to overcome multiple problems in the job for which he has no training—and for which he has no love... There is no actor who could have played the Negro teacher with such superb authority as Sidney Poitier."

Tony Mastroianni, reviewer for *The Cleveland Press,* called *To Sir, With Love* "a good movie made excellent by a towering and sensitive performance from Sidney Poitier... Sometimes playing with careful restraint, at other moments exploding with honest rage, his is a performance which realizes all that is best in the script and makes the rest better than it is. He is wonderfully alive to all the nuances of a complex character in a complicated situation."

The headline over Bosley Crowther's somewhat tepid review in *The New York Times* read: "Poitier Meets the Cockney," and the critique

itself went to lengths weighing this film against *Blackboard Jungle.* Crowther felt that "Mr. Poitier is much more startled and naive in the face of [his students'] academic and social recalcitrance than you would ever expect a graduate of *Blackboard Jungle* or even an average experienced person, to be... a nice air of gentility suffuses this pretty color film, and Mr. Poitier gives a quaint example of being proper and turning the other cheek [and] *To Sir, With Love* comes off as a cozy, good-humored and unbelievable little tale of a teacher getting acquainted with his pupils, implying but never stating that it is nice for the races to live congenially together."

*Time* spoke of the film as "a British expedition into the blackboard jungle... The plot is primer-simple [but] attempts to blend realism and idealism, an unstable mixture... Still, even the weak moments are saved by Sidney Poitier, who invests his role with a subtle warmth." In *The New Yorker,* Penelope Gilliatt concluded: "The star of *To Sir, With Love* is Sidney Poitier; he is a firm actor, and must be a right-minded man, but one hankers for the character he played in *Blackboard Jungle* instead of the point-making prigs he takes on now... If the hero of this Polly-

With Christian Roberts.

anna story were white, the pieties would have been whisked off the screen and his pupils blamed for cringing. The fact that he is colored draws on resources of seriousness in audiences which the film does nothing to earn."

*Hollywood Reporter* said, in defense: "Poitier's performance is near faultless, devoid of marring mannerisms, imbued with dignity. He is capable of projecting hurt and emotion through the eyes in a face which appears to be masking the betrayal of reactions. His increasing understanding of the minute topographical change needed to communicate feelings in facial close-up is superb."

Sparring with Christian Roberts.

With Rod Steiger.

# In the Heat of the Night

United Artists                1967

THE CAST:

*Virgil Tibbs*, SIDNEY POITIER; *Bill Gillespie*, ROD STEIGER; *Sam Wood*, Warren Oates; *Mrs. Leslie Colbert*, Lee Grant; *Purdy*, James Patterson; *Delores Purdy*, Quentin Dean; *Eric Endicott*, Larry Gates; *Webb Schubert*, William Schallert; *Mrs. Bellamy (Mama Caleba)*, Beah Richards; *Harvey Oberst*, Scott Wilson; *Philip Colbert*, Jack Teter; *Packy Harrison*, Matt Clark; *Ralph Henshaw*, Anthony James; *H. E. Henderson*, Kermit Murdock; *Jess*, Khalil Bezaleel; *George Courtney*, Peter Whitney; *Harold Courtney*, William Watson; *Shagbag Martin*, Timothy Scott; *Dr. Stuart*, Fred Stewart; *Ted Ulam*, Arthur Malet.

CREDITS:

A Norman Jewison/Walter Mirisch Production. *Producer*, Walter Mirisch; *director*, Norman Jewison; *screenplay*, Stirling Silliphant; based on the novel by John Ball; *photography*, Haskell Wexler; *music*, Quincy Jones; *title song*, Quincy Jones and Marilyn and Alan Bergman; *sung* by Ray Charles; *assistant director*, Terry Morse, Jr.; *art director*, Paul Groesse; *editor*, Hal Ashby. Color by De-Luxe. Running time: 109 minutes.

In the second of his three roles making 1967 a memorable year, Poitier became Virgil Tibbs, the cool, methodical black detective of novelist John Ball's bestseller, *In the Heat of the Night*, and in this crackling screen adaptation by Stirling Silliphant, he etched an unforgettable screen portrait which ranks alongside his Noah Cullen of *The Defiant Ones* and his Homer Smith of *Lilies of the Field*. Filmed in Dyersburg, Tennessee, and directed by Norman Jewison, *In the Heat of the Night* is compelling contemporary drama, less a murder mystery ("routine and arbitrary," is the way Bosley Crowther viewed that aspect) than a

As Virgil Tibbs.

With Warren Oates.

stunning motion picture confrontation by two splendid actors playing an arrogant, insecure, bullnecked Southern sheriff and a sophisticated, efficient black cop from the North who, in the end, develop subtly a mutual feeling of respect.

Opposite Poitier, as the gum chewing Sheriff Bill Gillespie, was Rod Steiger, creating a bril- liant performance which he never again matched in films. Blessed with a more flamboyant role than Poitier's, Steiger won the Oscar as the Best Actor of 1967, and the film itself was selected as Best Picture of the Year. To the dismay of many—especially the black establishment, Poitier was completely overlooked when the Oscar nomi-

With Quentin Dean, James Patterson and Rod Steiger.

With Rod Steiger.

nations were announced, failing to receive the ultimate screen acclamation for any of the three movies in which he starred that year—the three biggest grossing films of the year!

*In the Heat of the Night* opens with the murder of Philip Colbert (Jack Teter), a wealthy industrialist who had come to the small Mississippi town of Sparta to build a factory. Sam Wood (Warren Oates), the local deputy, had just finished his swing around the outskirts of town and his nightly sport of watching Delores Purdy (Quentin Dean), a nubile teenager who is in the

With Larry Gates and Rod Steiger.

habit of parading nude at her window. At 2:30 A.M. on this particular hot night, Sam stumbles over Colbert's body, and within the hour, he has arrested a well-dressed Negro whom he had found at the railroad station. To the consternation of Bill Gillespie (Steiger), the zealous police chief, the suspect turns out to be Virgil Tibbs (Poitier), a top ranking homicide detective on the Philadelphia police force, who had been in town merely to visit his mother and was awaiting the first train out that morning.

Disgusted with Gillespie's swaggering arrogance, Tibbs cannot get out of town fast enough, but soon becomes interested in the solution of the murder when Gillespie jails a second suspect, Harvey Oberst (Scott Wilson), a frightened young man whom Tibbs quickly concludes is innocent. And when the murdered man's widow (Lee Grant) decides that Gillespie, new on the job and working his first homicide, is bumbling the investigation, Tibbs reluctantly accepts Gillespie's "offer" to help with the case. Tibbs soon proves that Oberst, who had been found with the dead man's wallet, had picked it up after finding Colbert already dead. On the other hand, Tibbs becomes over-anxious to establish the guilt of Eric Endicott (Larry Gates), the local plantation owner who runs the town. An insolent, bigoted conservative who opposed Colbert's progressive plans for a modern factory, Endicott is affronted by being questioned by a Negro and slaps Tibbs in the face. Tibbs responds by reflexively slapping Endicott back and angrily threatens to destroy the man, a suspect in the murder. Tibbs regrets the false accusation later, realizing his own motives had been heavily prejudiced.

Gillespie, dumbfounded by the slapping scene, gradually develops a grudging respect for Tibbs. The other local whites, though, take a different view and form a vigilante gang with plans to go after the Negro cop. Undeterred, Tibbs continues his investigation—with and without Gillespie's assistance. After Gillespie wrongly charges his own deputy, Sam Wood, with the murder on learning that Wood's bank account had been growing substantially in recent weeks, Delores Purdy, the local chippie, is dragged to the police station by her brother (James Patterson), who claims that she is pregnant by Wood.

Tibbs, meanwhile, seeks out a local abortionist, Mama Caleba (Beah Richards), and learns that Delores is due there momentarily.

When she shows up, she is accompanied by her boyfriend, Ralph Henshaw (Anthony James), the counterman at the roadside diner where Sam Wood makes his customary midnight stop during his rounds. Confronted by Tibbs, Henshaw tries to shoot his way out, but when he admits that he had attacked and robbed Colbert, Delores' brother and his buddies come to Tibbs' aid. With the case closed, Gillespie drives Tibbs to the railway depot. They sit together quietly until the train arrives, and then shake hands. Tibbs boards the train, as Gillespie advises him: "Take care—ya hear?"

Philip T. Hartung wrote in *Commonweal* of the Poitier dilemma when he reviewed *In the Heat of the Night:* "Undoubtedly, the actor of the hour is Sidney Poitier. And about time. Although general moviegoers woke up to his charm, graceful strength, and warm humor several years ago in *Lilies of the Field* and the critics praised his acting even earlier in *The Defiant Ones* and *A Raisin in the Sun,* Poitier has piddled along in recent years in such bilge as *The Long Ships* and *The Bedford Incident,* and in repetitive portraits of the Noble Negro being kind to Whites . . . Poitier is by no means cinema's only Negro star, but, because of his many films and fine performances, he is certainly the pace setter, and his future roles will no doubt be the most important in his distinguished career . . . The great advantage of *In the Heat of the Night,* not only for Sidney Poitier but everyone else connected with the project, is that it is such a good movie."

In *Newsweek,* critic Joseph Morgenstern felt: "A film that is as fresh as this one deserves to be seen by fresh eyes and savored by fresh minds . . . [it] is such an admirable achievement that its faults as well as its virtues merit close attention . . . Poitier, who could be ruling the American roost if parts were handed out on the basis of talent instead of pigment, gets a rare opportunity to demonstrate the full sweep of his powers."

In *The New York Times,* Bosley Crowther thought that "it is in the magnificent manner in which Mr. Steiger and Mr. Poitier act their roles, each giving physical authority and personal depth to the fallible human beings they are," while Wanda Hale, in her four-star *Daily News* appraisal, exclaimed: "It's a pleasure, all too rare, to watch two splendid actors pitted against each

As Virgil Tibbs.

other with equal force such as Sidney Poitier and Rod Steiger in the exceptional murder mystery, *In the Heat of the Night* . . . I seldom go out on a limb by declaring that no other actor could have played a certain role but in this case I'm doing it with impunity. Nobody but an actor of Poitier's stature could have characterized John Ball's Negro detective with any amount of forcefulness."

Hollis Alpert said in *Saturday Review:* "Both Sidney Poitier and Rod Steiger are splendid as they subtly establish [their] relationship . . . Of course, the rules must be observed. Poitier must remain a prideful, lonely figure at the end, and Steiger, too, must pay the price of loneliness, because he can no longer share the majority [of his community's] point of view." Tony Mastroianni of *The Cleveland Press* saw the film as "a magnificent drama of racial and individual tensions . . . a great measure of the success must be credited to its principal players—Poitier and Steiger. Their performances have an integrity, a genuineness that transcends the script, an honesty that prevents them from striving for effects."

Judith Crist, then a reviewer for NBC-TV's Today Show, commented: *"In the Heat of the Night* is an American movie of great distinction [and] Sidney Poitier adds a new dimension to the Noble Negro he has been portraying recently, providing a streak of bigotry and tension that gives superb complement to Steiger. Theirs is a remarkable duet." And this from the *Christian Science Monitor:* "Mr. Poitier has been consistently fortunate in finding—or demanding—films which maintain a realistic perspective, thus allowing his talents to speak positively and convincingly on behalf of humanity's fundamental oneness. Films like this one make it plain that it is the dignity of mankind, not simply the rights and status of a single race, which is at stake."

*In the Heat of the Night* won five Academy Awards: In addition to those for Best Picture and Best Actor, it was honored for its screenplay (Stirling Silliphant), editing (Hal Ashby), and sound (Samuel Goldwyn Studio sound department).

With Rod Steiger.

With Katharine Houghton, Katharine Hepburn and Spencer Tracy.

# Guess Who's Coming to Dinner

Stanley Kramer-Columbia Pictures        1967

## THE CAST:

*Matt Drayton*, SPENCER TRACY; *John Prentice*, SIDNEY POITIER; *Christina Drayton*, KATHARINE HEPBURN; *Joey Drayton*, Katharine Houghton; *Monsignor Ryan*, Cecil Kellaway; *Mrs. Prentice*, Beah Richards; *Mr. Prentice*, Roy Glenn, Sr.; *Tillie*, Isabel Sanford; *Hilary St. George*, Virginia Christine; *Carhop*, Alexandra Hay; *Dorothy*, Barbara Randolph; *Frankie*, D'Urville Martin; *Peter*, Tom Heaton; *Judith*, Grace Gaynor; *Delivery Boy*, Skip Martin; *Cab Driver*, John Hudkins.

## CREDITS:

A Stanley Kramer Production. *Producer/director*, Stanley Kramer; *associate producer*, George Glass; *screenplay*, William Rose; *photography*, Sam Leavitt; *music*, Frank DeVol; *song* "The Glory of Love" by Billy Hill; *sung* by Jacqueline Fontaine; *assistant director*, Ray Gosnell; *art director*, Robert Clatworthy; *special effects*, Geza Gaspar; *editor*, Robert C. Jones. Technicolor. Running time: 108 minutes.

In Stanley Kramer's sophisticated comedy drama about interracial marriage, Sidney Poitier—cast between Spencer Tracy and Katharine Hepburn—had his third standout role of the year and found himself with the unique distinction of starring in two of the year's Academy Award nominated Best Pictures of the Year and acting with both the Best Actress (Katharine Hepburn) and Best Actor (Steiger) while he himself did not receive a nomination. His acknowledged elegantly graceful performance as Dr. John Prentice and his

With Katharine Houghton.

towering presence in *Guess Who's Coming To Dinner* were somewhat downplayed because of the Tracy-Hepburn screen reunion (their ninth film together and their first in fourteen years) and because the movie marked Spencer Tracy's final acting job (he died ten days after filming was completed).

Most critics scoffed that Poitier's role of a world famous, well-tailored, brilliant, incredibly handsome doctor and outstanding medical researcher, was somewhat inflated, leading *Time* to print its now classic comment that John Prentice's professional credits "make Ralph Bunche feel like an underachiever," while calling the film itself "integrated hearts and flowers."

Producer/director Stanley Kramer answered: "This was a courageous step for Sidney Poitier. He took the part before he saw the script and was willing to risk his star status on a film about intermarriage. I think some of the criticism of the role as being oversimplified was unwarranted. It had to be. The perfect black man—good looking and of substantial means—meets the perfect girl from a liberal family. They marry—Should there be any objection, it can only be because he is black. That was the point of the film and it worked . . . emotionally and intellectually—and it reached the millions who might have been in partial disagreement but were able to accept it quite satisfactorily."

The movie occupies a special place in screen history as the first major film not only to give serious attention to the question of interracial marriage but also to permit a mixed couple to hug and kiss—even though the breakthrough is seen through the rear view mirror of a taxicab. The sequence remains a landmark of cinema.

As the film opens, Joey Drayton (Katharine Houghton, niece of Katharine Hepburn making her screen debut) has just flown into San Francisco from Honolulu where she plans to introduce her fiancé, Dr. John Prentice (Poitier), to her parents, Matt (Spencer Tracy), the publisher of a liberal newspaper, and Christina (Katharine Hepburn), owner of a fashionable art gallery. Although she and John have known each other for only ten days, Joey has fallen in love and now

With Spencer Tracy and Katharine Hepburn.

has come to ask her socially prominent parents for their blessing. They, of course, have not been told in advance that John is black.

Because John must leave the next day for Switzerland on behalf of his work for the World Health Organization, Joey is determined that their wedding take place immediately. Once over her initial shock, Christina enthusiastically supports the marriage, but her husband, suddenly confronted by a test of his longtime idealistic beliefs, and despite John's impeccable credentials, is unable to reach a decision and spends the entire day debating with himself and others. Less involved observers, however, do not hesitate to voice their opinions. Christina's business associate, Hilary St. George (Virginia Christine), is quick to reveal her innate bigotry; long time family friend, Monsignor Ryan (Cecil Kellaway), feels assured that John and Joey will overcome their initial obstacles; and the Draytons' shocked Negro maid, Tillie (Isabel Sanford), vociferously berates John for his "uppity" impertinence, call-

With Cecil Kellaway and Katharine Houghton.

As Dr. John Prentice.

ing him "a smooth-talking, smart-ass nigger" and feeling that "this is carrying integration too far." John himself secretly confides to Matt and Christina that he will not marry Joey without their consent.

The dilemma is compounded when the impulsive Joey persuades John's parents to fly up from Los Angeles on the next plane and join the Draytons for dinner. (The Prentices, too, are not informed that Joey is white.) On their arrival, Mrs. Prentice (Beah Richards) sides with Christina but her husband (Roy Glenn, Sr.), a retired postman, takes a dim view of the situation and clashes in a violent argument with his son. Mean-

while, Mrs. Prentice has a terrace chat with Matt Drayton and appeals to his heart and memory by recalling the days when they too stood on the threshold of a youthful marriage. Finally, in the cool of the evening, Matt gathers his wife and daughter, their friend, Monsignor Ryan, John and his parents, and Tillie, the maid, and gives a long, heartfelt speech, coming down on the side of liberalism, and consents to the wedding. Moved by the wisdom of Matt's words, John's father also relents, and all concerned adjourn for a family dinner.

In *Films and Filming,* reviewer Roy Moseley called the William Rose story "an original screen-

With Isabell Sanford.

play which will rank as one of the best of all time. It is sincere, dramatic, amusing, clever . . . Stanley Kramer has directed his film with great and loving care, not only giving us an excellent movie but a human document of great importance for the future of all free thinking people [and] Sidney Poitier as Dr. Prentice gives his usual excellent performance."

Bosley Crowther, in *The New York Times,* found it "a most delightfully acted and gracefully entertaining film, fashioned much in the manner of a stage drawing room comedy that seems to be about something much more serious and challenging than it actually is . . . Mr. Rose has written a deliciously swift and pithy script, and Mr. Kramer has made it spin brightly in a stylish ambience of social comedy. Mr. Tracy and Miss Hepburn are superior . . . Mr. Poitier is also splen-

did within the strictures of a rather stuffy type." Wanda Hale's four star review in the New York *Daily News* also was cheer-laden. She spoke of the film as "an important contribution to motion pictures" and thought that "Poitier is excellent as the doctor, a man of honor and dignity."

Arthur Knight decided in *Saturday Review* that "the adroit interplay of such seasoned performers as the radiant Miss Hepburn, the graceful Poitier, and the stalwart, irreplaceable Tracy . . . provide the film's greatest satisfactions." Critic Knight also considered that "the Poitier character is so noble that one suspects a little racism in reverse [although he] has sufficient innate elegance and poise to sweeten the interracial pill for all but the most ardent fanatics."

*Variety* ran on with praise, calling the movie "an outstanding Stanley Kramer production, superior in almost every imaginable way" and "a landmark in its tasteful introduction of sensitive material to the screen . . . for Poitier, the film marks a major step forward, not just in his proven acting ability, but in the opening-up of his script character. In many earlier films, he seemed to come from nowhere; he was a symbol. But herein, he has a family, a professional background, likes, dislikes, humor, temper. In other words, he is a whole human being. This alone is a major achievement in screenwriting, and for Poitier himself, his already recognized abilities now have expanded casting horizons."

Slightly less kind was Brendan Gill, who

With Katharine Houghton, Katharine Hepburn and Spencer Tracy.

said in *The New Yorker:* "The screenplay is so ingeniously plotted that one almost forgives it for being, in effect, a drawing room comedy, better suited to the stage than to the screen . . . The movie insidiously charms us into ignoring its defects, and for this the credit must go to a superb cast . . . The Negro swain is handsome, brilliant, affectionate, loyal, persevering, unselfish—a paragon . . . The paragon is played by Sidney Poitier."

On the thumbs-down side were, among others, Stanley Kauffmann and Joseph Morgenstern. In *The New Republic,* critic Kauffmann carped that "Sidney Poitier, the surgeon, cuts one more slice off his by-now slightly stale performing loaf," and in *Newsweek,* reviewer Morgenstern sniffed that "The Negro is not merely a man, faulted and quirky like the rest of us, but a brilliant, famous, distinguished physician, a candidate for the Nobel Prize in niceness, a composite Schweitzer, Salk and Christ, colored black for significance." And while Archer Winsten, in the *New York Post,* was calling *Guess Who's Coming To Dinner* "a truly splendid film" and raving that "Sidney Poitier is brilliant," *Time* was complaining that the film "again proves Stanley Kramer's ability to put together cinematic bouquets of platitudes about important-sounding social issues . . . the characters and casting are all but archetypical [and] the situation is carefully stacked by the screenwriters." In *The Reporter,* writer Andrew Greeley dubbed the movie *"Abie's Irish Rose* in blackface."

With Katharine Houghton.

Poitier himself has said of the film's racial implications: "I have no way of determining how important it will be in a racial sense. It's awfully complex and we are not in the business of addressing ourselves directly to, nor exclusively to, the racial issue. In this film, we are first and foremost, it seems to me, interested in presenting entertainment with a point of view—entertainment that will first be accepted as such, then as a premise, a side of the issue."

*Guess Who's Coming To Dinner* won ten Academy Award nominations (actor, actress, supporting actor, supporting actress, picture, director, screenplay, editing, art direction, and musical score), but only Katharine Hepburn, for her acting, and William Rose, for his original screenplay, received Oscars.

With Roy Glenn, Sr., and Beah Richards.

With Lauri Peters and Beau Bridges.

# For Love of Ivy

Palomar Pictures International/
Cinerama Releasing Corporation                    1968

## THE CAST:

*Jack Parks*, SIDNEY POITIER; *Ivy Moore*, Abbey Lincoln; *Tim Austin*, Beau Bridges; *Doris Austin*, Nan Martin; *Gena Austin*, Lauri Peters; *Frank Austin*, Carroll O'Connor; *Billy Talbot*, Leon Bibb; *Jerry*, Hugh Hird; *Harry*, Lon Satton; *Eddie*, Stanley Greene.

## CREDITS:

*Producers*, Edgar J. Scherick and Jay Weston; *associate producer*, Joel Glickman; *director*, Daniel Mann; *screenplay*, Robert Alan Aurthur; based on an original story by Sidney Poitier; *photography*, Joseph Coffey; *music*, Quincy Jones; *title song*, Quincy Jones and Bob Russell; *sung* by Shirley Horn; *assistant director*, Steve Barnett; *art director*, Peter Dohanos; *editor*, Patricia Jaffe. In Color. Running time: 102 minutes.

"For the student of cinema sociology," critic Vincent Canby wrote of *For Love of Ivy*, "it marks the final step in the metamorphosis of Sidney Poitier from a fine character actor into a Hollywood superstar, with all of the mythic cool and sexual prerogatives of a Clark Gable."

*For Love of Ivy*, based on an original story by Poitier and developed into a screenplay by Robert Alan Aurthur (who had written Poitier's earlier *Edge of the City* and *The Lost Man*, their next collaboration, as well as the play *Carry Me Back to Morningside Heights* which Poitier would direct on Broadway), has been categorized as Hollywood's first attempt to show a love affair between a modern, successful black man and a modern, gorgeous black woman. A charming, unpretentious, somewhat contrived little romantic comedy in the Doris Day-Rock Hudson vein, with ingratiating performances by suave Sidney Poitier, a successful businessman whose legitimate truck-

With Abbey Lincoln.

With Beau Bridges.

ing concern is the front for an elaborate mobile gambling operation, and stunning Abbey Lincoln (the jazz singer in her second screen role), the maid/cook/housekeeper/confidante of a white suburban family.

The film, marking the emergence of Palomar Pictures International, a filmmaking subsidiary of ABC Television, mixes humor, sentiment and (a Poitier first) a heavy breathing seduction scene—with sheets strategically placed—and details how

wheeler-dealer businessman Jack Parks (Poitier) is conned by Tim Austin (Beau Bridges) and his sister Gena (Lauri Peters) into romancing the family maid, Ivy Moore (Abbey Lincoln), who has decided to quit her job and go to secretarial school. The Austins are convinced that the household would fall apart without Ivy, especially since Mrs. Austin (Nan Martin), a career-minded lady, long has been out of touch with the kitchen and domestic life. Their hippie son Tim determines

As Jack Parks.

that what Ivy needs is a boyfriend, and he blackmails Parks into taking her out, under threat of exposing Parks' illegal gambling casino inside a giant truck that cruises about Manhattan at night.

Following an awkward first date, Parks and Ivy begin warming up to each other, but their romance cools when Ivy learns that Parks had been negotiated through blackmail by her "family." Despite his long standing aversion to marriage, though, Parks persists in wooing Ivy, turning up once again at the Austin house and confessing his love for her, even promising to give up the gambling operation. And, as the lovers depart arm in arm, the Austins are left to face their domestic problems.

Poitier claims he wrote *For Love of Ivy* to present a realistic portrait of Negro womanhood. "I wanted to make this film for my daughters and

With Abbey Lincoln.

[ 163 ]

other Negro women who never get to see themselves on the screen . . . I'm not interested in having a romantic interlude on the screen with a white girl. I'd much rather have romantic interludes with Negro girls." (The statement was made on the heels of his onscreen romance with Katharine Houghton in *Guess Who's Coming To Dinner*.) Unfortunately, establishment film critics and impatient black writers failed to be enthused by Poitier's vision, complaining generally that despite the film's intentions the character of the maid—along with the patronizing of the white family—promoted the very racial stereotype he had tried to destroy.

Judith Crist, critic for *New York*, felt: "Sidney Poitier has gone onward, if not upward, with *For Love of Ivy*, the kind of romantic comedy that Hollywood specialized in 30 years ago . . . maybe we're back because Mr. Poitier was simply in search of a romantic comedy vehicle and is younger in moviegoing than some older folk.

What he has come up with is a slick, pat piece of pie, slightly stale around the crust but with a topical filling of racial comment and, for topping, Mr. Poitier in his most lighthearted and romantic role to date (hey there, Cary) with Abbey Lincoln as his partner . . . [It] offers us two very talented and beautiful professionals doing their best by a run-of-the-mill romance—and they both deserve better."

In *Saturday Review*, Hollis Alpert complained: "The story, I'm sorry to say, bears all the marks of mechanical contrivance. If it weren't for the ingratiating performance given by Sidney Poitier, the film might have been worse than it actually turns out to be." *The New Republic* critic, Stanley Kauffmann, called the film "one more bonbon from Never-Never-Land except—and the exception is the whole point—this time the lovers are black . . . Unlike Stanley Kramer's picture, it does not temporize fantastically with grave issues; it opts completely for the fantastic." Reviewer

With Leon Bibb and Beau Bridges.

With Abbey Lincoln.

With Abbey Lincoln.

Kauffmann also thought: "Poitier leveled off as an actor quite a while ago, but it is a good level, always forceful and credible. As a star, he has entered into the tacit sex-dialogue that is a requisite between a star and his audience. I saw the film at a matinee attended by lots of ladies of both colors and all ages. When Poitier stepped from his car to make his entrance, a sigh went around the theatre, an embrace of welcome."

In *The New York Times,* Vincent Canby observed: "With so many things going against it, it's a De Mille-sized miracle that *For Love of Ivy* is so entertaining and, on occasion, affecting . . . Poitier, being a powerful screen personality, gives it unusual dimension [and] gives this movie dream its moments of honesty."

From *Variety,* this: "Don't underestimate Sidney Poitier: lesser stars than he have carried poorer films than *For Love of Ivy* to boxoffice success . . . *Ivy,* however, would seem to offer little to filmgoers not infected with the Poitier mystique [and] what little force the picture has stems from Poitier's clear enjoyment of a role cut from Cary Grant cloth and from the novelty value of a black-on-black romance that culminates in a discreet but innovatory sex scene."

Among the least enthusiastic viewers was Penelope Gilliatt of *The New Yorker,* who wrote of it as "an immensely affable and well-calculated conventional comedy that happens to be about race [but] is practically indistinguishable from the most sedate, snobbish and cushioned Shaftsbury Avenue or Broadway comedy about the servant problem."

With Joanna Shimkus.

# The Lost Man

Universal                                    1969

THE CAST:

*Jason Higgs*, SIDNEY POITIER; *Cathy Ellis*, Joanna Shimkus; *Dennis Laurence*, Al Freeman, Jr.; *Carl Hamilton*, Michael Tolan; *Eddie Moxy*, Leon Bibb; *Dan Barnes*, Richard Dysart; *Photographer*, David Steinberg; *Sally*, Beverly Todd; *Orville*, Paul Winfield; *Reggie Page*, Bernie Hamilton; *Ronald*, Richard Anthony Williams; *Police Captain*, Dolph Sweet; *Terry*, Arnold Williams; *Theresa*, Virginia Capers; *Diane*, Vonetta McGee; *Michael Warren*, Frank Marth; *Miss Harrison*, Maxine Stuart; *Plainclothesman*, George Tyne; *Grandma*, Paulene Myers; *Willie*, Lee Weaver; *Miller*, Morris Erby; *Teddy*, Doug Johnson; *Minister*, Lincoln Kilpatrick.

CREDITS:

*Producers*, Edward Muhl and Melville Tucker; *associate producer*, Ernest B. Wehmeyer; *director*, Robert Alan Aurthur; *screenplay*, Robert Alan Aurthur; based on the novel *Odd Man Out* by Frederick Laurence Green; *photography*, Jerry Finnerman; *music*, Quincy Jones; *songs*, Quincy Jones, Ernie Shelby and Dick Cooper; *assistant director*, Joseph Kenny; *art*

As Jason Higgs.

As Jason Higgs.

directors, Alexander Golitzen and George C. Webb; *costumes,* Edith Head; *editor,* Edward Mann. Panavision and Technicolor. Running time: 122 minutes.

Sidney Poitier's portrayal of a black militant, glowering sullenly from behind modish sunglasses, in *The Lost Man* provided a jarring break from his previous supercool, superdecent, superstar roles. Working again with writer Robert Alan Aurthur (here doubling for the first time as director), Poitier is the radical organizer of a payroll heist to help the families of seventeen jailed "brothers." Screenwriter Aurthur adapted the memorable British film, *Odd Man Out,* Carol Reed's classic movie about the IRA that had starred James Mason, and transposed the original theme to the Black Revolutionary move-

ment of the late 1960s. Following closely on the ultra-violent *Uptight,* which Jules Dassin had "blackened" from John Ford's *The Informer,* another Irish cause classic, the Poitier film suggested that disgruntled black militants are merely hired henchmen for an unidentified criminal organization. It begins as a serious study of the conflicts between militant and non-violent advocates but slips rapidly into a melodramatic cops and robbers chase with the hero-criminal on the run and the devoted girl friend (here white) in tow toward the traditional tragic ending. Added is a miscegenation angle that simply would not have been tolerated by the militants, and the whole enterprise is self-defeating.

*The Lost Man* opens with Jason Higgs (Poitier) and "brothers" Eddie Moxy (Leon Bibb) and Reggie Page (Bernie Hamilton) watching

With Joanna Shimkus.

impassively from a nearby car as police disperse a non-violent demonstration by blacks outside a factory practicing discrimination. Several hours later, Jason contacts Dennis Laurence (Al Freeman, Jr.), the protest leader, and urges him to stage another demonstration as a diversionary tactic for a payroll heist he (Jason) is planning for the next day. After obtaining Dennis' reluctant cooperation, Jason meets Cathy Ellis, a white social worker whose romantic interest in him is baffled by his mysterious pose.

The robbery goes off smoothly while Dennis has his non-violent demonstrators keeping the police occupied elsewhere. Jason, Eddie Moxy, Reggie Page and Orville (Paul Winfield) seize the payroll of a major factory and take the plant director (Frank Marth) and his secretary (Maxine Stuart) hostage. When the group reaches the getaway car, though, the director gambles that Jason will not shoot and makes a break. In the ensuing scuffle, Reggie is killed and Jason is wounded in a shootout with his friend's assailant. Left to flee on foot with the money, Jason takes refuge in a movie theatre and begs a pretty manicurist (Beverly Todd) he meets there to help him. She takes him to her apartment, treats his wounds, and then contacts Dennis who agrees to assist Jason in getting the money to his organization

and to make his getaway by ship. Eddie and Orville, meanwhile, have made their way to a brothel run by Theresa (Virginia Capers), who betrays them by calling the police. They are killed in an ambush as they try to flee.

Jason and Dennis manage to get through to Cathy Ellis, who picks them up and hides them at her home. When Barnes (Richard Dysart), her liberal lawyer father, learns that she is harboring criminals, she breaks with him and agrees to take Jason to the waterfront. Barnes watches them leave and then calls police inspector Carl Hamilton (Michael Tolan), who trails the fugitives to the piers. There Jason again is wounded in another skirmish, and when Cathy finds him, he is so weak from his wounds that she has to support him as he tries to make his way to a waiting ship. Only a wire fence separates them from the ship, but the police are closing in, and realizing that Jason is doomed, Cathy takes his gun and draws police fire by shooting two bullets into the ground. Dennis rushes through the police lines to look at the dead bodies of his two friends, glares for a moment at Inspector Hamilton, and then walks from the pier.

In *The Lost Man*, Sidney Poitier plays the role James Mason had in the original; Joanna Shimkus (as of January, 1976, Mrs. Sidney Poitier) takes the part portrayed by Kathleen Ryan; and Al Freeman, Jr., as Poitier's compatriot, is in the role done by Robert Beatty. Comedian David Steinberg, in a part all but eliminated in the release print, is a hippie photographer (similar to Robert Newton's mad artist in the earlier version) who ghoulishly plans to catch death in Poitier's eyes.

"The first time we see Sidney Poitier in *The Lost Man*," critic Roger Ebert wrote in the *Chicago Sun-Times*, "we understand that this is going to be a different Poitier role, perhaps a key role in the development of the Poitier image. And it is. Poitier is not precisely a bad guy, but he is a long way from the milksop (if engaging) hero of *Lilies of the Field* or even of *In the Heat of the Night* . . . On balance, *The Lost Man* is a better film [than *Uptight*]. It has the Poitier performance, for one thing, and Poitier has seldom been stronger or more human. He has just about obliterated the good-behavior conduct of *Guess Who's Coming To Dinner*. Instead of a movie star, he seems much more inside his character." Ebert concluded: *"The Lost Man* presents a villain we could get to like, which is perhaps the idea in any movie featuring a No. 1 box-office star."

In *The New York Times,* Vincent Canby declared: "Sidney Poitier does not make movies, he makes milestones. It is not necessarily his fault, but rather it is the result of an accident of timing combined with his affinity for working with second-rate directors. Because he is black, as well as a major movie star, his movies require social interpretations that have nothing to do with cinema, which is ironic since Poitier has never made a movie that revealed anything as important about America as his success in it. He is a good actor, but it is his career that's important . . . *The Lost Man* is Poitier's attempt to recognize the existence and root causes of black militancy without making anyone—black or white—feel too guilty or hopeless [and] is a succession of compromises in style and content, including . . . Poitier's portrayal of a militant as a cool brother in shades but whose dress is less Afro than Brooks."

*Time* felt that "the film's sincerity is varnished with artifice . . . After *Guess Who's Coming To Dinner,* many black critics found Poitier in the pink of condition. Now outfitted with shades and a scowl, tersely barking orders for social upheaval, Poitier may be playing Superman, but it is a black fantasy this time, not a

With Beverly Todd.

With Joanna Shimkus.

white one [that] begins in an atmosphere of racial tension and of inner tension between activist and non-violent blacks, quickly fizzles into just another hunted man thriller."

Charles Champlin, critic for the *Los Angeles Times,* said: "The question urgently provoked by Sidney Poitier's latest starring film is whether urgent social issues and content can be used to serve the purposes of a movie melodrama which has no message to deliver (or no message which we can accept as valid). The sharp answer is no. As a result, *The Lost Man* is a notably offensive work, demeaning and damaging to the causes of social justice and social understanding . . . The realities of ghetto misery and the earnest sacrifices of genuine leaders are cheaply made to serve the ends of what in its own terms is a trivial and de-

rivative little charade. Violence would seem to have been repudiated in the blood-soaked finale, but the organization got away with the loot and Poitier's death looks not like irony but noble sacrifice."

*Variety* commented: "Poitier comes across in his strongest role in years, shedding the goodie-two-shoes characteristics of his recent pictures and moving into the tumult of the times by interpreting a Malcolm X-type leader intent on plotting robbery of an all-white factory . . . [His] purpose for the robbery is revealed. It's not militancy but to help feed the children of soul brothers in jail. This redeeming quality, belatedly added, weakens plot and characterization, but Poitier's performance overcomes it . . . It is Poitier's film and a strong bid for awards attention."

Shorter notices came from Stanley Kauffmann in *The New Republic,* who said: "Poitier is tense, but he must have difficulty these days remembering just which picture he is being tense in;" Paine Knickerbocker in the *San Francisco Chronicle,* who noted: "[It] purports to introduce Sidney Poitier in a new role, that of a black militant, but he is as civilized as ever, and the film is essentially an uninvolved white man's glance at current disorders;" Philip T. Hartung in *Commonweal,* who inscribed: "Sidney Poitier is another Negro-in-films from whom we expect too much. He is a star and generally considered one of the best of moviedom's actors . . . but Poitier makes mistakes, too, and one of them is *The Lost Man.*"

With Joanna Shimkus.

With Martin Landau.

# They Call Me MISTER Tibbs!

United Artists                                    1970

## THE CAST:

*Lt. Virgil Tibbs,* SIDNEY POITIER; *Rev. Logan Sharpe,* MARTIN LANDAU; *Valerie Tibbs,* Barbara McNair; *Rice Weedon,* Anthony Zerbe; *Capt. Hank Marden,* Jeff Corey; *Lt. Herbert Kenner,* David Sheiner; *Mealie (Janitor),* Juano Hernandez; *Marge Garfield,* Norma Crane; *Woody Garfield,* Edward Asner; *Sgt. Deutsch,* Ted Gehring; *Puff,* Beverly Todd; *Joy Sturges,* Linda Towne; *Andrew Tibbs,* George Spell; *Ginny Tibbs,* Wanda Spell; *Medical Examiner,* Garry Walberg; *Bikell,* Jerome Thor; *Reporter,* John Alvin.

## CREDITS:

A Mirisch Production. *Executive producer,* Walter Mirisch; *producer,* Herbert Hirschman; *director,* Gordon Douglas; *screenplay,* Alan R. Trustman and James R. Webb; *story,* Alan R. Trustman; based on the character created by John Ball; *photography,* Gerald Finnerman; *music,* Quincy Jones; *assistant director,* Rusty Meek; *art director,* Addison F. Hehr; *editor,* Bud Molin. Color by DeLuxe. Running time: 108 minutes.

In his second screen portrayal of homicide detective Virgil Tibbs, Poitier—now working out of San Francisco—is again up to here in a complex killing, but despite the militant tone of the title, and having gotten sainthood off his back, he does nothing more than methodically solve the murder of a hooker strangled in her flossy apartment, and demonstrate he's really just a plain cop with a wife, a mortgage, and two kids who fight and give mommy a headache.

Under director Gordon Douglas, *They Call Me MISTER Tibbs!* never rises far above being just a detective potboiler like the two Tony Rome movies Douglas recently had made with Frank Sinatra, with far too much footage devoted to Virgil Tibbs' domestic life. Poitier himself was unable to inject the needed zip into the proceedings, perhaps being somewhat preoccupied with pursuing new goals: directing and producing. According to *Variety,* he was permitted by Gordon Douglas to try his hand on the directorial reins in the scenes where his presence was not needed in front of the camera. *They Call Me MISTER*

With Barbara McNair.

*Tibbs!* was nothing more than a tepid followup to *In the Heat of the Night.*

In the new film, Tibbs (Poitier) is looking forward to an evening at home with his wife Valerie (Barbara McNair) and his two children after a dull day down at the department. An anonymous phone call shatters his plans, though. The tipster reports that a girl has been murdered and adds that the Reverend Logan Sharpe (Martin Landau), crusading local minister and campaigner for community rights, had been seen leaving the girl's apartment. It's more than a police matter: it's personal and it's political. Sharpe is one of Tibbs' closest friends and is the leader of an incipiently violent ghetto fight for self-government. Reluctantly, Tibbs questions Sharpe and learns that he had visited the girl, Joy Sturges (Linda Towne), that afternoon, just as he had visited several others in this parish.

Preliminary investigation turns up several prime suspects. The murder weapon bears the fingerprints of Mealie (Juano Hernandez), the building's janitor; the owner of the apartment house, Rice Weedon (Anthony Zerbe), a known pusher, has fled; wealthy realtor Woody Garfield (Edward Asner) has paid the murdered girl's rent. And there is the possibility, too, that Woody's jealous wife, Marge (Norma Crane), may have been aware of her husband's extra-curricular amours.

Torn between his duty as a policeman, his concern for Sharpe, and the ever-present threat of a town in turmoil, Tibbs decides to concentrate his inquiries on Weedon, but loses him after a chase when he (Tibbs) arrives in the middle of a drugs deal. With the help of one of Weedon's hooker friends, Puff (Beverly Todd), Tibbs is led to Mealie whose information leads back to Sharpe. Under close questioning, Sharpe eventually confesses to the murder after the girl had taunted him about his virility. He asks Tibbs to postpone the arrest until polling is completed on a local community issue for which he had been campaigning. When Tibbs refuses, Sharpe throws himself under a truck. After that, for Tibbs, it's

With Juano Hernandez.

With George Spell.

back to his personal problems, his loving wife and his lively youngsters.

Several critics stressed the point that the script by Alan R. Trustman (who previously had written *Bullitt)* was misguided in having a white minister holding control of masses of blacks, and perhaps Poitier and Landau should have switched roles—which then would have scuttled the entire project as a Virgil Tibbs story.

Among the best notices for both Poitier and the film was the one from Wanda Hale, who gave the movie 3½ stars in the New York *Daily News* and called it "a good, solid murder mystery, kept tightly together by Gordon Douglas." Critic Hale felt: "We all know why Tibbs made such a good impression on us. He was played by Sidney Poitier, whose continually fine acting, wonderfully expressive face and graceful gestures are a pleas-

With Anthony Zerbe.

[ 175 ]

ure to watch as he goes about coolly and conscientiously solving a murder."

Vincent Canby, meanwhile, wrote: "With *They Call Me MISTER Tibbs!*, Poitier establishes another inalienable right, that of the black movie star to make the sort of ordinary, ramshackly entertaining, very close to pointless movie that a white movie star like Frank Sinatra has been allowed to get away with for most of his career. Actually, this may be one of the most important rights of all, for eventually it should allow Poitier to behave less like a solemn abstraction and more like a real, vulnerable man . . . Poitier's performance is mostly one of presence—wise, kind, just, tough, almost supernatural." Paul D. Zimmermann of *Newsweek* found it "the right movie in the wrong medium. It is, from start to finish, a slick television product . . . The fault is not in the star but in the script, for Sidney Poitier plays Tibbs with every grimace, pregnant pause, win-

With Martin Landau.

With Jerome Thor, Edward Asner and David Sheiner.

ning smile, downcast look and upturned pair of hands an actor can call upon to summon humanity where none exists. Tibbs is a type without being a person. He is the Good Black Cop, a role Poitier already played with fine artistic and financial results in *In the Heat of the Night.*"

Critic William Collins complained in *The Philadelphia Inquirer:* "Poitier doesn't seem to make much of an effort any more. Although he is one of the most expansive and powerful actors of his generation, he keeps getting these parts which practically freeze him into deadpan, and director Gordon Douglas certainly hasn't encouraged him to do otherwise in this film."

Jim Meyer said in *The Miami Herald:* "Poitier has earned his reputation as a fine, hardworking actor and so it's his misfortune that here he has nothing worthwhile to work with. Although long a great personal favorite, I'd be less than honest if I said he's great in this film. If any-

thing, this could be his weakest characterization ever."

From Penelope Gilliatt in *The New Yorker:* "The picture is an amiable and mildly idiotic one that would have done better, I should think, chopped up as soap opera on television . . . the direction job is perfectly pleasant, and there are some acting scenes that come off well, simply because everyone involved is unblinkingly convinced of the high seriousness of each turn of events, as in good soap opera."

The British view came from David Wilson in *Monthly Film Bulletin:* "An untidy script—which may once have included an explanation of the title—gives Sidney Poitier no chance to flesh out a skeletally written character, the intermittent scenes from family life being no more than a clumsy unobtrusive attempt to demonstrate that as a family man Tibbs has problems like any other."

With Beverly Todd.

With Lani Miyazaki, Raul Julia, Demond Wilson, Billy Green Bush, James J. Watson, Jr., and Ron O'Neal.

# The Organization

United Artists                    1971

THE CAST:

*Lt. Virgil Tibbs,* SIDNEY POITIER; *Valerie Tibbs,* Barbara McNair; *Lt. Jack Pecora,* Gerald S. O'Loughlin; *Mrs. Morgan,* Sheree North; *Bob Alford,* Fred Bier; *Benjy,* Allen Garfield; *Lt. Jessop,* Bernie Hamilton; *William Martin,* Graham Jarvis; *Juan Mendoza,* Raul Julia; *Joe Peralez,* Ron O'Neal; *Stack Baker,* James A. Watson, Jr.; *Night Watchman,* Charles H. Gray; *Larry French,* Jarion Monroe; *Annie Sekido,* Lani Miyazaki; *Sgt. Chassman,* Dan Travanty; *Dave Thomas,* Billy Green Bush; *Rudy,* Maxwell Gale, Jr.; *Chet,* Ross Hagen; *Tony,* Paul Jenkins; *Zack Mills,* John Lasell; *Capt. Stacy,* Garry Walberg; *Charlie Blossom,* Demond Wilson; *Andy Tibbs,* George Spell; *Ginny Tibbs,* Wanda Spell; *Dan,* Richard Colin Adams; *John Bishop,* Johnny Haymer.

CREDITS:

A Mirisch Production. *Producer,* Walter Mirisch; *director,* Don Medford; *screenplay,* James R. Webb; based on the character created by John Ball; *photography,* Joseph Biroc; *music,* Gil Melle; *art director,* George B. Chan; *special effects,* Sass Bedig and Norman O. Skeete; *editor,* Ferris Webster. Color by DeLuxe. Running time: 107 minutes.

The third Sidney Poitier-Virgil Tibbs movie,

With Gerald S. O'Loughlin and Dan Travanty.

while several pegs below *In the Heat of the Night,* was superior to *They Call Me MISTER Tibbs!* both in ingenious plotting and the wise decision to play down Tibbs' domesticity. This outing altered the Tibbs character slightly, making him a sort of rebel cop who helps a group of vigilante-minded Third World idealists bust an international drug ring, and even having him bounced from the force for his independent ways.

The film begins with a lengthy, pre-title heist of a furniture factory, front for a crime ring, and the seizure of a five-million-dollar heroin cache.

With Bob Orrison.

With Barbara McNair.

Virgil Tibbs (Poitier) enters the case when, during the robbery investigation, the factory manager is found murdered. All leads draw a blank until Tibbs learns that a dedicated band of young radicals led by Juan Mendoza (Raul Julia) had pulled off the heist. They disclaim, though, responsibility for the killing, insisting that they simply intend to hold the heroin until the syndicate's drug trafficking is stopped by the police. The group asks his assistance, leaving them free to try their own methods, and Tibbs agrees, without revealing what he knows to his superiors.

When the factory watchman, Morgan (Charles H. Gray), is murdered as he is being taken in for questioning, Tibbs and his partner, Jack Pecora (Gerald S. O'Loughlin), question Morgan's wife (Sheree North) and discover that he had stock in the furniture company. Meanwhile, Joe Peralez (Ron O'Neal), one of the vigi-

With Wanda Spell.

[ 180 ]

With James J. Watson, Jr.

lantes holding the heroin, is beaten up by syndicate thugs. He agrees to make a private deal with the mob, but their suspicions are aroused and both he and Annie Sekido (Lani Miyazaki), another member of the group, are killed before Tibbs can intervene.

Tibbs is suspended when his superiors discover that he had been withholding information, and his own suspicions about corruption in the police narcotics division convince him to turn in his gun and badge. Pursuing the investigation on his own, Tibbs finds that Mrs. Morgan has been working as a runner for the syndicate and that Benjy (Allen Garfield), a small-time hood, is about to make a drop. With the assistance of Juan Mendoza and his friends, Tibbs goes after the local pushers, capturing them after a lengthy chase through the then under construction BART subway tunnels under San Francisco. The syndicate's chiefs are arrested when the police close in, but before they can be questioned, they are shot down by killers imported by the mob.

Arthur Knight, in *Saturday Review,* called the film "a combination of Mr. Tibbs and *Mod*

With Sheree North.

*Squad* [that] ingeniously aligns Poitier with a sextet of former users and dealers who have their own reasons for fighting the drug syndicate. As in earlier Tibbs episodes, this connection places him outside the law, even to the extent of turning in his badge, but his instincts, it transpires, are sound, leading him to ever higher echelons of organized crime. There is a nice sense about this film—due in part to the writing and in no small part to the casting—of never quite knowing in whom to believe."

In the *Boston Herald-American,* critic John Kronenberger said: *"The Organization* is primarily a star vehicle, an art form that's supposed to be dying out in this post-studio age, but looks healthy enough from this distance. One of the distinguishing marks of star vehicles is that minor incongruities, things that would otherwise be eliminated, tend to be overlooked out of deference to the lead . . . Poitier is a superstar, a magnitude reached after long years of paying dues most of us can't imagine and one to which he is absolutely entitled. If, at the present point in his career, he wants to underline the fact that he has taste—

custom-tailored suits, elegant sports jackets, Burberrys trenchcoats as well as money—and he does have taste—nobody has the right to deny him this . . . *The Organization* is a professionally made picture that gives its audience most of the things they go to see: a couple of unpleasant murders, split-second robbery and efficient suspense."

In the view of Donald J. Meyerson of *Cue,* "Sidney Poitier, fuller of cheek and belly, is once more Virgil Tibbs, a pleasantly middle-class San Francisco police officer who runs and chases across the famed hill of the California city to apprehend the leaders of *The Organization* . . . Poitier is undeniably bland and the acting is generally uneven, but under director Don Medford's skilled hands, the pace is lively and the action is continuous. Much better than *They Call Me MISTER Tibbs!,* this film indicates there is more box-office gold in them thar Tibbs hills."

A. H. Weiler, reviewing the film for *The New York Times,* wrote: "Our reigning black superstar, Sidney Poitier, who, as detective Virgil Tibbs, has been majestically impervious to criminals and the white Establishment in *In the*

*Heat of the Night* and *They Call Me MISTER Tibbs!*, retains his imperious cool . . . But despite his smooth restraint, this dizzying complex of a king-sized heroin heist, shootings and chases evolves largely as surface action and reaction so dear to TV's cops and robbers . . . Poitier is unflappable and tough but he does occasionally show signs of weariness and a desire to spend more time with Barbara McNair and George and Wanda Spell . . . He can't be blamed, since *The Organization* can be rough on super city sleuths as well as moviegoers who've been through much the same melodramatics before."

The view from Judith Crist in *New York Magazine:* "*The Organization* is the third film offering us Sidney Poitier as the close-mouthed, family-loving, crime-fighting-with-cool-man, Virgil Tibbs . . . Poitier et al, and particularly Sheree North, do well." *Variety* spoke of the film as "suspenseful, packed with violent action and enough excitement to make for strong box-office appeal . . . As usual, Poitier plays it cool and delivers handily in his role."

British critic David Wilson, writing in *Monthly Film Bulletin,* called the movie "an absolutely routine piece of work, directed by Don Medford with the kind of anonymous efficiency which will guarantee a television airing. As before, Sidney Poitier (here only incidentally black, for which we must be grateful) is incorruptibility incarnate, bending the rules only when a higher purpose is involved, but at least we're spared all but a small dose of those soporific interludes from family life that punctuated *They Call Me MISTER Tibbs!*"

With Gerald S. O'Loughlin (in white trenchcoat).

With Will Geer.

# Brother John

Columbia Pictures                    1971

THE CAST:

*John Kane,* SIDNEY POITIER; *Doc Thomas,* Will Geer; *Lloyd Thomas,* Bradford Dillman; *Louisa MacGill,* Beverly Todd; *Sheriff Orly Ball,* Ramon Bieri; *George,* Warren J. Kemmerling; *Charley Gray,* Lincoln Kilpatrick; *Rev. MacGill,* P. Jay Sidney; *Frank Gabriel,* Richard Ward; *Henry Birkhardt,* Paul Winfield; *Miss Nettie,* Zara Cully; *Cleve,* Michael Bell; *Jimmy Gabriel,* Howard Rice; *Marsha Gabriel,* Darlene Rice; *Turnkey,* Harry Davis; *Sarah Gabriel,* Lynn Hamilton; *Calvin,* Gene Tyburn; *Perry,* E. A. Nicholson; *Bill Jones,* Bill Crane; *Lab Deputy,* Richard Bay; *Henry's Friend,* John Hancock; *Nurse,* Lynne Arden; *Motel Owner,* William Houze; *Neighbors,* Maye Henderson and Lois Smith.

CREDITS:

An E & R Production. *Producer,* Joel Glickman; *associate producer,* Herb Wallerstein; *director,* James Goldstone; *screenplay,* Ernest Kinoy; *photography,* Gerald Perry Finnerman; *music,* Quincy Jones; *assistant directors,* Tom Schmidt and Charles C. Washburn; *art director,* Al Brenner; *editor,* Edward A. Biery. Eastman Color. Running time: 94 minutes.

"SIDNEY POITIER is BROTHER JOHN"—as the ads for the film, Poitier's first for his own E & R Productions, announced. After being accorded the ultimate screen billing (in league with "Paul Newman is Hud" and "Frank Sinatra is Tony Rome"), Poitier then had his "superhero" stereotype brought to full fruition—thanks to Ernest Kinoy's mystical screenplay—literally playing God's messenger. It was the ultimate step, as one writer noted, in a career of progressive role-deification, wrapped in an obtuse melodrama that starts engrossingly with a mystery with sociological overtones and winds up a doomsday parable.

Poitier is enigmatic John Kane, "an impeccably tailored, world traveled, multilingual angel who, born some years before in Hackley, Alabama, has returned to his home town to make one final audit before Judgement Day." (The descrip-

With Beverly Todd.

tion is Vincent Canby's.) Kane has come back ostensibly to visit his dying sister, but the suddenness of his arrival provokes considerable anxiety throughout the small community. They recall how he had appeared previously after the deaths of his mother and father.

Louisa MacGill (Beverly Todd), a lovely black schoolteacher who recently had abandoned her career in New York City, finds herself falling for the man she remembers as a childhood friend. Doc Thomas (Will Geer), the town's general practitioner, recalls delivering Kane during a thunderstorm 35 years ago and later witnessing his unexpected reappearance every time death visited his family—even though no one ever summoned him. Doc's ambitious son, Lloyd (Bradford Dillman), the aggressive district attorney,

suspects that Kane is an outside agitator sent in to help Charley Gray (Lincoln Kilpatrick), leader of a strike by blacks against the town's major industrial plant. Lloyd Thomas and Orly Ball (Ramon Bieri), the redneck sheriff, search Kane's belongings and discover some blank diaries and a passport stamped with visas from several countries off-limits to Americans. After checking with federal agencies and finding that Kane is not a known subversive, Sheriff Ball, under Lloyd's coercion, assigns his racist deputy, George (Warren J. Kemmerling), to keep Kane under surveillance. When George attempts a physical confrontation though, and humiliates Kane's brother-in-law, Frank Gabriel (Richard Ward), in front of the latter's children, Kane subdues the deputy with a karate chop, and later uses the same technique to

With Beverly Todd.

handle three young black toughs who challenge him.

When Kane announces he intends to leave town, the sheriff has him jailed on a bogus charge, but with the sudden death—prophesied by Kane—of strike leader Charley Gray and the threat of erupting violence, Doc Thomas, convinced that Kane is no longer the same person he had known as a child, frees him from jail and confronts him with his suspicion that somehow he is now the embodiment of the angel of death, an emissary from an alien planet. While violence in the town—the apocalypse embodied in the greed, hatred and ambitions of the bi-racial community—becomes increasingly imminent, Kane leaves as suddenly as he first had appeared.

Charles Champlin, critic for the *Los Angeles Times,* considered: "Having offered larger-than-life heroes as dream figures for its (largely white) audiences all these years, Hollywood in *Brother John* appears to be trotting out the old formulas again, this time to appeal specifically to the black audience which is now (rightly) regarded as highly lucrative. Nothing wrong with this, except that *Brother John* smacks more of calculation than conviction . . . Poitier is not simply heroic,

he is evidently superhumanly heroic. It would be easy to identify him as a heavenly messenger right away, except for the romantic interlude with the schoolmarm . . . In its own terms, *Brother John* is skillfully done. Poitier acts with great dignity and, when he has a chance, with great charm."

In the *Chicago Sun-Times,* Roger Ebert rambled on about Poitier's screen development over the previous two decades, noting: "He was one of the best actors in movies, period, and he may be that again, but at the moment I believe Poitier is going through a crisis not unlike those affecting Rod Steiger and Marlon Brando. He has become too . . . transcendental is the word, I guess. He has become so heroic and so ethical, such a figure of persecution in an intellectual liberal way, that he's been cut off from the roles he should be playing, the roles of real men with failings as big as their virtues . . . Recently, [his acting] has gotten so self-conscious, so introspective, that's he's actually been dissipating his personal magnetism. Perhaps it's no coincidence that *In the Heat of the Night* was his last film with a strong director and that the later films have lacked any directorial point of view."

In *New York* Magazine, Judith Crist com-

[ 186 ]

plained: "As if we needed more to add to the muddle-headedness of our social-statement movies, there's Sidney Poitier's latest vehicle . . . we ought to suspect the fakery early on by James Goldstone's heavy-handed direction [with] the constant concentration on Poitier's deadpan holier-than-thou immobility, his stoney-faced bemusement [as] a karate-chopping Christ figure. Perhaps Poitier has indeed become larger than life."

Vincent Canby felt: "Here was Sidney Poitier, wearily acknowledging the apotheosis by which a good actor is being transformed into an exalted public figure, a man more or less forced into second-order movies *(They Call Me MISTER Tibbs!, The Lost Man)* that demand, not performances, but visitations . . . In *Brother John,* Mr. Poitier couldn't be more disengaged [and] if the film is a disaster—and it is—the responsibility is Mr. Poitier's, whose company produced the movie and hired everyone connected with it. It's too late to believe that he's still a passive participant in his own premature deification."

David Skerritt, reviewing for *The Christian Science Monitor,* decided: *"Brother John* is fraught with evidence of an artistic struggle between two conflicting aspects of James Goldstone's directorial personality: the mystic and the sentimental . . . Sidney Poitier stars, in his usual smooth fashion [and] is as coolly skillful as ever in the central role." Gary Arnold, critic for *The Washington Post,* disagreed, calling the film "probably the weakest starring vehicle Sidney Poitier has ever been persuaded to hitch his star

With Ramon Bieri.

to . . . [he] ends up with a sort of rickety soapbox of melodrama, trapped by a script that expresses things smugly when it bothers to articulate social problems at all and trapped inside a role that encourages a lot of inscrutable, self-righteous pose-striking."

The New York *Daily News'* Kathleen Car-

With Lincoln Kilpatrick and Beverly Todd.

[ 187 ]

With Beverly Todd.

roll objected to "Poitier attempting to play a Christ-figure" in scenes where "the sun's rays seem to form a crown around his head." She further held that the reason "why Sidney Poitier's movies tend to look alike . . . is that Poitier himself always looks too perfect, as if he were wearing some kind of special superstar glow that sets him apart from everyone else and allows him to accomplish the impossible."

And from Britain's *Monthly Film Bulletin*. "Poitier's talents as an actor have so often been employed in the service of prevailing social myth-ology that it was perhaps inevitable, with the current vogue for Apocalyptic Warnings, that he should find himself portraying a planetary alien sent to catalogue the self-destruction of the human race. Fortunately, the silly mystical mystery around which the plot of *Brother John* revolves is not suggested until the end of the film."

In *Life,* critic Richard Schickel bemoaned that "Mr. Poitier's acquiescence in the process of his own canonization continues to mystify me. He's really too good an actor and too valuable a figure to be abused in this fashion."

With Harry Belafonte.

# Buck and the Preacher

Columbia Pictures                    1972

THE CAST:

*Buck,* SIDNEY POITIER; *The Preacher (Willis Oakes Rutherford),* HARRY BELAFONTE; *Ruth,* Ruby Dee; *Deshay,* Cameron Mitchell; *Floyd,* Denny Miller; *Madam Esther,* Nita Talbot; *Kingston,* James McEachin; *Uncle Cudjo,* Clarence Muse; *Sinsie,* Julie Robinson; *Indian Chief,* Enrique Lucero; *Sheriff,* John Kelly; *Headman,* Tony Brubaker; *Sarah,* Lynn Hamilton; *Sam,* Doug Johnson; *Joshua,* Errol John; *Little Henry,* Ken Menard; *Delilah,* Pamela Jones; *Elder,* Drake Walker; *Little Toby,* Dennis Hines; *Mizoo,* Fred Waugh; *Tom,* Bill Shannon; *Frank,* Phil Adams; *Earl,* Walter Scott; *George,* John Howard; *Deputy Marcus,* Jerry Gatlin; *Brave,* Jose Carlos Ruiz; *Express Agent,* Ivan Scott; *Man in Express Office,* Bill Cook; *Bank Teller,* John Kennedy; *Esther's Girls,* Shirleena Manchur, La

Markova, Hannelore Richter, Valerie Heckman and Stephanie Lower.

CREDITS:

An E & R Productions/Belafonte Enterprises Film. *Producer,* Joel Glickman; *associate producer,* Herb Wallerstein; *director,* Sidney Poitier;* *screenplay,* Ernest Kinoy; *story,* Ernest Kinoy and Drake Walker; *photography,* Alex Phillips, Jr.; *music,* Benny Carter; *performed* by Sonny Terry and Brownie McGhee; *second unit director,* Chuck Hayward; *assistant directors,* Sheldon Schrager and Jesus Martin; *editor,* Pembroke J. Herring. In Color. Running time: 103 minutes.

Sidney Poitier's second Western *Buck and the Preacher* reunited him with his longtime friend,

* Replaced Joseph Sargent.

With Harry Belafonte.

Harry Belafonte, whose comradeship and rivalry dates back to their days with the American Negro Theatre of the mid-1940s. The film, for their own E & R Productions and Belafonte Enterprises, went into production in Durango, Mexico, on February 4, 1971, with Joseph Sargent directing. Within five days, Poitier himself took over for Sargent after firing him, and began another phase of his screen career. "It was at the insistence of Belafonte, with my concurrence," Poitier told an interviewer for *Ebony*. "I thought that Sargent was not giving us what we wanted and it was certainly too late to ask Columbia to wait and send us another director."

While not the first "soul western," *Buck and the Preacher* stands as the most important one—primarily because of its stars. Mixing comedy and drama, it spins the yarn of how a dedicated wagonmaster (Poitier), guiding freed slaves to homesteads in the Far West and keeping them out of the clutches of white labor recruiters from southern plantations, becomes involved with bogus preacher/conman (Belafonte). "Mister Tibbs and the Angel Levine go West," as *Variety* described the film.

Following the Civil War, a black ex-Union cavalryman named Buck becomes wagonmaster to a trainload of former slaves. His main concern is to protect the migrants from a band of night riders, led by the unscrupulous Deshay (Cameron Mitchell), a white man hired by plantation owners to drive the Negroes back to the cotton fields. After destroying one wagon train, Deshay sets a trap for Buck at the ranch house of his woman, Ruth (Ruby Dee), but Buck escapes and rides off to join the next group of migrants, stopping only to trade horses—at gunpoint—with a seedy black preacher who introduces himself as Reverend Willis Oakes Rutherford, of the High and Low Orders of the Holiness Persuasion Church

With Ruby Dee.

As Buck.

With Harry Belafonte.

(Belafonte). This preacher, it turns out, carries a pistol in his Bible, which helps him collect "charity" contributions.

Caught riding Buck's horse, the Preacher smooth-talks his way out of a lynching and then sets out to get himself a $500 reward that Deshay is offering for the capture of Buck. Finding his way to the St. Anne Parish Wagon Train with the help of a black lad named Little Toby (Dennis Hines), the Preacher locates Buck, who has just

concluded a deal with a local Indian tribe for the safe passage of his train. That night, Deshay's raiders, who have followed the Preacher, attack and loot the wagon train, killing, among others, Little Toby.

Enraged, Buck and the Preacher track Deshay's men to a bordello run by Madam Esther (Nita Talbot), and while the Preacher comes in the front door and creates a diversion with a flamboyant Bible reading, Buck sneaks in the back

With Harry Belafonte and Ruby Dee.

With Ruby Dee.

way and guns down Deshay and most of his men. The revenge killing is too late, though; the stolen money has disappeared. As the sheriff's posse and Deshay's second-in-command, Floyd (Denny Miller), are hunting for Buck and the Preacher, they have picked up Ruth and doubled back to the nearly deserted town to hold up the bank and the express office.

The trio then takes a short cut back to the train and Buck attempts to bargain with the Indians for guns and ammunition. He is turned down, however, with the Indians maintaining that what they have is needed for their own fight against the white man. When the Sheriff (John Kelly) decides not to attack the ex-slaves, he is killed by the murderous Floyd, and a siege is mounted. But Buck and the Preacher lure Floyd and his gang into the hills—and into the hands of the waiting Indians. With the threat to safety removed, the wagon train resumes its westward trek.

Critics found *Buck and the Preacher* a comedy Western, a message film; a hard-riding adventure story; "a kind of *Wagon Train* in blackface" (Arthur Knight, *Saturday Review);* a

long-overdue history lesson, a serious commentary on freedom, and/or an opportunity for a large number of fine black actors to work in an important and non-militant (or "exploitation") movie. In *Cue,* Donald J. Meyerson wrote: "Sidney Poitier achieves a personal triumph directing and starring in this impressive Western. The talented actor has been saddled and trammeled of late by a series of routine films, so it is an occasion for rejoicing to see him at his acting best. As a new director, he establishes himself well. His film is nicely paced and packed with enough action, laughs and tears to satisfy the most demanding moviegoer . . . [He] expertly handles the traditional elements of the Western film idiom, and adds the novel twist of having Indians aid the blacks . . . This is a stirring film."

Vincent Canby observed that *"Buck and the Preacher,* Sidney Poitier's first film as director as well as star, is a loose, amiable, post-Civil War Western with a firm though not especially severe black conscience. The film is aware of contemporary black issues but its soul is on the plains once ridden by Tom Mix, whom Poitier, astride his

[ 193 ]

With Harry Belafonte.

galloping horse, his jaw set, somehow resembles in the majestic traveling shots given him by the director."

In *New York* critic Judith Crist said: ". . . in spite of the fact that the credits say it was written by Ernest Kinoy (of the disastrous *Brother John)* and directed by Sidney Poitier, in his debut no less, nobody can convince me that it wasn't scripted by a machine named Slicko and brought to the screen by a computer . . . Face it. The three [leads] are skilled performers and charming per-sonalities. Poitier is nobler than ever, Belafonte is naughty-lovable, Miss Dee an enchantress. And they breeze through this clunking predictable bang-bang-you're-dead-but-unbloodied clinker with a professionalism to be admired."

Jay Cocks of *Time* Magazine felt that "Poitier mostly contents himself with dispensing his standard Captain Marvel characterization . . . even so, there are a couple of scenes in which [he] reminds us that he is still a superb actor." In the *Chicago Sun-Times,* Walter Lowe, Jr. dis-

With Harry Belafonte.

[ 194 ]

cussed the film in terms of the vibrations he experienced: "Among the vibes communicated by Poitier as a director is one of supreme confidence. You can sense that man's many years in the film industry have enabled him to conduct his little epic with ease as though he had run it through his head for maybe twenty years . . . Poitier established that this film is owned and operated, lock, stock and barrel, by a black man [and] the black actors thrive under Poitier's touch, and even the minor roles are so sharply delineated that one cannot help but notice how much talent has been wasted by Hollywood's insistence on using blacks mainly in cab driver and butler roles."

*Variety* noted: "Never let it be said that Sidney Poitier and Harry Belafonte will sit still for being typecast. Ever since they've been in films, both black actors, particularly Belafonte, have been experimenting with versatility. Although they still haven't found their proper niche with their first Western, their efforts do provide an evening of generally entertaining comedy and drama . . . Poitier also directed, which may explain his occasional air of not really being involved in the acting [and] it is Belafonte who dominates the film."

For Kevin Thomas of the *Los Angeles Times,* "the initial joint appearance of Poitier and Belafonte on the screen" was "an auspicious first" that "even takes on the comic aspects of *Butch Cassidy and the Sundance Kid,*" while in *Commonweal,* reviewer Colin L. Westerbeck, Jr., expressed his opinion that "the themes of exchange are obviously what appealed to Mr. Poitier when he chose the script for this Black Western . . . [He] plays Buck as the latest word in self-reliant, soft spoken, straight-shooting cowboys. At one point, while escaping a trap laid by his white nemesis, [he] even executes a running mount that would have made Yakima Canutt proud. Yet I don't want to give the impression that Buck and his unscrupulous sidekick, the Preacher, are just Roy Rogers and Gabby Hayes in blackface. There is also an undertone in the film whispering benignly, 'Up against the wall, m—f—, this is a stick-up!' "

With Ruby Dee and Harry Belafonte.

As Matt Younger.

# A Warm December

First Artists/National General Pictures     1973

THE CAST:

*Matt Younger,* SIDNEY POITIER; *Catherine,* Esther Anderson; *Stefanie Younger,* Yvette Curtis; *Henry Barlow,* George Baker; *Myomo,* Johnny Sekka; *George Oswandu,* Earl Cameron; *Marsha Barlow,* Hilary Crane; *Burberry,* John Beardmore; *Carol Barlow,* Ann Smith; *Janie Barlow,* Stephanie Smith; *Singer in Club,* Letta Mbulu.

CREDITS:

A First Artists/Verdon Production. *Producer,* Melville Tucker; *director,* Sidney Poitier; *screenplay,* Lawrence Roman; *photography,* Paul Beeson; *music,* Coleridge-Taylor Perkinson; *assistant directors,* David Tomblin and Brian Cook; *art director,* Elliot Scott; *editors,* Pembroke J. Herring and Peter Pitt. Technicolor. Running time: 101 minutes.

As both director and star of *A Warm December,* described by its makers as "a topical and touching love story set against the background of intrigue

[ 196 ]

in London and in an emergent East African State's Embassy there," Sidney Poitier made his first contribution to First Artists, the independent production outfit in which he was partnered with Paul Newman, Barbra Streisand, Steve McQueen and Dustin Hoffman to gain creative as well as financial control over film projects from initial pre-planning to final distribution.

The film, invariably referred to as "Sidney Poitier's *A Warm December*," is romantic drama which, because of its theme (the leading lady is dying of an incurable disease), universally has been compared to *Love Story,* exploited for black audiences, along with a touch of *Roman Holiday,* transposed to London. With two beautiful people in the leading roles, graceful Sidney Poitier and stunning newcomer Esther Anderson, *A Warm December* attempts to say something meaningful about emergent Africa while framing its message against the generally fail-safe soap opera film-making genre.

*A Warm December* starts out like a cloak and dagger movie with a beautiful young woman being followed through London by an assortment of sinister looking characters. Happening along is Matt Younger (Poitier), a widowed Washington doctor who has brought his ten-year-old daughter, Stefanie (Yvette Curtis), to Great Britain for a holiday and a visit to his old friend, Henry Barlow (George Baker). Matt has a series of encounters with the lovely girl (Esther Anderson) and on two occasions, helps her elude a man who is trailing her. She is grateful, but declines his offer to take her to an African gala night at the Drury Lane Theatre, saying she is going there anyway. Then she gets into a big limousine chauffeured by a black man with tribal scars, later identified as Myomo (Johnny Sekka). Later, at the theatre, Matt sees her arrive in the company of the Torundan Ambassador, George Oswandu (Earl Cameron), and learns that she is Oswandu's niece, Catherine, a member of her country's Economic Development Council.

Although she continues to be followed everywhere, Catherine and Matt start meeting erratically, and soon become lovers. When she becomes ill during a helicopter trip planned as a treat for Stefanie, Matt suspects that her health is the reason for the constant surveillance. He attempts to

With Esther Anderson.

call on her at the embassy but is brushed off by the Ambassador and Myomo. He finally discovers that she has sickle cell anemia, an incurable disease transmitted from her mother. In the helicopter, she had gone into crisis.

Undeterred, Matt asks Catherine to marry him. She refuses, but agrees to spend a few days with him and Stefanie in the country. During their stay in an old country cottage, as their relation-

Director Poitier discussing a scene with Esther Anderson.

ship deepens, Catherine suffers a severe attack and is rushed to a local hospital for emergency treatment. On her recovery, she tells Matt that she will marry him after all. Back in London, her uncle tries to persuade her to change her mind, but she tells him: "It's December for me, and I know there's not much time left, but I want a husband and child before I die."

Matt waits in vain for her at the home of his friend, Barlow, and in the mounting panic at her non-appearance, he finally goes after her and traces her to a reception at the Russian Embassy where she is promoting a hydroelectric plant for her country. There she says goodbye to him, explaining that although she loves him, in view of the short time she has left she feels that her obligations to her country are more important. Her final words to him: "Goodbye, my husband, thank you for a warm December."

Critic Roger Greenspun wrote in *The New York Times:* "Sidney Poitier's *A Warm December* is the latest in the grand tradition of non-disfiguring incurable-illness movies. But there is a twist. He and she are black, and the illness now is sickle-cell anemia . . . The real reasons for *A Warm December* (besides a good cry) are kindness to children, homely virtues, sentimental sex, touristy travel and unforgettable personality. It is like opening some impossibly typical, transcendentally

awful issue of *Reader's Digest* . . . For the romance in this game, Sidney Poitier, now almost 50 years old, is a little past his prime. As a good actor, it seems especially cruel that he should suffer one of his silliest roles in his own movie."

In *The Washington Post,* Gary Arnold conceded that "it's not really that bad or that distinctive. The problem with the film is that it's not much of anything, including anything significantly annoying . . . Poitier has no more character to play than Miss Anderson does, but he is a star, and his presence helps to fill the void from time to time. He's quite charming, particularly when he doesn't try to run on the charm, and his direction is certainly adequate [but] Poitier gives us precious little to warm up to in *A Warm December."*

Judith Crist said: "It's a dashing, slick, old-Hollywood romance—and the sort of movie that the popcorn-and-Kleenex crowd can really wallow in . . . Militants may scoff at schmaltz . . . but this is exactly what Poitier had in mind, to my mind, some years ago when he said he made *For Love of Ivy* so that his children could identify with characters in a middle-class movie."

Reviewing in the *St. Louis Post Dispatch,* Joe Pollack complained: "Poitier is getting a little too old to play a romantic lead, even though he does pose as an American doctor on vacation.

[ 198 ]

As Matt Younger.

With Esther Anderson.

His age shows in the closeups . . . Poitier's direction shows numerous flaws. The scenic shots seem inserted in a number of areas [with] little reward for pace and the growth of the story and the characters." Critic Pollack decided: "*A Warm December* really isn't a bad film. It's a love story with some warm moments, a generally good performance by Poitier and considerable tenderness, but it is unfortunately too much soap opera without enough reality."

*Variety,* uncharacteristically, gave an unremittantly negative notice to *A Warm December,* calling it "poorly written by Lawrence Roman, sluggishly directed by Poitier himself (who heads the cast as well), and awkwardly paced . . . Poitier's direction has moments of seeming forced and too-aware of the plot's faults . . . [it] runs most of its length as an apparent suspenser, then shifts to its terminal disease theme, effect of which is not so much suspense as a feeling of tease and cheat."

And *Time* Magazine's conclusion: "[It] is no angry social document. It is very much in the old tradition of star-crossed Ruritanian romance, with overtones of *Love Story*. Poitier deals with grave matters, but in such a cushy way that he makes them all seem frivolous," while this from Britain's *Monthly Film Bulletin:* "Saddled with an aimless script, Poitier is marginally more effective in front of the camera than behind it."

To compensate for the parade of downbeat reviews was Ann Guarino's rave in the New York *Daily News*. She gave the film 3½-stars and declared: "Sidney Poitier directs himself and his cast so deftly in *A Warm December* that one is not aware that he is pulling the strings on both sides of the camera. He does a splendid job as actor and director. The tender, bittersweet love story . . . captures interest and holds it throughout because of fine performances [and he] is to be commended for choosing a story that does not exploit his race and one with which others can empathize."

With Rosalind Cash.

# Uptown Saturday Night

First Artists/Warner Bros.          1974

## THE CAST:

*Steve Jackson*, SIDNEY POITIER; *Wardell Franklin*, BILL COSBY; *Geechie Dan Beauford*, HARRY BELAFONTE; *The Reverend*, FLIP WILSON; *Sharp Eye Washington*, Richard Pryor; *Sarah Jackson*, Rosalind Cash; *Congressman Lincoln*, Roscoe Lee Browne; *Leggy Peggy*, Paula Kelly; *Madame Zenobia*, Lee Chamberlin; *Geechie's Henchman*, Johnny Sekka; *Slim's Henchman #1*, Lincoln Kilpatrick; *Slim's Henchman #2*, Don Marshall; *Irma Franklin*, Ketty Lester; *Little Seymour*, Harold Nicholas; *Silky Slim*, Calvin Lockhart.

## CREDITS:

A First Artists/Verdon Production. *Producer,* Melville Tucker; *director,* Sidney Poitier; *screenplay,* Richard Wesley; *photography,* Fred J. Koenekamp; *music,* Tom Scott; *title song,* Tom Scott and Morgan Ames; *sung* by Dobie Gray; *second unit director,* Harry F. Hogan, Sr.; *assistant direc-*tor, Charles C. Washburn; *art director,* Alfred Sweeney; *editor,* Pembroke J. Herring. Technicolor. Running time: 104 minutes.

Poitier's *Uptown Saturday Night* moved the actor-turned-director to the next plateau. Using his superstar clout in the industry, he was able to assemble, for his 1974 contribution to First Artists, a sensational cast of the top black talent available to demonstrate, as *Sounder* and *Claudine* had done previously, that black performers need not be supercool assassins in mindless exploitation films. With buddies Harry Belafonte, Bill Cosby, Flip Wilson, Roscoe Lee Browne, Richard Pryor, Calvin Lockhart and others, Poitier made a laudable attempt to stage a small scale version of Stanley Kramer's *It's a Mad, Mad, Mad, Mad World,* bringing to mainstream America the type of black comedy—not to be confused with black humor—that long had been the staple

With Johnny Sekka, Harry Belafonte and Bill Cosby.

of Harlem's Apollo Theater and others like it in urban areas, and what has been called "the chitlin circuit."

*Uptown Saturday Night* is laced with raffish good humor and rollicking observations on life, along with put ons of the stereotypical Negro attitudes that had been the backbone of the primarily white film industry from its beginnings. Added elements include standard fillips of action adventures: a caper, a brawl, a shootout, a car chase. All the violence expected in cinema of the Seventies, minus the bloodshed. The film's comic potential, unfortunately, failed to take it out of the realm of a TV situation comedy and its individual standout gems (Belafonte's campy imitation of Marlon Brando in *The Godfather,* Flip Wilson's swaggering reverend sermonizing on loose lips, Richard Pryor's con man gumshoe, Roscoe Lee

Brown's hypocritically mellifluous politician) remain merely bits which director Poitier was unable to develop into the zany momentum, let alone the outrageousness, the tale desperately needed. It had the ingredients to have become as nutty as *Blazing Saddles* of the same period.

The misadventures of Steve Jackson (Poitier), hardworking factory hand, and his fun loving buddy, Wardell Franklin (Bill Cosby), a high spirited cab driver, begin when the two manage to sneak away from their wives (Rosalind Cash and Ketty Lester) for a few hours of booze, broads and gambling on a Saturday night uptown at the exclusive club run by Madame Zenobia (Lee Chamberlin). While they are enjoying themselves, though, the club is raided by a gang of masked men on the payroll of Silky Slim (Calvin Lockhart). When Steve later realizes that a

With Bill Cosby and Roscoe Lee Browne.

$50,000 winning lottery ticket had been in his wallet, among the items ripped off, he and Wardell, wary of the police, decide to go after the crooks themselves.

First they hire a fumbling investigator, Sharp Eye Washington (Richard Pryor), but he just takes their money and skips. Next they go for help to pompous Congressman Lincoln (Roscoe Lee Browne), something of a slicker himself, and learn inadvertently that Leggy Peggy (Paula Kelly), the tootsie who is married to the slimy politician, is one of Madame Zenobia's ladies. She puts them in touch with Little Seymour (Harold Nicholas), a small time hood, who has them worked over. In desperation, they go to Geechie Dan (Belafonte), a ghetto ganglord currently organizing a gang war against his rival, Silky Slim. At first Geechie Dan thinks Steve and Wardell are hit men after him, but then begins to put some credence in their story of the ripoff.

When Silky Slim happens to pay a call on Geechie Dan during the boys' visit, they recognize Slim as the leader of the raid on Madame Zenobia's. Hurriedly, they concoct an elaborate plan to retrieve the missing lottery ticket and convince Slim that they have $300,000 in diamonds which they'd be happy to split with him. The boys talk both Slim and Geechie Dan into assembling their gangs at a charity mountaintop picnic, where the police are ready to swoop in and round up the various criminals. Slim, however, attempts a get-

away with the suitcase containing the ticket. Steve and Wardell take off after him, but during the struggle for the prize, when they catch him, the suitcase is tossed off a high bridge. Without a thought, the boys dive into the river below to recover the ticket so that they can return to their incredibly patient wives.

Vincent Canby gave the film a favorable notice in *The New York Times,* calling it "essentially a put-on, but it's so full of good humor and, when the humor goes flat, of such high spirits that it reduces movie criticism to the status of a most nonessential craft . . . You've never seen so much eye-popping fear and unwarranted braggadocio used in the service of laughs. Yet the result is not a put-down comedy but a cheerful jape that has the effect of liberating all of us from our hangups. . . . Mr. Poitier's intelligence and taste are most noticeable in the film's casting, in the leeway he gives his actors, and in the ability at times to make himself seem physically small and downright intimidated. For a man of his stature, that cannot be easy."

In her review in *The New Yorker,* Penelope Gilliatt spoke of some of the recent revolutionary black films, and then considered: *"Uptown Saturday Night,* directed by Sidney Poitier, demonstrates something more revolutionary—black is fun. [It] is a larky story that nobody but blacks could have pulled off . . . Poitier, who must be

With Harry Belafonte and Bill Cosby.

With Bill Cosby, Harry Belafonte and Calvin Lockhart.

With Rosalind Cash.

well over six feet, has somehow made himself look smaller. Splendidly erasing his pious recent past in films, he acts here an aging and inefficient lounger who ordinarily dreams of booze and girls' legs in front of the television but suddenly finds himself in a startling uptown world where men are thrown out of gang saloons as if they were chewed-up cigar stubs."

Ann Guarino also reviewed the film favorably, giving it 3½ stars in the New York *Daily News,* calling it "a lively, entertaining comedy," and reporting that "the pacing is uneven, but Poitier draws good performances from the entire cast." On the critical fence was Donald J. Meyerson of *Cue,* who felt that "the stars communicate some of the fun they had making this film, but it is mostly a labored black situation comedy with the look of a TV pilot in search of a series . . . The real pleasure of the film comes from its performers. Poitier is fine as the popeyed oaf, and Cosby is delightful as a sloppy sharpy who gets his friend into trouble . . . The film lacks the maniac merriment of a Mel Brooks movie, but it does have some hilariously zany scenes to make it an audience pleaser. What it needed was a funnier script and tighter control, which Poitier as director was unable to provide."

Unamused was Paul D. Zimmermann, critic for *Newsweek,* who said: "An all-star game is rarely played for esthetics. Instead, it's intended as a showcase for personality. Such is the case with *Uptown Saturday Night*—a *Sting* style yarn

. . . Poitier is not an inventive comic talent—he is erratic behind the camera and amiable but not funny in front of it. When the funny set pieces stop, the film sputters—but not before delivering a carnival of fine comic characters."

Downright hostile was the critic for *Variety,* who tagged it: "Great black talent, some funny ideas and breezy charm almost nullified by Sidney Poitier's own tepid performance and routine direction." The paper's review listed among the film's debits "a helter-skelter screenplay, Poitier's lifeless performance, and Poitier's unimaginative comic direction . . . too much of the time, *Uptown Saturday Night* just lies there, waiting impatiently for more inventive comedy business and a zippier pace than the sober Poitier seems able to provide. If the soundtrack were turned off, a nearsighted viewer could mistake the picture for a gangland meller, so melancholy and measured is Poitier's *mise-en-scene.* Actor Poitier also dampens the proceedings with a bland, comically mistimed performance that suffers greatly in comparison to Cosby's zesty rendition of his carefree buddy."

In a similar thumbs down report, David McGillivray wrote in Britain's *Monthly Film Bulletin:* "One is forced to the conclusion that had it been filmed with a white cast, this collection of atrophied comedy routines would have been virtually indistinguishable from a Monogram farce of the Forties. Everyone tries hard to affect a happy-go-lucky air, but the material is so feeble and Sidney Poitier's direction so uninspired that the performances . . . look depressingly mediocre. It is difficult to see in *Uptown Saturday Night* anything but a colossal waste of talent."

With Michael Caine and Prunella Gee.

# The Wilby Conspiracy

United Artists                    1975

THE CAST:

*Shack Twala,* SIDNEY POITIER; *Jim Keogh,* MICHAEL CAINE; *Major Horn,* NICOL WILLIAMSON; *Rina Van Niekirk,* Prunella Gee; *Persis Ray,* Persis Khambatta; *Mukerjee,* Saeed Jaffrey; *Van Heerden,* Ryk De Gooyer; *Blane Van Niekirk,* Rutger Hauer; *Wilby Xaba,* Josef de Graf; *Shepherd Boy,* Freddy Achiang; *Cape Town Police Commandant,* Patrick Allen; *Judge,* Brian Epsom; *Headman in Masai Village,* Abdullah Sunado; *Gordon,* Archie Duncan; *Highway Policeman,* Peter Pearce; *Prosecuting Counsel,* Helmut Dantine.

CREDITS:

An Optimus and Baum/Dantine Production. *Executive producer,* Helmut Dantine; *producer,* Martin Baum; *director,* Ralph Nelson; *screenplay,* Rod Amateau and Harold Nebenzal; based on the novel by Peter Driscoll; *photography,* John Coquillon; *music,* Stanley Myers; *song* "Geliefde Man" by Stanley Myers and Jeremy Taylor; *sung* by Jean Hart; *second unit director,* Rod Amateau; *assistant director,* Ivo Nightingale; *special effects,* Kit West and Phil Stokes; *editor,* Ernest Walter. Color by DeLuxe. Running time: 105 minutes.

Working for the first time in several years under someone else's direction, Sidney Poitier was reunited with Ralph Nelson *(Lilies of the Field, Duel at Diablo)* in a slick chase thriller that revived memories of the actor's roles in both *The Defiant Ones* and *The Mark of the Hawk* of an earlier day. *The Wilby Conspiracy,* from Peter Driscoll's bestselling novel, follows the flight of a black South African revolutionary and a reluctant white companion, forced to flee together in a desperate dash for the border with a racist cop and his sadistic deputy in pursuit. The parallels to Poitier's *The Defiant Ones* are quite obvious, although the action and the dialogue are varnished to a mid-Seventies sheen in the chunks of graphic violence and flip banter. More than one critic noted that *The Wilby Conspiracy* marked another step in director Ralph Nelson's attempt to take the title of cinema's liberal polemicist from Stanley Kramer, who had been its spokesman during the two previous decades.

Filmed in the spring of 1974 in Kenya (with the blessings, it was reported, of President Jomo Kenyatta, who personally invited Poitier to make his movie there), with stock shots of Cape Town and Johannesburg to simulate South African authenticity, *The Wilby Conspiracy* is thought to be the first major studio motion picture starring top international actors to come out squarely against apartheid. More unusual was the fact that top billed Sidney Poitier would agree once again to play a black African agitator (as in *The Mark of the Hawk* and *Something of Value*) at this point in his career. Regardless, he and Michael Caine, a couple of old pros, helped disguise with their presence and charm the reality that *The Wilby Conspiracy* is a routine potboiler spiced with lots of action as well as an undetermined point of view (the ending, to confuse matters, has three sharp twists in a row).

Poitier is Shack Twala, a Bantu extremist who is acquitted in a Cape Town court on a fresh charge of terrorism and released after serving ten years in a prison colony. His white lady lawyer, Rina Van Niekirk (Prunella Gee), and her lover, Jim Keogh (Michael Caine), a British min-

With Michael Caine.

ing engineer, head for her place with Shack for a celebration drink when they are stopped in a routine police roadblock/search. Shack, seated in the back seat of Rina's car, is ordered out and manacled. When one of the blacks caught in the roundup is bludgeoned, the enraged Shack knocks down the police officer, and in the ensuing brawl, he and Keogh make a hasty getaway in Rina's car. The two flee toward Johannesburg where Rina has an apartment and Shack has friends in the Black Congress movement who will help him get out of the country.

Hot on their heels is Major Horn (Nicol Williamson), chief of State Security, who is paranoically possessed by visions of three million whites surrounded by eighteen million blacks ("No Zulu twenty years out of the tree is going to give me 50¢ and put me onto a freighter to shoot me out of the country *we* built!" he tells his aide Van Heerden). Horn relentlessly dogs their steps but allows them to reach Johannesburg and meet Shack's contact, Mukerjee (Saeed Jaffrey), a "dedicated" Indian dentist. While Shack is negotiating with Mukerjee, Keogh is dallying with Rina in her tub when Horn and Van Heerden burst in, sadistically dangle an electric hair dryer over their tub, and intimidate Keogh into double-crossing Shack at the border after explaining that Shack had been vice president of the Congress at the time of his arrest and that he is eager to return a cache of diamonds—held in safekeeping by Mukerjee—to revolutionary leader, Wilby Xaba (Josef de Graf), encamped just beyond the South African border.

With Nicol Williamson.

As Shack Twala.

With Prunella Gee, Persis Khambatta, Michael Caine and Saeed Jaffrey.

At Mukerjee's place, meanwhile, the security police stage a raid, as Shack and Mukerjee's lovely assistant, Persis Ray (Persis Khambatta), engage in a little stand-up sex in a cramped closet nearby. When Shack and Keogh finally get together once again, there is an angry scene between the two before they decide to cooperate in retrieving the diamonds from Mukerjee's hiding place— a 200-foot sink hole in a nearby swamp. At the site, Mukerjee is killed by Persis Ray, who attempts to steal the cache, and she in turn is shot down by Shack. With Keogh and Rina, he then races for the border, fighting off a police patrol and finally blackmailing Rina's playboy husband, Blane (Rutger Hauer), into flying them across. In Wilby's encampment, though, they are surprised by the arrival of Horn, who announces that he had planned from the start to have Shack and Keogh lead them to Wilby. Horn tells Shack, Keogh and Rina that they are free.

Shack is seen as a traitor by Wilby's men, and he has trouble talking them into helping stop Horn from taking off in his helicopter with Wilby. Shack's desperate efforts, along with a pitched battle among the villagers and Horn's soldiers, interrupt Horn's flight. With his men killed, Horn is persuaded to hand over Wilby, and he is then shot dead by Keogh.

Vincent Canby reported in *The New York Times* that the film is "a sort of light-hearted *The Defiant Ones* played for a good many laughs as well as for suspense and of course social comment

With Freddy Achiang.

... it does take itself as seriously only as the plot demands, but never too solemnly ... Mr. Caine and Mr. Poitier are never unaware that their material may not be the greatest, but that doesn't spoil their good spirits, and when a good line comes along they get maximum results without stomping on it or us [and] giving them excellent support, acting, in effect, as straightman to the two leading comics, is Nicol Williamson."

Ann Guarino felt in the New York *Daily News* that "Apartheid attitudes in South Africa get quite a going over in *The Wilby Conspiracy,* a taut, thought provoking chase adventure [and] Sidney Poitier is in top form ... As directed by Ralph Nelson, the film maintains interest and suspense, but its best part easily is the humorous contrast between an indignant Michael Caine and a cheeky Poitier."

"A political thriller set in South Africa," is how Stanley Kauffmann described the film in *The New Republic.* "There is not one credible moment in it but there is not one boring moment.

With Prunella Gee and Michael Caine.

Such a suspension of disbelief, without the slightest reference to logic or probability, bespeaks the power of conversation [although] I don't know whom to praise for the bright dialogue or to blame for the mechanically shunted plot . . . Poitier, whom I haven't seen in several years, has lost none of his emotional strength and equally effortless charm."

In *Time,* Jay Cocks observed that "Among the more pressing issues addressed in *The Wilby Conspiracy* is the manner of how Sidney Poitier, shackled by handcuffs, manages to—well, relieve himself. Mr. Poitier often finds himself in dilemmas of this kind [and] such odd, frivolous moments make *The Wilby Conspiracy* a surprisingly breezy diversion . . . a reasonable level of satire is maintained throughout even while everyone clowns."

While Penelope Gilliatt wrote a lengthy précis in *The New Yorker* praising the work of Nicol Williamson and mentioning Poitier only once in the plot context, William Wolf was commenting in *Cue:* "There is cause for special anger at the messing up of a film with strong points to make about racism in South Africa. A sure, knowing hand would have kept the film taut, tough and credible, [but instead] the impact is vitiated by horrendous dialogue, silly bits of melodrama and unbelievable relationships."

In *Saturday Review,* Karl E. Meyer wrote: "What can happen in a spy thriller *cum* politics, when the elements fail to cohere, is sadly evident in *The Wilby Conspiracy,* a well-intended film set in apartheid ridden South Africa. Sidney Poitier plays a black revolutionary so virtuous that we cannot believe in him; Michael Caine, his English accomplice, obviously doesn't, because Caine goes through the motions with his tired reflex mannerisms. In fact—and this was not the intention of director Ralph Nelson—we find ourselves exulting in the villain."

And John Crittenden, critic for New Jersey's *Bergen Record,* spoke of the film as "a routine little chase movie that could have been filmed almost anytime in the last decade—it's that nondescript in everything but its politics . . . almost everything about the film is preposterous, but it does move along quickly, and Caine, Poitier and Williamson do admirably in their two dimensional parts. *The Wilby Conspiracy* adds up to much less than it might have been. Its director, Ralph Nelson, who guided Poitier's *Lilies of the Field,* chose slickness over substance."

With Nicol Williamson, Joseph De Graf (in helicopter) and Michael Caine.

With Bill Cosby.

# Let's Do It Again

First Artists/Warner Bros.          1975

THE CAST:

*Clyde Williams*, SIDNEY POITIER; *Billy Foster*, BILL COSBY; *Bootney Farnsworth*, Jimmie Walker; *Biggie Smalls*, Calvin Lockhart; *Kansas City Mack*, John Amos; *Beth Foster*, Denise Nicholas; *Dee Dee Williams*, Lee Chamberlin; *Ellison*, Mel Stewart; *Bubbletop Woodson*, Julius Harris; *Jody Tipps*, Paul E. Harris; *Lt. Bottonley*, Val Avery; *Elder Johnson*, Ossie Davis; *Zack*, Billy Eckstine; *Fish 'n' Chips Freddie*, Morgan Roberts; *Biggie's Girl*, Talya Ferro; *Biggie's Gang*, Doug Johnson, Richard Young and Cedric Scott; *Hotel Detective*, Med Flory; *Fortieth Street Black*, Rodolfus Lee Hayden; *Factory Secretary*, Jayne Kennedy; *Telephone Operator*, Hilda Haynes.

CREDITS:

A First Artists/Verdon Production. *Producer*, Melville Tucker; *director*, Sidney Poitier; *screenplay*, Richard Wesley; *story*, Timothy March; *photography*, Donald M. Morgan; *music*, Curtis Mayfield; *songs sung* by The Staple Singers; *as-sistant director*, Reuben L. Watt; *production design*, Alfred Sweeney; *special effects*, Charles Spurgeon; *associate producer and editor*, Pembroke J. Herring. Technicolor. Running time: 112 minutes.

The unqualified success of *Uptown Saturday Night* led Sidney Poitier to round up much of the team responsible for it, including producer Melville Tucker, writer Richard Wesley, and co-star Bill Cosby (plus Calvin Lockhart and Lee Chamberlin, et al.), and do it again in *Let's Do It Again*. Whatever blockbuster business the first of these films did as a smash "crossover" movie (a black film that appeals to white as well as black audiences), the second rapidly eclipsed it in popularity. Less a sequel than merely a continuation of its top grossing predecessor, *Let's Do It Again* is a somewhat better conceived vehicle in the free form substance of classic Hal Roach comedy or prime Harold Lloyd, with Poitier (again working both sides of the camera) and Cosby doing unin-

With Bill Cosby.

hibited farce in the grand Bing Crosby-Bob Hope manner of three decades earlier.

This time, the pair play blue collar buddies once more—an Atlanta milkman (Poitier) and his factory worker pal (Cosby)—who go to New Orleans with their wives, become involved with a gangly, would-be prize fighter, outfox a couple of warring mobsters, and come home with enough money to construct a new meeting hall for their lodge. In its first three months of release, *Let's Do It Again* quickly became the most successful black movie made to that time, eventually grossing more than $10 million. Even the soundtrack album of the Curtis Mayfield score and the title song by The Staple Singers became No. 1 smashes.

Breezing along on a string of conventional gags, outrageous situations, and their personal charm, Poitier and Cosby are, respectively, Clyde Williams and Billy Foster, lodge buddies. They learn that their lodge, the Sons and Daughters of Shaka, has lost its lease and needs $50,000 for a new meeting place. Scooping up the lodge's building fund, Clyde and Billy gather their wives (Lee Chamberlin and Denise Nicholas), scoot down to New Orleans, and hatch a scheme to raise the needed money. The boys dude themselves up, place some heavy bets with two big-time rival bookies: Kansas City Mack (John Amos), an oldtimer, and Biggie Smalls (Calvin Lockhart), a dapper kingpin trying to muscle in on Mack's territory. Then, using Clyde's talents as an amateur hypnotist, they go to work on Bootney Farnsworth (Jimmie Walker), a puny pugilist who has just been battered by bruising Fortieth Street Black (Rodolfus Hayden). Clyde puts a hex on Bootney, who becomes a temporary Superman under the spell—long enough for the boys from Atlanta to fleece the gamblers in a big "sting." Clyde and Billy grab their winnings, collect their wives, and get out of town before the gangsters realize they've been ripped off.

(At this point, the picture virtually runs out of plot, but with a generous supply of unshot film still in the camera, it seems, the cast and crew apparently decided: "Let's do it again!" (And they do.)

The time is six months later. At the dedication of the new lodge hall, Elder Johnson (Ossie Davis) is showering Clyde and Billy with praise for their fund raising efforts, as Mack and his gun

With Bill Cosby, Denise Nicholas and Lee Chamberlin.

With Bill Cosby.

toting friends call the honored guests aside. Wise to what had happened in New Orleans, but willing to make a deal with the boys who took him, Mack "persuades" Clyde and Billy to make a return trip with him and put the whammy on Bootney again for his rematch with Fortieth Street Black. Before the fight, he tells them, he wants Clyde to take off the spell after all bets are down so that Mack and his boys can collect on Fortieth Street Black while the suckers are betting on Bootney. Dee Dee Williams and Beth Foster accompany their husbands, believing that this trip

With Bill Cosby

is to raise money for the lodge's child care center.

Attempts to accomplish this new mission put Clyde and Billy into various predicaments involving window escapes on ropes of sheets, rooftop chases, and hassles with the law, as fast talking Billy comes up with a new three-pronged scheme to save his and Clyde's hides and pull another con on the hoods. While their wives, posing as a pair of worldwise hookers, pay visits to the establishments of Kansas City Mack and Biggie Smalls, and place sizeable, anonymous bets, Clyde and Billy manage to hypnotize both fighters, who meet in the center of the ring on fight night and simultaneously blast away with sizzling, deadly left hooks . . . and both go down. Not so coincidentally, the outcome of the bout is what the disguised ladies had bet $5000 on at twenty-to-one odds. They collect their winnings only moments before Mack and Biggie realize that they had been ripped off once again and take off in hot pursuit of Clyde and Billy. Fleeing the furious gangsters, the boys decoy them into the police station where the outfoxed bookies reluctantly are forced to donate to the Policeman's Fund much of what Clyde and Billy had conned from

them, as the two couples from Atlanta head home much wiser and considerably wealthier.

Much of the same criticism of *Uptown Saturday Night*–particularly about Sidney Poitier's intrinsic lack of comedic abilities–was repeated in appraisals of *Let's Do It Again*. "It is apparent why Sidney Poitier set this project in motion and directed it: his making films for black audiences that aren't exploitation films," Pauline Kael wrote in *The New Yorker*. "Poitier is trying to make it possible for ordinary, lower middle class black people to see themselves on the screen and have a good time. The only thing that makes the film remarkable is that Poitier gives an embarrassed, inhibited performance. As casual, lighthearted straightman to Bill Cosby, he is trying to be something alien to his nature. He has too much pride, and too much reserve, for low comedy [ and ] for an actor of Poitier's intensity and grace to provide this kind of entertainment is the sacrifice of a major screen artist."

Ms. Kael felt: "As a director, Poitier is overly generous with the actors; he isn't skilled enough to shape sequences so that the actors can benefit from their closeups [ but ] what a strange

With Bill Cosby and Val Avery.

phenomenon it is that the actor who rose through sheer skill and became as elegant as a black Cary Grant should now, out of his deep conviction, be playing a milkman, bug eyed with comic terror, hanging outside a window by a sheet. And looking sick with humiliation . . . Poitier is fighting what he's doing with every muscle of his body; he's fighting his own actor's instinct which is telling him that his cartoon role is all wrong for him."

*Cue's* Donald J. Meyerson also was disappointed by Poitier, finding that "this rollicking new farce is wonderfully old-fashioned, totally improbable comedy and much better than its predecessor . . . adroitly directed by Sidney Poitier [although he] lacks an intrinsic sense of comedy as an actor and looks awkward next to the free-wheeling Cosby." Fran Weil, critic for the *Boston Herald-American,* agreed, noting first that "although some of *Let's Do It Again* works, most of it suffers from forced hilarity," and then that "it is Sidney Poitier who disappoints in the film. His performance as Cosby's affable straightman is a lusterless, thankless task. And the problems seem to have been further aggravated by the fact that Poitier's concentration had to be divided between the portrayal and the direction of the movie. The result, unfortunately, is that Poitier

has been upstaged by his directing and his co-stars."

In *The New York Times,* reviewer Richard Eder found that "some of it is pretty funny. The movie's main strength is Bill Cosby, who looks like a starved sheep in wolf's clothing . . . Mr. Poitier is no comedian but makes an adequate straightman." His fellow critic, Ann Guarino, giving the film three-and-one-half stars in her New York *Daily News* notice, spoke of the movie as "a fast, funny, entirely entertaining antic. If the plot is light, at least the incidents are hilarious," and noted that "Poitier, who doubled as director, surrounds himself with a top cast of black peers—and permits them to steal his thunder [while he] does get off some colorful moments of his own."

And while Jay Cocks of *Time* was calling *Let's Do It Again* "another comedy full of tired jokes and fairly high spirits . . . by the time Poitier and Cosby have rerun their plot, the meager supply [of jokes] has been totally exhausted and so has the audience," Stephen Klain was observing in the *Independent Film Journal:* "Poitier's direction moves things along as briskly and broadly as the material permits. As he did in the previous film, Poitier has given himself relatively little to do as an actor, preferring to let the camera linger on Cosby, who lets all stops out."

As Clyde Williams.

[ 215 ]

As Manny Durrell.

# A Piece of the Action

First Artists/Warner Bros.                    1977

THE CAST:

*Manny Durrell,* SIDNEY POITIER; *Dave Anderson,* BILL COSBY; *Joshua Burke,* JAMES EARL JONES; *Lila French,* Denise Nicholas; *Sarah Thomas,* Hope Clarke; *Nikki McLean,* Tracy Reed; *Bruno,* Titos Vandis; *Bea Quitman,* Frances Foster; *Ty Shorter,* Jason Evers; *Louie,* Marc Lawrence; *Nellie Bond,* Ja'net DuBois; *Willie Maunger,* Edward Love; *Barbara Hanley,* Sheryl Lee Ralph; *Denise O'rville,* Tamu; *Mrs. McLean,* Gammie Burdette; *Reverend McLean,* Wonderful Smith; *Mr. Theodore,* Cyril Poitier; *Cookie,* Sherri Poitier; and Eric Laneuville, Ernest Thomas, Dianne Dixon, Bryan O'Dell, Pat Renella, Rudy Diaz, Kurt Grayson, John Rivera, Raoul Anthony, Jack Brami, Martin Azarow, Andre Lacorbiere, James Fraracci, East Carlo, Martin Sherbanee, Dominic Barto.

CREDITS:

A First Artists/Verdon Production. *Producer,* Melville Tucker; *director,* Sidney Poitier; *screenplay,* Charles Blackwell; *story,* Timothy March; *photography,* Donald M. Morgan; *music,* Curtis Mayfield; *arranger/conductor,* Gil Askey; *songs sung* by Mavis Staples; *assistant director,* Dwight Williams; *second unit director,* Malcolm Atterbury; *production design,* Alfred Sweeney; *ballet sequence,* Dance Theatre of Harlem; *choreography,* Arthur Mitchell; *associate producer and editor,* Pembroke J. Herring. Panavision and Metrocolor. Running time: 135 minutes.

Equally as entertaining and successful, if a touch less farcical, as its two predecessors that also teamed Sidney Poitier and Bill Cosby and utilized much of the same creative talent, *A Piece of the Action* wisely followed producer/director Poitier's now-proven formula of making classy, enjoyable movies for the family trade, black and white. The latest provided another winning dose of comedy/action—a contemporary caper movie in the mold of *The Sting,* with several chunks of a previous Poitier hit, *To Sir, With Love,* shoehorned into the hijinks, allowing the star to make a few pertinent, if sugar-coated, social comments. Woven into this fun-filled tapestry are such elements as a pair of endearingly larcenous heroes, a cool, streetwise ex-cop who has their number, some mighty unhappy syndicate types who've been bamboozled by them, a bunch of ghetto dropouts in need of recycling, and a couple of foxy ladies to provide romantic diversions, plus a hip, soul-sizzling score by Curtis Mayfield.

In the midst of the light-hearted, often incredible proceedings, Poitier manages to slip in his public service message—several thought-provoking sequences describing what it's like to be young, black and unemployed, as one of the dropouts ruthlessly attacks her teacher as a black bourgeoise making her living off the destitution of other blacks, and another revealing the agonizing extent of his desperation about finding a job.

The scene: Chicago of the Seventies. Dave Anderson (Cosby) is deftly knocking over an office vault stuffed with laundered Mafia loot and making an ingenious getaway by leaping from a 12th-story ledge into a well-padded truck. Across town, in an unrelated scam, Manny Durrell (Poitier) is masterminding a plot to part an underworld bigwig named Bruno (Titos Vandis) from $375,000. The local constabulary is perplexed by these independently executed and seemingly clueless crimes, but detective Joshua Burke (James Earl Jones), about to retire from the force, solves the capers on his own, lures Dave and Manny to a hotel room where they meet one another for the first time, and then proceeds to anonymously blackmail them into volunteering their services as social workers. They are coerced into reporting to a South Side community im-

With Bill Cosby.

provement center run by Lila French (Denise Nicholas) where they will donate five years each —until the statute of limitations runs out—doing penance in a ghetto job corps. Their initial assignment: turn their first batch of thirty youngsters into employable citizens in just three weeks and get them jobs.

The reluctant new social workers flip a coin and it is decided that Manny will prepare the incorrigibles for employment and Dave will hunt up the job leads—while romancing Lila in his spare moments. Between whipping their charges into shape and locating willing employers, the pair endeavor to unmask their blackmailer and keep a step or two ahead of Bruno and his men who've gotten one of Manny's ex-associates to finger him. In the classroom, meanwhile, Manny has assessed the problems of Sarah Thomas (Hope Clarke), the center's beleaguered counselor, and, confronting his menagerie of unemployables

With Tracy Reed, Denise Nicholas and Bill Cosby.

and speaking their language, he concocts a few modern Aesop fables. Then, as incentives, he gives each half of a torn $100 bill and offers object lessons about self-esteem, consideration for others, simple courtesy, and a way to pay some of life's dues—to get a piece of the action.

Dave, in the meantime, finally has unraveled the mystery of their blackmailer, and the two confront Burke who admits that the center had been his dead wife's pet project. When Manny then gets word that his live-in girlfriend, Nikki McLean (Tracy Reed), has been kidnapped by Bruno, Burke agrees to give Manny and Dave inside police information on Bruno, allowing Manny to ransom Nikki by pulling off another elaborate "sting." He then returns to his class in time to share with Dave going-away gifts and a surprise commission from their graduates.

In the *Los Angeles Times,* critic Kevin Thomas judged: "With each picture, Poitier becomes a more assured director . . . *A Piece of the Action* is a joyful, humorous fantasy [and] everyone in the film excels under Poitier's generous, spirited direction . . . With [it] and his two previous pictures, Poitier has effectively tried to counterbalance the now-waning deluge of 'blaxploitation' pictures. In doing so, he's made the kind of movies with appeal for audiences both black and white."

David Ansen said in *Newsweek:* "There aren't many stars today who take it upon themselves to be role models, but Sidney Poitier, actor, director, producer, has been walking this esthetic tightrope for many years and making box-office gold out of the dilemma [and] *A Piece of the Action . . .* allows director Poitier to touch just about every commercial base—action, comedy, romance, sentiment—while capping it all with an uplifting message on the virtues of self-improvement." Reviewer Ansen also allowed that "Poitier has two things going for him: his own sincerity and the ingratiating spontaneity of its cast. Corny and hip, cynical and sentimental, formulaic and funky, *A Piece of the Action* may have a medicinal intent, but it goes down like ice cream soda."

Ann Guarino awarded the film three stars in her New York *Daily News* critique, reporting that "Sidney Poitier's *A Piece of the Action* is an entertaining comedy with elements of mystery, suspense and pertinent comments that will have reviewers reacting with 'Right on!' . . . Like Newman and Redford, Poitier and Cosby are an engaging team, and there's some lively music by Curtis Mayfield calculated to have the audiences dancing out the doors."

Generally, critical opinion more or less matched that of Michael Buckley, who, in *Films in Review,* found *A Piece of the Action* "an excellent film with performances to match. Bill Cosby has never been better than herein, directed by his co-star, Sidney Poitier, whose behind the camera work is his best to date . . . There should be *A Piece of the Action, Part II.*"

With Cyril Poitier, Denise Nicholas, Bill Cosby, Tracy Reed and James Earl Jones.

# Other Film Appearances by Sidney Poitier

## From Whence Cometh Help (1949)

Produced by the U.S. Army Signal Corps
Directed by Broder Peterson.
Written by Bruce Wagler.
(Filmed March 30, 1949–May 3, 1949).

Cast includes: Si Oakland, Phil Robinson, Leila Urnst, Blair Davies, Elza Poehsgen, Eric Lawrence, John Leighton, Gloria Strook, Fred Cotton, Leo Needham, Paul Langton, Pat Dexter, Eddie Waglon, Pat McVey, Jack Cottrell, Bill Layton, Garrit Walberg, Robert Dwight, Sidney Poitier, Earl Syndor, Martin Baum, Milo Boulton, Lee Richards, William Beal, John Arlis, Sid Renoir, Jack Carron, Charles Holt, Sandy Kenyon, Hal Alexander, James Jannett, Bill Myers, Bill Bly, Norman Bliestein.

## King: A Filmed Record... Montgomery to Memphis (1970)

Released by Maron Films, Ltd., on behalf of the Martin Luther King Foundation.

Produced by Ely Landau.
Directed by Joseph L. Mankiewicz and Sidney Lumet.

Appearances by Harry Belafonte, Ruby Dee, Ben Gazzara, Charlton Heston, James Earl Jones, Burt Lancaster, Paul Newman, Sidney Poitier, Anthony Quinn, Clarence Williams III and Joanne Woodward.

# Sidney Poitier on the Stage

## Lysistrata

The Aristophanes play adapted by Gilbert Seldes in two acts. Staged by James Light; choreography by Felicia Sorel; music by Harry Bryant. Revived with an all-Negro cast by James Light and Max J. Jelin.

Belasco Theatre, New York 10/17/46 (four performances).

Pearl Gaines (Leader of Old Women's Chorus)
Etta Moten (Lysistrata)
Fredi Washington (Kalonika)
Mildred Smith (Myrrhina)
Mercedes Gilbert (Lampito)
Leigh Whipper (Leader of Old Men's Chorus)
Rex Ingram (President of the Senate)
Maurice Ellis (Spartan Envoy)
Emmett Babe Wallace (Kineslas)
John de Battle (Trygeus)
Larry Williams (Nikias)
Sidney Poitier (Polydorus)
Emory S. Richardson (Lykon)

"Sidney Poitier has a few comic utterances as the sex-starved Polydorus."
—Ward Morehouse, *New York Sun*

## Anna Lucasta

A play in three acts by Philip Yordan; staged by Harry Wagstaff Gribble. Revived by John Wildberg.*

National Theatre, New York 9/22/47 (32 performances).

>Wesleen Foster (Katie)
>Rosette Le Noire (Stella)
>Laura Bowman (Theresa)
>Roy Allen (Stanley)
>Warren Coleman (Frank)
>Frank Wilson (Joe)
>Ralf Coleman (Eddie)
>Slim Thompson (Noah)
>Claire Jay (Blanche)
>Merritt Smith (Officer)
>Isabelle Cooley (Anna)
>Lance Taylor (Danny)
>Sidney Poitier (Lester)
>Duke Williams (Rudolf)

## Freight

A one act play by Kenneth White; staged by John O'Shaughnessy. Produced by the American Negro Theatre.

Harlem Children's Center, 28 W. 134th St., New York 2/4/49.

>Maxwell Granville (Roty)
>Lance Taylor (Fast Boy)
>Roy Allen (Oz)
>William Greaves (Pug)
>Kenneth Manigault (Bucket)
>Sidney Poitier (Lottie)
>Raymond Hill (Mish)
>Dots Johnson (Samp)
>Maurice Thompson (Peg-Leg)
>Glen Gordon (Jake)

* original production: 8/30/44-11/30/46.

With Ruby Dee and Diana Sands.

With Claudia McNeil.

## A Raisin in the Sun

A three act drama by Lorraine Hansberry; staged by Lloyd Richards; presented by Philip Rose and David J. Cogan.

Shubert Theatre, New Haven 1/21/59-2/8/59.
Blackstone Theatre, Chicago 2/10/59-3/7/59.
Ethel Barrymore Theatre, New York
   3/11/59-10/17/59.
Belasco Theatre, New York 10/19/59-6/25/60.

>Ruby Dee (Ruth Younger)
>Glynn Turman (Travis Younger)
>Sidney Poitier (Walter Lee Younger)*
>Diana Sands (Beneatha Younger)
>Claudia McNeil (Lena Younger)
>Ivan Dixon (Joseph Asagai)

* succeeded by Ossie Davis on 8/31/59.

With Ruby Dee and Diana Sands.

Louis Gossett (George Murchison)
Lonnie Elder 3rd (Bobo)
John Fiedler (Karl Lindner)
Ed Hall (Moving Man)
Douglas Turner (Moving Man)

"Sidney Poitier established himself as the finest of all Negro actors."—Tom Prideaux, *Life Magazine*

"Sidney Poitier's performance as the vociferous son sparkles like a fireworks display."—*Variety*

With Claudia McNeil.

## Carry Me Back to Morningside Heights

A comedy in three acts by Robert Alan Aurthur; staged by Sidney Poitier; presented by Saint Subber in association with Harold Loeb.

John Golden Theatre, New York 2/27/68 (one preview and seven performances).

> Louis Gossett (Willie Nurse)
> David Steinberg (Seymour Levin)
> Johnny Brown (Henry Hardy)
> Cicely Tyson (Myrna Jessup)*
> Diane Ladd (Alma Sue Bates)

*succeeded by Beverly Todd

"... a very sad, very sick, self-styled comedy ... a lengthy racist farce. The kindest thing I could do to the play's director, Sidney Poitier, would be to avoid mention of his name."
— Clive Barnes, *The New York Times*

"It has been known for some time that Mr. Poitier has ambitions to be a director. That being accurate as a report, he would have to start somewhere. He would have to serve up his first professional attempt. This play is it, and I have to say that he has a hard, hard row to hoe."
—Whitney Boulton, *New York Morning Telegraph*

# Sidney Poitier on Television

## Philco Playhouse (NBC 11/16/52)

"Parole Chief" Directed by Delbert Mann. Based on the autobiography of David Dressler.

> Harry Townes (David Dressler)
> Donald Foster (Pat Byron)
> Sidney Poitier (Ernest Adams)
> Allen Nourse (Townsend)
> Perry Wilson (Belle Dressler)

> Mario Gallo (Louie Dabit)
> Terry Becker (Larry)
> Leo Penn (Roy)

and: Charles Thompson, Robert Armstrong, Dick Sanders, Bob Mermann, Charles Mendick, Anna Mindt, John Stephen, Ann Dere, Tiger Andrews, Andy Sabilia, Gene Gross.

With director Delbert Mann during Philco Playhouse rehearsal (1952).

## Pond Theatre  (ABC 6/23/55)

"Fascinating Stranger" by Booth Tarkington.

Sidney Poitier (Clifford Hill)
Larry Gates (Alfred Tuttle)

## Philco Playhouse  (NBC 10/2/55)

"A Man Is Ten Feet Tall" directed by Robert Mulligan. Teleplay by Robert Alan Aurthur.

Sidney Poitier (Tommy Tyler)
Don Murray (Axel)
Martin Balsam (Charley)
Michael Strong (Foreman)
Hilda Simms (Lucy Tyler)
Kathleen Murray (Katherine)
Don Gordon (1st man)
Joe Comadoro (2nd man)
Johanna Douglas (Mother)
Meg Wylie (Operator)
Florence Anglin (Landlady)
Ed Walsh (Policeman)
Sid Raymond (Checker)
Lou Frizzell (2nd Policeman)

## Sunday Showcase  (NBC 10/25/59)

Tribute to Eleanor Roosevelt on Her Diamond Jubilee.

Arthur Godfrey, host, with Marian Anderson, Lauren Bacall, Ralph Bellamy, Gertrude Berg, Milton Berle, Eddie Cantor, Art Carney, Maurice Chevalier, Jimmy Durante, Henry Fonda, Cedric Hardwicke, Helen Hayes, Bob Hope, Jose Iturbi, Henry Morgan, Sidney Poitier, Elizabeth Taylor.

## The Strollin' 20s  (CBS 2/11/66)

A musical special recapturing Harlem during its glory days, produced by Harry Belafonte and written by Langston Hughes.

Sidney Poitier as narrator/host, with Harry Belafonte, Diahann Carroll, Sammy Davis, Jr., Duke Ellington, Langston Hughes, Paula Kelly, George Kirby, Gloria Lynne, Nipsey Russell, Joe Williams.

The cast of *The Strollin' 20s* (1966): (front row) George Kirby, Gloria Lynne, Diahann Carroll and Paula Kelly; (second row) Poitier, Langston Hughes, Joe Williams, Nipsey Russell and Duke Ellington. Harry Belafonte, the producer, oversees the gathering.

## ABC Stage '67: A Time for Laughter (ABC 4/6/67)

A special tracing the development of Negro humor and its effects on American life, produced by Harry Belafonte.

Sidney Poitier as narrator/host, with Harry Belafonte, Godfrey Cambridge, Diahann Carroll, Redd Foxx, Dick Gregory, George Kirby, Moms Mabley, Pigmeat Markham, Richard Pryor, Diana Sands.

## Black History: Lost, Stolen or Strayed (CBS 7/2/68)

First program in seven part CBS News special, "Of Black America."

Bill Cosby, host.

## Three Young Americans In Search of Survival (ABC 3/17/69)

Two hour study of trio devoting their lives to ecological, natural and human values.

Paul Newman, host, and Sidney Poitier (seen touring Philadelphia's ghettos while there filming *The Lost Man*) offering views about the black man's life in urban centers.

## Soul! (PBS 3/22/72)

Sidney Poitier and Harry Belafonte discuss *Buck and the Preacher* with Ellis Haizlip, producer and host of the Public Television program about Black culture.

## The Merv Griffin Show (May, 1972)

Sidney Poitier and Harry Belafonte promoting *Buck and the Preacher*.

## The New Bill Cosby Show (CBS 9/11/72)

Sidney Poitier and Harry Belafonte as themselves in the series premiere.

## ABC Wide World of Entertainment: A Tribute to Stanley Kramer (ABC 8/21/75)

Sidney Poitier among the actors discussing with Kramer the various films on which they worked together. Poitier told Kramer: "I did three very important pictures for you, and at the time we made them, they were all revolutionary films."

## The Merv Griffin Show (November, 1975)

Sidney Poitier and Bill Cosby promoting *Let's Do It Again*.

## The Merv Griffin Show (September, 1976)

Sidney Poitier among presenters at the 1976 *Ebony* Music Awards.

## The Stars Salute America's Greatest Movies: The American Film Institute 10th Anniversary Gala (CBS 11/21/77)

Sidney Poitier co-hosts with Charlton Heston and Henry Fonda.